THE DISCOVERY
OF CANADA

Edward W. Nuffield

Haro Books

ISBN 0-9680288-0-2
Copyright © 1996 Edward W. Nuffield

Cataloging in Publication Data

Nuffield, E. W. (Edward W.)
The discovery of Canada

Includes bibliographic references and index.

    1. Canada—Discovery and exploration. 2. America—
Discovery and exploration. 3. Canada—History—To 1663 (New France)*
I. Title.
FC300.N83 1996   971.01'1   C95-911161-1
E101.N83 1996

Production: Lorna Brown
Cover: Bakker Plumbe Graphic Designers, Burnaby, B.C.
Printed and bound by Hignell, Canada

HARO BOOKS

1603 - 1835 Morton Avenue, Vancouver, B.C. Canada V6G 1V3

Contents

List of Maps and Figures

Dedication

To Islay,
and
Rosemary, Patrick and Ashley

Acknowledgments

I am indebted to Professor D. D. Hogarth of the University of Ottawa for discussions of his research into the voyages of Martin Frobisher. My daughter Joan read the manuscript and made many suggestions for improving it.

Preface

The history of the discovery of Canada by Europeans is commonly thought to have begun with the Viking invasion of North America from Greenland, about A.D. 1000. The Vikings may not have been the first Europeans to reach America. Some historians believe they were preceded into the Gulf of St. Lawrence, about A.D. 800, by Irish monks searching for a safe haven in which to practice their way of life.

The Vikings abandoned their settlements in North America early in the eleventh century and they withdrew from Greenland two or three hundred years later. But they clung to Iceland and Europeans continued to visit that island regularly and in large numbers—to fish and trade. Occasionally their small sailing ships would have been driven off course in the stormy North Atlantic and then some of them probably sighted the lost island of Greenland and even the American mainland.

The Scandinavian experience in America was kept alive in Iceland by tales passed from one generation to the next, and by a few historians who recorded the tales. Visiting seamen heard the stories and carried them abroad, and by this means there developed a body of knowledge about lands in and beyond the North Atlantic Ocean—knowledge that was unpublished but common to mariners who frequented these waters. Records show that in the decade before the 1492 Columbus voyage to the West Indies, English adventurers were lured by this lore to sail out onto the Atlantic, specifically to search for new lands. There is some evidence to believe that at least one of these voyages touched the shores of North America before 1492.

Within a few years after John Cabot's rediscovery of mainland North America in 1497, he was followed to Newfoundland by fishermen from England, France, Portugal and Spain, attracted by his report that the ocean off its east coast swarmed with cod. And as these waters became crowded, the fishermen entered the Gulf of St. Lawrence and began fishing and trading with native Americans. This commerce had probably reached and become established in the lower regions of the St. Lawrence River in the first decade of the sixteenth century, well before Jacques Cartier "discovered" the river in 1535.

Part One

The Discovery of America

The shortest distance between the continents on opposite sides of the Atlantic Ocean is at the equator. About 1300 miles (2100 km.) of open sea, straddling the equator, separates the northeastern tip of Brazil, in South America, from Sierra Leone in Africa. Columbus could have covered the distance in about fifteen days in one of the Portuguese caravels of his time. Yet this was not the scene of man's first crossing of the Atlantic—at least not his first recorded crossing. The people that faced each other across this stretch of water apparently felt no need or urge to venture far out onto the uncharted ocean and thus there were no chance or unplanned crossings or meetings. The first crossing of this part of the Atlantic was made in 1500 by a Spaniard, Vicente Yañez Pinzón, the man who commanded Columbus' *Niña* in 1492.

The earliest recorded crossing of the Atlantic was in the far north. The Vikings—"the men of the North," inhabitants of Denmark, Sweden and Norway—are generally conceded to have been the first Europeans to reach North America although they were not the first Europeans to purposefully sail out onto the Atlantic, out of sight of shore, in search of new lands. The Vikings were seafarers, a venturesome and daring people. They lived in a time of expanding travel and trade and it led them to breast the open seas in search of new lands to plunder and occupy. They seemed to have an inexhaustible supply of men and leaders of great ability to organize the men into formidable fighting forces. They forged westward from one island to the next and eventually these "stepping stones" brought them to North America, by accident as it happened.

Some historians dispute that the Vikings were the first Europeans on North American soil. The Irish were just as courageous and enterprising on the ocean as the Vikings. They went abroad with a different purpose, searching for peace and the freedom to worship the new Christianity. They fled before the Vikings and they may have reached North America before the Norsemen.

1

The Way to North America

The mythical islands of the Atlantic Ocean

Legends and myths about the Atlantic Ocean, the islands that were thought to lie in it, and what lay beyond the ocean formed a part of the folklore of European man from ancient times. This early speculation about the Atlantic was common in countries like Norway, Ireland and Portugal that border the open ocean, but it was present also in the old civilizations ringing the Mediterranean Sea.

Perhaps the oldest known tale about the Atlantic is the story of "Lost Atlantis."[1] Atlantis was said to be an island, the center of a powerful kingdom, situated in the Atlantic Ocean just off the Pillars of Hercules (the two promontories on opposite sides of the Strait of Gibraltar). An archipelago of lesser islands was supposed to lie beyond Atlantis. According to the legend, the island's rulers undertook to conquer the world and its armies succeeded in overrunning most of the Mediterranean countries. Eventually, after a long war, they were defeated by a coalition of nations led by Athens. Then, about 9500 B.C., Atlantis was destroyed by an earthquake and the island sank into the sea leaving only shoals to mark the location; most of its people were lost. The earliest reference to Atlantis is attributed to Plato who related the legend to illustrate a proposition in political philosophy. He may have invented it for that purpose but he claimed that the story came from the Athenian sage, Solon, who had heard it from Egyptian priests.

The evidence for the existence of another legendary island, Thule[2], is imputed to Pytheas, a Greek explorer and geographer, who is said to have visited the Atlantic coast of Europe and the British Isles about 300 B.C. Pytheas' own report of this voyage is lost and we have to rely on references in the works of more recent writers to deduce the itinerary of his travels. The accounts of these later authors differ one from the other, and their narratives do not lead to a consistent story; however, it seems certain that Pytheas visited some of the northern countries along the Atlantic. The English monk and historian, Bede[3], writing in the eighth century, is the author of some of the references to Thule. In his book *De Ratione Tem-*

porum, he wrote that Pytheas reached Thule by sailing north from England for six days. Bede referred to Thule as the most northerly of the inhabited islands and said the island had neither daylight in winter nor darkness on the longest summer day. Bede's narrative led some early scholars to equate Thule with Iceland. Today the consensus has it that Bede's Thule was probably Norway.

Atlantis and Thule were only two of a number of the mysterious islands that figured in the pre-Christian beliefs held by people in the Mediterranean countries. The supposed locations of the islands were marked on ancient charts and the islands formed the basis of sagas and even voyages of discovery into the Atlantic Ocean. They included the Islands of the Blessed which featured an attractive version of the hereafter for practical-minded people. It was said the virtuous dead, retaining their faculties, lived carefree on these islands, enjoying the activities that had given them pleasure in life.

Another island that was prominent in more recent tales of the Atlantic was known as Brazil[4]. The name derived from a wood called brazilwood, used in the Middle Ages to obtain a red dye. The wood was said to grow in abundance on this mythical island which was identified on a fifteenth-century Venetian map with one of the larger islands of the Azores. When the Azores were colonized without discovering brazilwood, its supposed location was shifted to the fogbanks off the southwest coast of Ireland and was shown on maps well into the nineteenth century.

A tale that originated in Spain held that when the Moors overran that country early in the eighth century, an archbishop and a number of bishops and other Christian men and women fled by ship with their goods and livestock to the island of Antilia[5]. In the years before Christopher Columbus sailed to America, Spanish mariners undertook a number of voyages into the Atlantic, specifically to search for this island. As the eastern extremities of the Atlantic became better known, the location of the supposed island was moved westward and eventually the haven of the archbishop and his people became identified with the Spanish settlement known as the "Province of Seven Cities" in the southwestern United States.

The Irish, an imaginative people, living on an island, quite naturally developed an extensive folklore related to the sea. Their pre-Christian tales varied from the prosaic to a mixture of mythological and religious beliefs. They included fables of pagan heroes who sailed into the Atlantic in search of the Irish Heaven—mystical lands called the "Land of Youth" or the "Land of the Living" lying somewhere in the sea beyond their western horizon. If nothing else, the tales indicated that the Celts believed in a happy otherworld.

Small Christian communities existed in Ireland early in the fifth century but the large scale conversion from paganism to Christianity took place only after St. Patrick was sent as bishop to Ireland in 432. In the beginning the Christian movement was characterized by the development of an ascetic monasticism resulting in the founding of many small monasteries, some of them built on relatively inaccessible islands off the Irish coast or in isolated regions inland. Already in the sixth century there was much sea traffic around the British Isles. Fishermen and merchants were unafraid of the ocean and traveled widely and skillfully in their seaworthy ships. Ardent and devout monks took advantage of the opportunity this offered, to travel abroad. They went "beyond the impenetrable seas"—some to mainland Europe to preach, some to the Orkney Islands off the northern tip of Scotland and some to the more remote Shetland Islands, fifty miles (eighty km.) northeast of the Orkneys, to pursue a hermit's life.

In the middle of the seventh century, the Pope's decision to replace Celtic with Roman rites alienated many monks and prompted another migration, this time to the Faeroe Islands, 200 miles (325 km.) north of the Shetlands. It is fair to assume that the monks knew of the existence of these islands before they embarked. Other monks went out onto the Atlantic in their sea-going boats (covered with layers of greased hides to keep the water out) and let the winds carry them where they would, praying that God would guide them to the Fortunate Islands, an Irish concept of Heaven.

Irish sagas dating from about the seventh century tend to reflect the Christian doctrine. Thus, the fabled islands in the Atlantic Ocean became known variously as the "Land of Promise," the "Kingdom of Heaven," the "Land of Truth" and, apparently suiting some Irish concepts of Heaven, the "Land of Fair Women."

The tales include prosaic accounts of Irish saints voyaging in the dim past, out on to the Atlantic Ocean to distant lands. One of these tales concerns St. Brendan[6], an Irish monk who lived from about 484 to 578. He is said to have searched the Atlantic Ocean for the heavenly islands around 545. The tales of his adventures, told through the centuries, were drawn together, possibly early in the eighth century, into a legend of sea adventure. It was put down in Latin prose in the ninth century as the *Navigatio Brendani* (The Voyage of St. Brendan). It tells that St. Brendan and fourteen monks made a prolonged search for the heavenly islands, touching the Hebrides, the Shetlands and the Faeroe Islands. The account relates that they sailed westward from the Faeroes for forty days when they saw through a sudden clearing of the fog, an iceberg "the colour of silver, as hard as marble, and of the clearest crystal."[7] As they closed on the land, they saw strange creatures on shore with "catlike heads, boar's tusks and spotted bellies"— almost certainly walruses. They believed they had found the "promised land" of the saints (later it became known as Brendan's Isle) but, the story goes, they were not to enjoy it for Brendan was told he must return to Ireland and relate his adventures.

Undoubtedly, the Brendan sagas were embellished over the years to make the narrative more interesting, and likely the deeds of a number of adventurers were credited to Brendan. The sagas include enough credible detail that was not within the ordinary experience of the monks, or of other adventuring seafarers of the eighth century and earlier, or of the storytellers who described the adventurers, to conclude that they cannot be easily dismissed as mythical extravagance. Although legendary, the narrative of St. Brendan undoubtedly drew on authentic reports by seamen of sightings of lands in the Atlantic north and west of Ireland.

European mariners of the first millennium were probably more venture-some and skilled, and sailed the open seas more extensively, than is generally believed. Although the early navigator had no compass or charts, he used the sun and stars to sail an east-west course and to tell him if he was north or south of his home port. He noted the flight of birds, the color and flow of the water and the nature of weed and wood that drifted on its surface, and his observations told him where to search for land and when he was close to it.

If fishermen and merchants, and their Irish monk-passengers, were in the habit of ranging as far abroad as the Faeroe Islands in the seventh century, it is reasonable to assume that they had ventured or been storm-driven, even further afield. They had probably seen Iceland—about three days sail (240 miles or 385 km.) northwest of the Faeroes—and even Greenland as early as the sixth century (the time of the alleged St. Brendan voyages), centuries before the Norsemen settled in Iceland.

Iceland—first stepping stone from Europe to America

The classic image of Vikings—inhabitants of Scandinavia but mainly Norwegians—as barbaric ax-wielding marauders, raiding foreign shores in their ships, plundering churches, killing and enslaving people—represents only a fraction of these men of the North. Scandinavians embraced a pagan religion in the last centuries of the first millennium, but otherwise they were not basically different from people in neighboring countries. They showed the same degree of cruelty toward their enemies, they were no more violent in war, and they bestowed as much love on their families. Scandinavians were not just warriors; they were farmers, merchants, politicians and explorers. They were an ambitious people with important seafaring skills, living in an agrarian world at a time of expanding trade. It led the more adventuresome leaders among them to roam the known world and beyond it, engaging in trade in anything from slaves to honey and silver, searching for arable land, bent on accumulating wealth to make their own lives easier and to reward their followers and keep them loyal.

Beginning shortly before A.D. 800, a significant number of Scandinavians began undertaking a more certain way of realizing their ambitions. They went "Viking"—raiding foreign shores to take what they wanted with purposeful force and violence, seizing pasture and farm land, plundering wealth, burning for the mere sake of destroying, killing indiscriminantly, making off with prisoners for personal use or profit. The Viking age lasted three centuries and affected almost every part of the world the Vikings could reach with their ships.

Vikings traveled the seas in low-slung, shallow-draft ships built almost entirely of oak with some pine (judging from ships that have been recovered), and caulked with tarred animal hair or wool. A typical large ship might measure almost eighty feet (24 m.) in length, have a beam of nearly twenty feet (6 m.), and a height, from the keel to the gunwale midships, of more than six feet (2 m.)—big enough to transport seventy men, their weapons and all the supplies needed for an adventure. These ships had a draft of less than four feet (little more than a metre), enabling them to enter shallow rivers and disembark men near shore along shelving beaches. They were characterized by a high curved prow and stern ornamented with carvings and they carried a single mast that could be lowered for taking the ship under a low bridge or making it less conspicuous when undertaking a surprise attack; it carried a square sail. Some ships also had provision for two rows of oarsmen, thirty or more per side, who were used when the wind failed, or when it was necessary to maneuver near shore in confined waters. The ships were steered with a large oar near the stern on the right side. A Viking ship could reach speeds of more than ten knots although an average speed, under varying conditions, was more in the order of six knots.[8] They were so designed that when speed was attained, the bow lifted out of the sea thereby reducing the drag of the water. Modern reconstructions of these vessels have shown that they were easily maneuvered and could sail at an angle of up to 45° into the wind.[9]

The Vikings invaded the Faeroe Islands about 770; then, in rapid succession, they came to the Shetlands, the Orkneys and the Hebrides, burning churches and monasteries, sacking the towns and holding the inhabitants to ransom. They appeared off the coast of Ireland about 795 and thereafter there were frequent raids, some reaching far inland.

The Irish monks and hermits wanted no part of a life under these barbarians. About the year 800, those who were able, loaded their goods

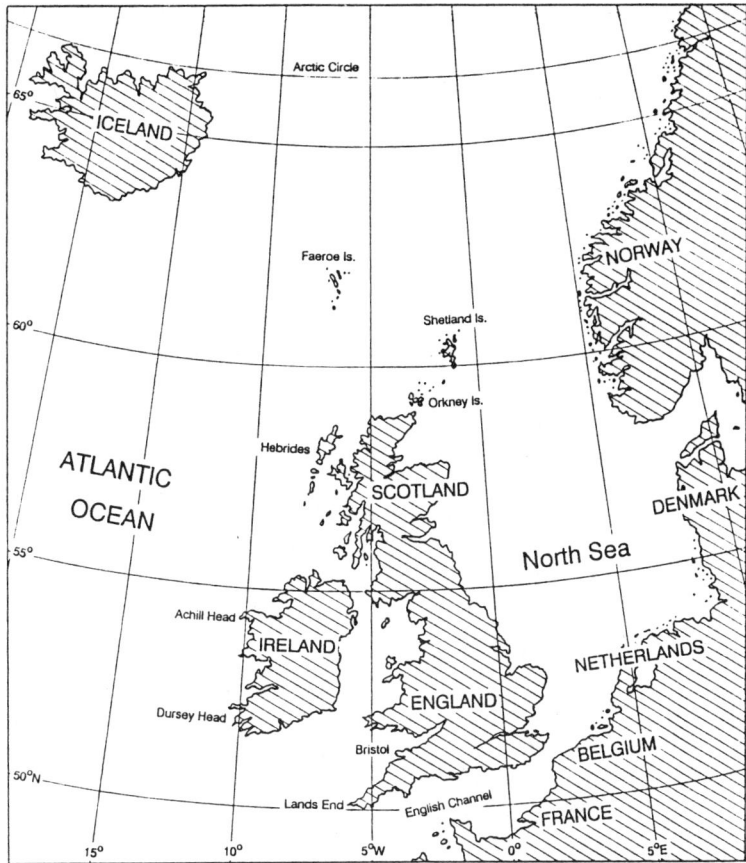

Figure 1.
The island
"stepping stones"
to Iceland.

into the leather boats of the day and guided by their fishermen who knew the seas northwest of Ireland, sailed to Iceland—some 600 miles (950 km.) from Ireland, and only 240 miles (385 km.) from the Faeroes. These Irish people settled in several places along the east coast—the first white settlers in Iceland. They were probably joined by other Irish over the years and this helped to extend the life of the first Christian community in Iceland, composed principally of celibate men, for a century—until the island was discovered by the Vikings.

The discovery of Iceland by Scandinavians

In the early part of the ninth century, a Norwegian ship bound for the Faeroes, was

> driven out to sea westwards, and came to a vast country. They went ashore...climbed a high mountain, and scanned the country in all directions looking for smoke or any other sign that the land was inhabited, but they saw nothing.[10]

15

The landing was probably in the Eastfjords on the east coast of Iceland. The Norsemen stayed the winter and

> in the summer they went back to the Faeroes, and as they were sailing away from the coast a lot of snow fell on the mountains, so they called the country Snowland.[11]

About the middle of the ninth century,

> A man called Gardar Svafarsson, of Swedish stock, went out in search of Snowland guided by his mother, who had second sight. He made land east of Eastern Horn [on the southeast coast of Iceland] where at that time ships could put in. Gardar sailed right round the country and proved it to be an island.[12]

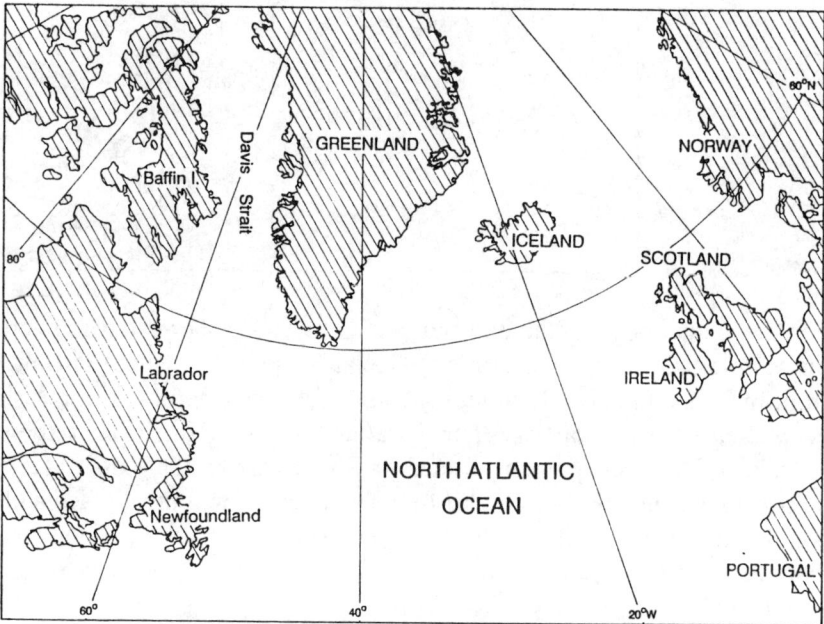

Figure 2. Iceland and Greenland—the "stepping stones" to mainland America around the north end of the Atlantic Ocean.

For a time after that, Iceland was known as Gardar's Isle. Gardar built a house and spent the winter in Iceland and in spring he set sail back to Norway.

> After he'd put out to sea, a boat drifted away from the ship with

a man called Nattfari aboard, and a slave and a bondswoman. Nattfari settled down there.[13]

Nattfari was probably the first Scandinavian settler in Iceland.

Floki Vilgerdarson, a Viking, went in search of Gardar's Isle, going first to the Shetland Islands. The sagas tell that Floki had three ravens to help him find the way and before he left the Shetlands he released them one after the other. The first raven flew to the stern of the ship and back, the second went straight up and came back down, and the third flew over the bow and did not return. Floki took the ship out to sea and steered in the direction of the third raven's flight; eventually, it brought him to Horn on the south coast of Gardar's Isle.

Floki went ashore and

> climbed a certain high mountain, and north across the mountain range he could see a fjord full of drift ice. That's why they called the country Iceland, and so it's been called ever since.[14]

Ingolf and Hjorleif found a settlement in Iceland

In 871, Ingolf and Hjorleif, blood-brothers and great-grandsons of Hromund Gripsson, went on a Viking expedition from Norway with Holmstein, Herstein and Hastein, the sons of Earl Atli, the Slender. They got on

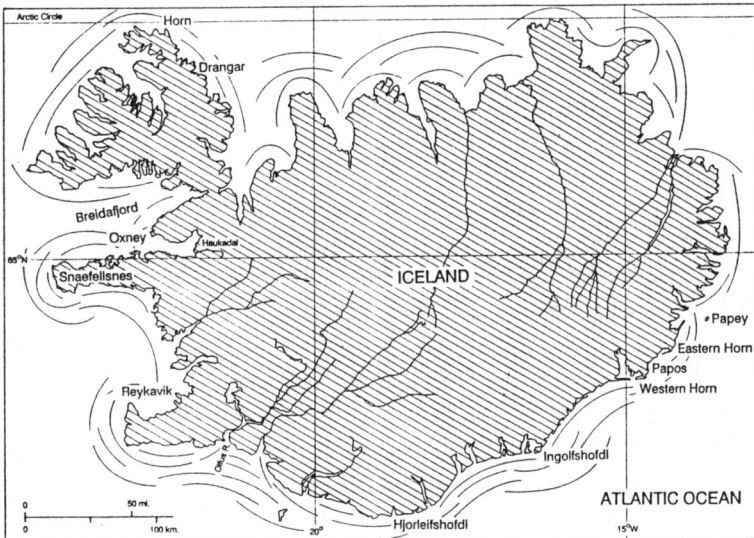

Figure 3. Iceland.

well together and their expedition prospered, and when they reached home the two blood-brothers gave a feast for their fellow Vikings. At that feast Holmstein swore he would marry Helga, Ingolf's sister. This angered Leif who wanted her for himself. The anger festered and in the spring of 872 the two blood-brothers went in search of Holmstein. When they found him and his brother Herstein, they fought; Holmstein was killed and Herstein was forced to flee.

The following winter (872–3), Herstein tried to kill the blood-brothers but he was killed instead. This resulted in much ill feeling between the families; to smooth the relations, messengers were sent to Earl Atli offering to compensate him for the death of his two sons. It was agreed that Leif and Ingolf would give him and his remaining son all the property they owned in Norway. Having concluded this business, the blood-brothers readied a ship and set out in search of Iceland, the land Raven-Floki had visited. They found it, stayed the winter (873–4) and returned to Norway where Leif and Helga were married.

Ingolf immediately began preparations for another voyage to Iceland but Leif went on a plundering expedition to Ireland. It is said he found an underground chamber that was dark until light started from a sword a man was holding. Leif killed the man and took the sword and great riches as well. Thereafter he was known as Hjorleif, meaning sword-Leif. Having accomplished all this, he sailed back to Norway to rejoin Ingolf.

The following spring—the year was about 874—the blood-brothers made final preparations to sail to Iceland with the purpose of settling there. They sailed close to each other until Iceland came into view. Then Ingolf threw some easily-recognizable wooden equipment overboard, saying he would settle where it came ashore. He landed at a place that is now called Ingolfshofdi, on the southeast shore. Hjorleif continued westward along the coast and wintered on its southernmost tip (today it is called Hjorleifshofdi).

In the spring (875) Horjleif set his slaves to plowing the soil. He had only one ox and consequently the slaves had to pull the plow. They resented this and plotted the death of their masters. They knew they would have to divide the Norse forces to beat them and to accomplish this they slaughtered the ox and told Hjorleif that a wandering bear had killed the animal. They persuaded Hjorleif to spread his men and search the woods for the bear. Then they ambushed the Norsemen, one by one, and killed them all. They took the Norsemen's women, their goods and a boat, and rowed over to some nearby islands and settled down to live there.

Meanwhile, Ingolf sent two slaves to search the shoreline for the equipment he had flung overboard. In the course of this search, the men happened on the bodies of Hjorleif and his men in the woods and brought the news to Ingolf. After he had seen to the burial of his blood-brother and the other men, Ingolf climbed a headland and from there saw islands lying to the southwest. He had observed that Horjleif's boat was missing, and he surmised the slaves had fled to one of these islands and were hiding there. He searched for them and one day he came upon them while they were eating a meal. At sight of the Norsemen, the slaves scattered in all directions, some even jumping off a cliff to escape, but Ingolf and his men found and killed them all.

Ingolf carried the widowed women back to Hjorleif's settlement and they wintered there. In the spring, he took all the people and goods in the two ships and sailed westward, following the shoreline. They stayed that third winter west of the Olfus River and in that year his slaves found Ingolf's equipment washed up on the shore at the site of Reykjavik. In the spring Ingolf moved everything west across the moor to this spot and there he set up the first permanent Scandinavian settlement in Iceland.

It did not take long for the Scandinavians to discover that they were not the first white people to settle in Iceland. Scandinavian sagas relate that

> before Iceland was settled from Norway there were other people there, called Papar [meaning Irish priests] by the Norwegians. They were Christians and were thought to have come overseas from the west [i.e. from west of Norway], because people found Irish books, bells, croziers, and lots of other things, so it was clear they must have been Irish. Besides, English sources tell us that sailings were made between these countries [Iceland and Ireland] at the time.[15]

The names with which the Scandinavians identified the papar settlements persist to the present day on modern maps (for example, Papey and Papos) and bear witness to their origin.

The papar—the earliest European settlers in Iceland—were the monks and hermits, numbering perhaps a hundred in all, who had fled Ireland and the islands that lie north and west of Scotland, beginning about 800, seventy years before Ingolf settled at Reykjavik. Whether they were dispossessed of their books and bells by Ingolf's followers, or they were forced to flee and their going was too precipitous to gather the articles is not known. The ancient Icelandic histories[16] contain no further mention of these people and we may assume if they were not killed by the Vikings, they quit the island just as they did Ireland, refusing to live with them. We can speculate that in the latter event, they organized a small fleet of fishing vessels about the year 900 and set sail, carrying from necessity only the bare essentials for their existence. Their destination was probably the next land (Greenland) to the west of Iceland—land their fishermen had probably seen, although perhaps not visited.

As the population of Europe grew and farm land became scarce, the Viking raids turned into waves of emigrants. Ingolf and his people were followed to Iceland by other Scandinavians, mostly Norwegians, in search of land and the opportunity to build a life free of the tyranny of war and poverty that ruled the old country. Some had been forced out of their homeland by Harrald Fine-Hair, king of Norway; others left of their own free will, anxious to escape this cruel despot. Some came from countries the Vikings now occupied—Ireland, Scotland and the nearby islands. Most of these latter settlers were Christian and they remained true to their faith, but this rarely held for their descendants who chose to embrace the dominant religious beliefs of their new country; Iceland was basically pagan for the first hundred years of Scandinavian occupation.[17] The settlers arrived in a steady stream and by the end of the tenth century, the population of Iceland was about 75,000.

Greenland—the second stepping stone

Early in the tenth century (between 900 and 930), about twenty-five to fifty years after Ingolf and Hjorleif settled in Iceland, a man named Gunnbjorn, sailing from Norway, was blown past Iceland and came within sight of the east coast of Greenland and its offshore islands. He did not land but he discussed the experience with his sons and his brother after he reached Iceland. The rapid influx of settlers had created a shortage of good farming land in Iceland. Yet, although the mysterious country lay only four days of daylight-sailing due west of Snaefellsnes, Iceland[18], no attempts were made to follow up on Gunnbjorn's report for half a century. It remained a mystery, the memory of it kept alive by tales told along Iceland's west coast until Erik the Red—red of hair and beard—appeared on the scene.

Shortly after 970, when he was still in his teens, Erik and his father, Thorvald, had to leave Norway in consequence of getting involved in some killings. They journeyed to Iceland with the intention of taking up farming land. The new country was already extensively settled and as a result, they were forced to homestead southeast of Horn at Drangar, on the rockbound northern coast. Horn is the closest approach to Greenland from Iceland—200 miles (320 km.) distant across Denmark Strait—visible only on an exceptional day. Greenland, usually shrouded in fog and cloud, was not a common sight but the knowledge of its existence to the west must have been widespread among the settlers near Horn.

Thorvald died here and Erik, who had married, moved his family south to Haukadal at the head of Breidafjord where his wife's mother's people lived and began clearing some of the family land for farming. In the course of this work his slaves inadvertently caused a landslide onto a neighbor's house. This angered a kinsman of the neighbor and he took it upon himself to kill the slaves. Erik retaliated by killing the kinsman and another man, and for this he was banished from Haukadal.

Erik now moved west and made his home at Oxney. In the course of time, a neighbor—a man named Thorgest—borrowed some equipment from Erik. When Erik asked for its return and did not get it back, he went and fetched it. Thorgest took offense at this action and he came after Erik and they fought. Two of Thorgest's sons and some other men were killed in the fighting. Erik was outlawed by the local assembly for this incident and he hid in the nearby islands while Thorgest and his men combed the countryside for him, bent on revenge.

In searching for a way out of his dilemma, Erik may have remembered the unknown land that lay northwest of Horn. Was this the same land Gunnbjorn had sighted some fifty years ago when he had drifted westward past Iceland? Was this a prudent time to leave Iceland and go in search of that land? Erik decided it was. He began readying his ship and he put out the word among his friends that he wanted volunteers for a voyage to find Gunnbjorn's discovery.

Erik the Red rediscovers Greenland

The principal sources of information about the discovery and settlement of Greenland by Scandinavians, and the subsequent Viking voyages to North America, are two compendia of sagas: the *Groenlendinga Saga* (the Greenlanders' Saga), and *Eiriks Saga Rauoa* (Eirik the Red's Saga).[19] The original transcripts, completed after 1200 and perhaps as early as the first quarter of the thirteenth century, are lost; the existing transcripts date from the fourteenth century. The two sets of sagas do not share a common source and were probably written independently, each in ignorance of the other, for there are important differences relating to the discovery and occupation of Vinland in America.

The authors of the compendia drew on the recitation of traditional tales and verses, and they interviewed the descendants of the Viking discoverers. As well, they examined the written history, genealogy and geography of the day. They appear to have been scholarly and well-informed, sifting and organizing the material available to them, not content to transcribe everything that came to ear or eye.

Erik and his companions put out from Snaefellsnes, a prominent peninsula that juts into Denmark Strait, and sailed west along the 65th parallel of latitude. The year was 981 or 982. Within four days' sailing, the east coast of Greenland came into view and soon they intercepted the island, probably near Ingolfsfjeld. It was an inhospitable-looking country, crowned by a desolate icecap. Erik turned southward, following the coastline, looking for habitable land. He rounded the southern tip of Greenland and stopped at Eiriksfjord on the west coast, just above Cape Farewell. He was entranced by the southern fjords that offered good anchorage for fishermen and stretched deep into the interior, past luxuriant pastures—farming land richer than anything he could have acquired in Iceland. Best of all, it was a land for the taking, a seemingly empty country with only the ruins of dwellings, boats and stone implements to show that he and his men were not the first people on these shores. This was a country to colonize. Here, at what became known as the Eastern Settlement, Erik passed his first winter in North America.

The company stayed two more winters in Greenland using the summers to explore the interior to the head of Eiriksfjord. They returned to Iceland, landing at Breidafjord on the west coast where Erik spent the winter with Ingolf. In the spring he again fought with Thorgest and he was beaten. Apparently, the victory satisfied Thorgest for thereafter the two men lived in peace. Erik began recruiting settlers. He called the new country Greenland to make it more attractive to prospective colonists but also because in places it was a green land. The grass was lush alongside all the fjords he had explored; he had even seen birch and willow trees. He was quite successful in attracting his countrymen; ten years previously, Iceland had suffered a severe famine that had killed some of the old and helpless people. Many of the poorer farmers had lost hope and were eager for a fresh chance.

Erik set out in the summer (the year was 985 or 986) with enough people to man about twenty-five ships, to make the voyage across Denmark Strait. The people—men, their wives and children, and their serfs—were drawn from the western part of Iceland. They carried everything they owned—household goods, cattle, implements and arms. Some ships were lost at sea, more were driven back by storms but fourteen ships, carrying about 400 Icelanders, reached Greenland and took up land and established the Eastern Settlement along the southwest coast. Erik made his home at Brattahlid on the Eiriksfjord.

2

The Scandinavian Episode in America
986 to about 1016

Bjarni Herjolfsson sees mainland North America

In 986 Bjarni Herjolfsson, a trader, left Norway with a cargo, intending to spend the winter in Iceland where his father lived. He was surprised to learn, on arrival, that his father had sold his property and had sailed with Erik the Red in the previous month as a prospective settler in Greenland. Bjarni decided to follow his father. There was no one to guide him or even to give him accurate directions (the compass was not known to the Vikings), but his crew was willing and they set off to find his father in the unknown land to the west. They began the voyage at the mouth of the Olfus River (latitude 64°N), a considerable distance south of Erik's point of departure.

Three days out at sea, the gradually-fading mountains of Iceland sinking below the horizon, they lost their following wind. The ship was engulfed in fog and then a north wind took charge. For "many days" they were carried southward by wind and current, with never a sight of land, the sun or the stars. At length the weather cleared, the sun came out and they were able to get their bearings. They raised a sail and set a westward course, and within a day they sighted land. They drew near and saw a shoreline backed by low, well-wooded hills. Bjarni had been told enough about Erik's snow and ice-clad island where trees grew mainly at the heads of fjords deep in the interior, to know this was not Greenland. Besides, this was an east-facing coastline and he knew Erik's settlement was on a west coast.

Despite the grumbling of his crew, Bjarni would not allow the men to go ashore for firewood and fresh water. The height of the sun told them they were well south of their destination and he took the ship out to sea and sailed northward. They sighted land again after two days but this country too, was forested and flat, and definitely not Greenland. The crew again agitated to go ashore to replenish supplies but Bjarni would not hear of it.

They turned seaward again and sailing before a southwest wind, they came to a third land after three days. It was mountainous and glaceated but

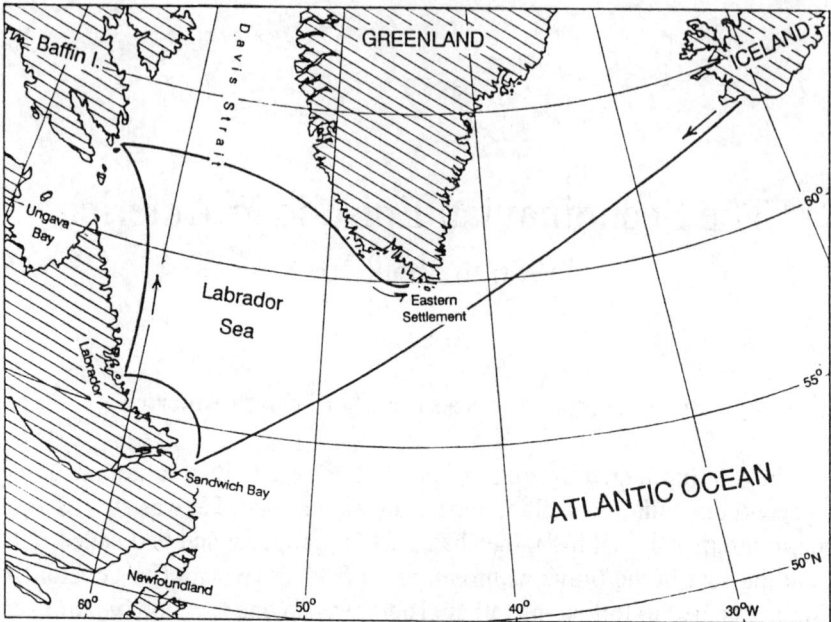

Figure 4. The probable route of Bjarni Herjolfsson's voyage,
in 986, from Iceland to America and Greenland.

when the men asked if this was their destination, Bjarni replied that the land looked to be good for nothing; therefore, it could not be the country Erik the Red had chosen for a settlement.

Bjarni moved the ship out to sea and ran before a freshening wind. After four days they saw a fourth land. The crew asked if this was Greenland and Bjarni replied it looked much like the Greenland that had been described to him and when they reached the coast, he followed it southward. Bjarni was right; they were alongside the western side of Greenland and eventually they came to the just-settled part (the Eastern Settlement) and Eiriksfjord where Erik had begun farming.

Bjarni learned that his father, Herjolf, had taken up land further south, on a fjord (Herjolfsfjord) marked by a prominent ness or promontory at its opening, and that is where Bjarni found his father. Bjarni gave up sailing after this experience and continued to live here after his father died.

Historians generally agree that Bjarni's first brush with land was in mainland North America but there is no consensus on the question of where he made his landfall. Locations ranging from Massachusetts to Labrador in the north have been advocated. If we accept the account in the Greenlanders' Saga[1], that only nine days elapsed from the time Bjarni first sighted land until he arrived at Herjolfsfjord, there was little time for him to make a long

24

voyage adjacent to the coast of North America before crossing Davis Strait to Greenland. Jones[2] places his landfall just south of latitude 54°N, in the vicinity of Sandwich Bay, in southern Labrador. This allows for a southward drift in the fog of about ten degrees of latitude or roughly 700 miles (1100 km.) on the outward voyage from Iceland.

The second sighting, also of low forested land, occurred after two days' sail—equivalent to about 200 miles (320 km.)—up the coast. This would place the location just below Nain (latitude 56°N), still in Labrador but well south of the tenth-century forest line.

Jones believes the third sighting was on the southern extremity of Baffin Island (latitude about 62°N).

Leif the Lucky, son of Erik the Red, lands in the New World

Bjarni's story of a wooded shoreline caught the attention of Greenlanders for their new country grew no timber suitable for building ships and homes. Curiously, more than a decade passed before someone followed up on the report.

In the year 1000, Erik the Red's son, Leif, undertook a voyage from Greenland to Norway. His ship was driven off course onto the Hebrides and he and his crew remained there most of the summer, ostensibly waiting for a favorable wind. Leif used the time to advantage with a well-born woman by the name of Thorgunna. When it was time to sail, she asked to come with him saying she carried his child. Leif refused to take her and tried to placate her with the gift of a gold ring, a cloak of Greenland wool and a walrus-ivory belt. She said she would send the boy (she was sure it was a male child) to Greenland and thought she might "come to Greenland myself before the game is played out."[3]

Leif reached Norway and was well received by King Olaf who instructed him in the Christian faith as was his habit with all heathens with whom he came in contact. Apparently Leif was easily converted and soon baptized, and his shipmates readily followed suit. At Olaf's invitation, Leif spent the winter in the king's court. This was considered a signal honor for the son of a remote-island chief.

In the spring, after Leif announced his intention of returning to Greenland, Olaf asked Leif to carry the Christian faith to Greenland and preach the gospel. The king had not had much success in spreading Christianity to the western islands. Some years previously he had sent a priest to Iceland but the holy man had got into a fight, killed two Icelanders and become quite ineffective as a preacher. Olaf thought he had never seen a man better fitted than Leif for the task. Leif agreed to the undertaking and returned to

Greenland accompanied by a priest and other holy men. He and his mission were welcomed on the island and he was instrumental in converting many people to Christianity. His father, Erik, "took coldly to the notion of abandoning his faith"[4] and always maintained that Leif had introduced a "shyster" (as he styled the priest) into Greenland.

There was still talk of Bjarni's new world and Leif, now a prominent man, was approached by a number of chieftains to organize a search for the new land. Leif was persuaded; he talked with Bjarni about the voyage and he purchased Bjarni's ship and got a crew of thirty-five men together. He asked his father to lead the expedition but Erik was reluctant saying he was too old for the adventure, Finally, however, he agreed but on the way to the ship Erik had the misfortune to fall off his horse and he broke a number of bones in his foot. He took this as a sign that it was not his destiny to discover more lands and he returned home; Leif continued on to the ship with the crew.

Leif set out from Greenland in 1002 with his thirty-five men to find the forested country, tracking Bjarni's course in reverse. They steered a west-

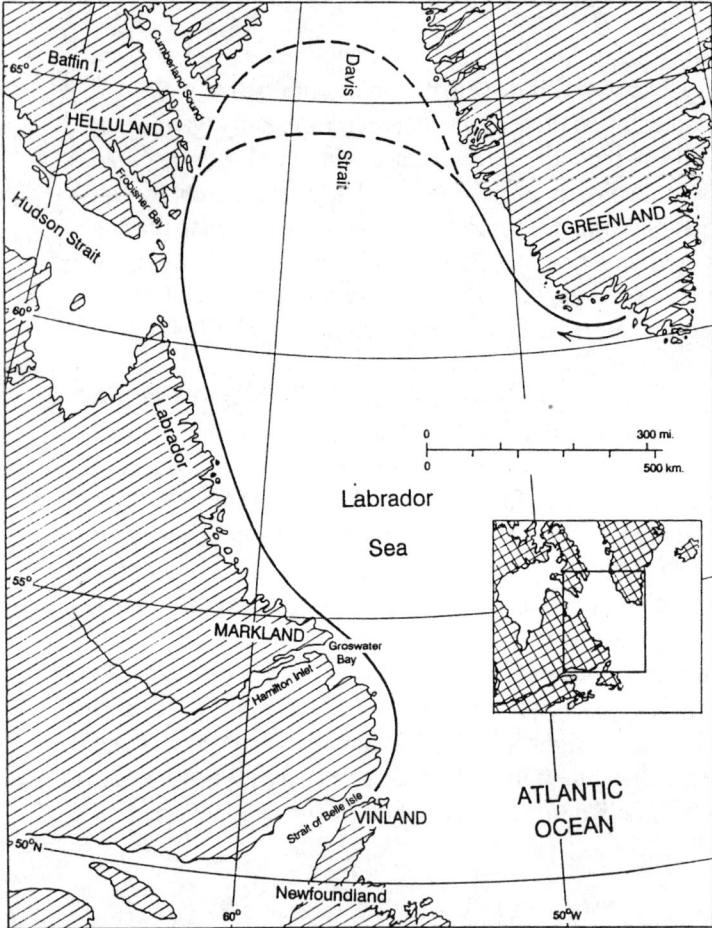

Figure 5.
The probable route of Leif Erikson's voyage from Greenland to Vinland in 1002.

northwesterly course across Davis Strait and reached Bjarni's third land discovery (Baffin Island) where they went ashore. The landscape at the landfall was marked by what looked to be a single slab of rock extending up from the sea to the glaciers that dominated the country. Leif named the region Helluland (Flatstone Land) for the strange outcropping and this is what Baffin Island was first called.

They put out to sea again and after several days they came to low, forested land with a white-sand shoreline sloping gently to the sea—the second new land of Bjarni's voyage. They cast anchor and spent a short time ashore. Leif decided to call the region Markland (Wood Land); it was probably Hamilton Inlet in Labrador[5] which is just north of latitude 54°N.

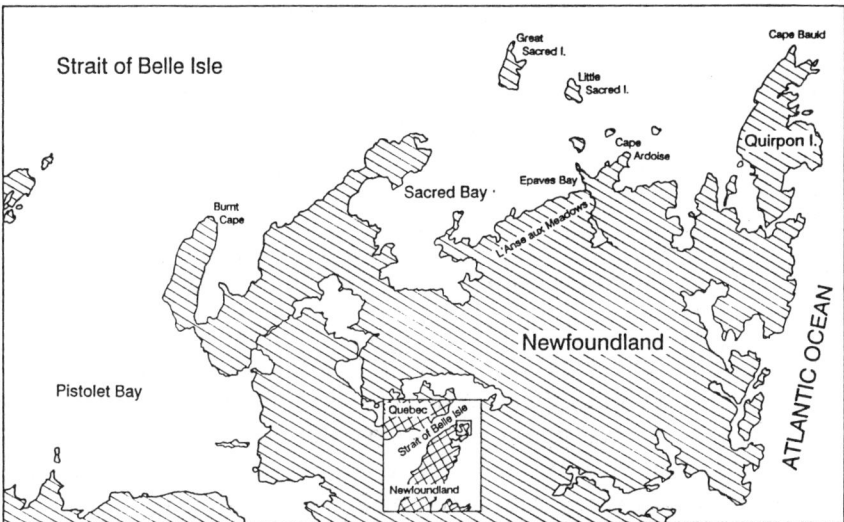

Figure 6. L'Anse aux Meadows, the site of the first Viking landing in North America.

They moved well out to sea and continuing southward across open water, they sighted land after two days. They went ashore on an island lying north of a cape projecting out from the mainland.[6] The island was a rich pasture land and it delighted them, and when they tasted the dew on the grass it seemed sweeter than anything that had ever touched their lips. They returned to the ship and sailed into a shallow bay on the mainland. The tide was out and the ship went aground, but they were so eager to see this land that they left her and rowed the ship's boat into a river flowing out of a lake. The area pleased them. The thick forest gave way in places to natural pastures with luxuriant grass for cattle. Nearby they found a species of wheat growing wild, and the lake and river teemed with salmon. Altogether it was

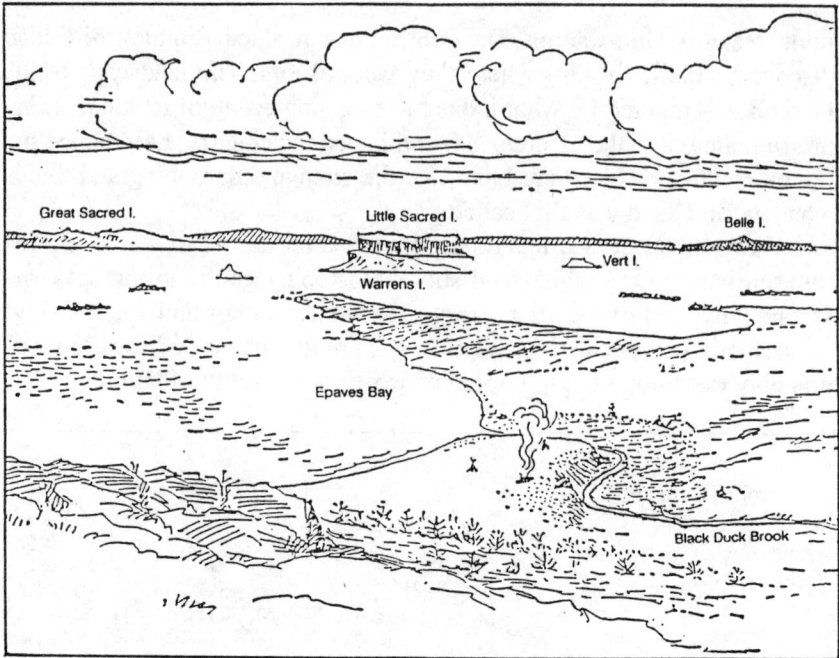

Figure 7. Panoramic sketch of the site of Vinland with the coast of Labrador in the background (after Jones: *The North Atlantic Saga*, 1964, pp. 120–1).

a pleasant place and it would provide ample food for man and beast. They decided to spend the winter here and when the tide rose, they brought the ship up the river and into the lake and began cutting timber to build shelters.

No frost came that winter, the grass on which the livestock fed hardly withered, and the river and lake continued to provide the men with fish. Leif divided his company in two and each day one group or the other explored the countryside, always returning before nightfall. They discovered grapes on one of these forays and Leif was pleased to make provision to carry grapes and vines as well as timber back to Greenland.

It is generally believed that the discovery of grapes led Leif to refer to the region of his discovery as Vinland (Land of Wine). The Norse word *vin* also means "grassy plain" and some historians have argued that the name Vinland should be translated Pasture Land. Leif may have reasoned it would be an attractive and useful name for the discovery. Extensive grass fields were an unusual sight for Norsemen; the name, conveying the thought of abundant rich pasturage in a mild climate, would be a powerful incentive for prospective settlers from Iceland and Greenland (although perhaps not as heady as the thought of grapes and the wine that could result). Later, back in Greenland, the camp where Leif spent the winter—the first Scandinavian

28

encampment in mainland North America—came to be called Leifsbudir (Leif's shelters).

Historians do not agree on the location of Leifsbudir and have postulated Leif's landfall in such widely separated areas as Cape Cod, the Bay of Fundy, Newfoundland and Labrador. The descriptions of Vinland in the Norse sagas point to the northern tip of Newfoundland as the most likely place for the encampment, and Great Sacred Island as the site of the initial landing. The northeastern seaboard enjoyed a temperate climate at the time and could have supported the growth of grapes and wild wheat.

In June 1961, the Norwegian-born navigator and explorer Helge Ingstad and his archaeologist wife, Anne Stine, began investigating a region between Pistolet Bay and Cape Bauld on the northeastern tip of Newfoundland, near the village of L'Anse aux Meadows where little Black Duck Brook meanders to its outlet into Épaves Bay. The Ingstads, searching for evidence of Norse habitation, were drawn to the location by the abundant meadow land; nowhere along the coast of Labrador had they found what they considered to be sufficient grazing land for the livestock a Viking

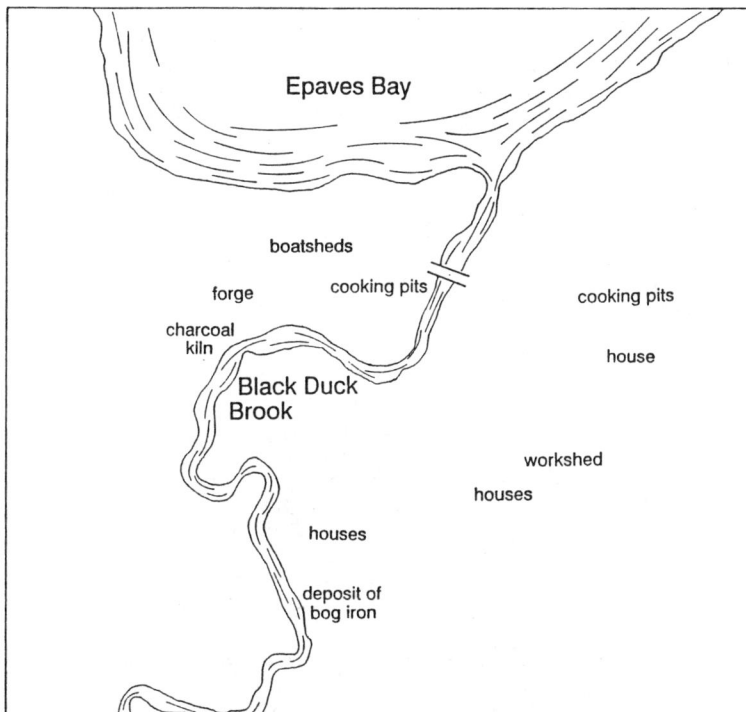

Figure 8. The Ingstad excavation site of Vinland (after Wahlgren: *The Vikings and America*. 1986, fig. 75, p. 123).

29

encampment would have to harbor over a winter. Another attraction lay in the presence of curious mounds found a mile south of the village, a feature that had intrigued its inhabitants for years. Were these humps the remnants of Leifsbudir? The Ingstads began excavating the site in 1962.

The work[7] has shown that the site was once occupied by people of Stone Age culture—probably Dorset Eskimo—but also, at another time, by people of European ancestry. The mounds are the ruins of their sod dwellings that included a work shed, a bath-house and boat sheds. The excavations also revealed a kiln for the production of charcoal, and a smithy used (judging by the charcoal, slag and metallic iron found in the vicinity) for extracting iron from local bog ore, a technique familiar to Norsemen and employed in Greenland. Carbon-14 analyses of various materials at the site are consistent with a date of about A.D. 1000 for these later artifacts and, therefore, compatible with the conclusion that the site is the remains of Leifsbudir.

The word Vinland is now generally used as a geographical term for a coastal region of northeastern North America, from Leifsbudir in New-

Figure 9. The 1579 map prepared by the Icelander, Sigurdar Stephanius, showing the region of the Viking travels in the North Atlantic Ocean.

foundland to the most southerly extent of Norse exploration in New England. The Vikings probably traveled many miles of coastline and lived in a number of locations during the Scandinavian episode in North America, and the tale of these adventures may have been conveniently condensed into a few dramatic stories. Some historians distinguish two Vinlands: Vinland I in northern Newfoundland including Leifsbudir and Straumsfjord (see below), and Vinland II in New England. There is no evidence that the Norsemen became familiar with the whole of the intervening territory.

Next summer (1003) Leif sailed for home, his ship loaded with timber and grapes. They were within sight of Greenland when Leif spied a ship with a cargo of timber, piled onto a reef and her crew standing nearby, stranded. Leif learned that the leader of the group was a man called Thorir. He took the men aboard his ship but he did not have space for the cargo and it remained on the reef. It is not known where Thorir cut the timber but likely, it was somewhere on the east coast of mainland North America and in that event, Leif may not have been the first Viking to land on the mainland.

Leif found lodgings for Thorir, his wife Gudrid and the crew. They fell sick in the winter and Thorir and most of his crew died. Gudrid, however, survived.

Leif prospered after the voyage and he became known as Leif the Lucky.

Thorvald explores the west side of Newfoundland

Leif and his men talked enthusiastically to their countrymen about their discovery of a bountiful land—a land that grew timber and grapes, and could support livestock. It caused much discussion in Greenland that winter. Leif's expedition had not ventured far afield from the original landfall and Greenlanders reasoned there was much more land to be explored. The prospect fascinated Thorvald, brother of Leif, and it induced him to make preparations to duplicate the voyage. Leif offered to lend Thorvald his ship but first he used her to collect the timber Thorir had left on the reef.

About 1004, Thorvald sailed with thirty men and wintered quietly in Leifsbudir, catching fish for food. In the spring, he sent a number of men in the ship's boat through the Strait of Belle Isle into the Gulf of St. Lawrence to explore the west coast of Newfoundland. They found it to be a beautiful and well-wooded land with the forest growing no great distance from the sea. They saw white sand beaches, quiet shoaling water and many islands.

The country seemed quite empty of human habitation but on one of the islands they found a wooden shelter that seemed to have been used for storing grain.[8] The discovery of this structure has been used as evidence to support a thesis by certain modern scholars, that the Scandinavians were preceded into the Gulf of St. Lawrence by other Europeans.

Thorvald spent a second winter in Leifsbudir and early in spring he took the ship and a part of the crew north to examine the Labrador coast. The keel of their ship was broken when a heavy sea drove them ashore off a cape along a stretch of sandy beaches, somewhere south of Hamilton Inlet. Thorvald had the men erect the broken keel on the headland and he named the headland Kjalarnes (Keelness).

They repaired the ship and continued northward and came to Hamilton Inlet marked by a forested headland jutting out into the sea. Thorvald turned into the opening and took the ship in to the vicinity of Lake Melville. The Norsemen went ashore to examine the country and Thorvald was so pleased with the region, he said he wanted to make his home here. In the course of wandering about, they came upon nine native Americans—the first people they had seen in this country—asleep under their boats. They promptly killed all except one who managed to escape.

The Norsemen had a good look around and saw in the distance, various mounds which they took to be human habitations. Then, back at their ship, they lay down to sleep after their exertions. They were wakened by the shout of one of their men, warning them that the lake was covered with countless natives in skinboats coming, without doubt, to revenge the killing of their companions. The natives attacked the Europeans and Thorvald was fatally wounded by an arrow before they withdrew. He thought the natives would soon renew the attack and he instructed his men to speed preparations for a return to Leifsbudir. He knew he was about to die from his wound and he asked to be carried to the forested headland which he had admired. It would become his home sooner than expected for this is where he wanted to be buried.

His men did everything Thorvald asked of them and then returned to Leifsbudir where the remainder of the crew waited. They used the winter to gather grapes and vines, and cut timber, and in the spring they loaded the ship and sailed back to Greenland.

Thorsteinn, brother of Thorvald and a Christian, felt he had to retrieve Thorvald's body and give it a proper burial in consecrated ground. He sailed from Greenland with his wife and twenty-five men, in search of the Kjalarnes headland but the weather was not kind. The ship was blown back and forth and finally back to Greenland without ever reaching the Labrador coast. Apparently Thorsteinn's voyage was one of many undertaken by Scandinavians to the new world. The rich forests and pastures of Vinland lured them to make the voyage that became familiar although probably not routine, with the ships of the day.

Thorfinn Karlsefni's Straumfjord settlement

In the spring of 1011 or 1012, Thorfinn Karlsefni, a well-to-do Icelandic trader, and his partner Snorri Thorbrandsson, arrived at Eiriksfjord in Greenland and began buying and selling. Thorfinn lodged the winter with Leif Eiriksson. Gudrid, the widow of Thorir whom Leif had rescued from a reef, had remarried and after she had been widowed a second time, Leif took her to live in his household. She was a beautiful, clever woman with an attractive personality and Thorfinn was immediately drawn to her. Shortly after the Yule he proposed marriage. Gudrid was willing but she left the decision to Leif. Leif had heard nothing but good about Thorfinn; he thought it would be a good match and the couple was married that winter.

The rich fields and abundant forests of the new world continued to attract the Scandinavians and merchants sponsored voyages to bring back cargoes of timber which earned handsome profits. As yet there had been no attempts to establish a permanent settlement in Vinland. Influential Green-landers now approached Thorfinn and Snorri to outfit a ship and lead an expedition to Vinland the Good, as it had come to be called, to found a colony there. Urged on by Thorfinn's lovely wife, Gudrid, the two men were readily persuaded and they assembled a company of about sixty men and five women. The group included Gudrid, Erik the Red's daughter Freydis and her husband, and Erik's son-in-law Thorvald.

Two other Icelanders, Bjarni Grimolfsson and Thorhall Gamlason, decided to accompany the expedition in their ship, manned by a crew of forty. Finally, Thorhall the Hunter, who had been on the Thorvald voyage to the new world, joined the expedition with a third ship.

The convoy of three ships sailed in the spring of 1012 or 1013, carrying about 160 men, and a variety of livestock including cows and one bull, ewes and a ram, and perhaps pigs and goats. Thorfinn followed the route used by Leif and his brother Thorvald, sailing up Greenland's west coast, across Davis Strait to Baffin Island and then southward to mainland North Amer-ica. In doing so, he conformed to a Norse practice of avoiding long ocean passages, hugging the coastline where he could be guided by established landmarks. In the absence of scientific navigational aids, it was a more certain way of reaching a chosen destination. A north wind carried them south from Baffin Island and after two days they sighted mainland North America in a forested part of Labrador—presumably Leif's Markland. They beat past a shoreline of long sand beaches and on a headland they found the keel of a boat; they thought this must be Thorvald's Kjalarnes. They continued southward and on a coastline indented with bays, they moored the ships—probably in Sandwich Bay.

The sagas tell that Thorfinn had two Scots with him, a man and a woman, who were noted for being fleet of foot. He put them ashore, instructing them to spy out the land to the south during the next three days. When they returned to the ships, one had a bunch of grapes and the other some wild wheat to show him. Thorfinn concluded this was a choice productive country and he ordered the ships to continue down the coast. The tale of the two Scots suggests a Labrador that was too bountiful to be real.

They came next to a coastline that was indented with fjords. Thorfinn halted the ships at a broad opening (which he took to be the entrance to a large fjord) with an island at its mouth. They went ashore on the island and found it was so crowded with nesting birds it was difficult to avoid treading on their eggs. They called the "fjord" Straumfjord and the island Straumey. The description of the two features is consistent with the Strait of Belle Isle (the northern entrance to the Gulf of St. Lawrence), and Belle Isle or perhaps Great Sacred Island[9] at its entrance. Still, the location of Straumfjord is a matter of dispute; places as far south as the Hudson River have been postulated but it seems unlikely that Vikings, familiar with fjords, would have applied the word "fjord" to any part of the coastline of North America south of Newfoundland.

The Norsemen took the ships into the opening and went ashore on its south side where they saw abundant pasture for their livestock. The region seemed to be a good place to spend the winter and establish the settlement, and so they carried their goods ashore. If the "fjord" was the Strait of Belle Isle, they had landed on the northern tip of Newfoundland, near or at the site of Leif's encampment.

That first autumn Thorfinn's wife, Gudrid, gave birth to a son—the first known birth in mainland North America of a child of European parents. They named him Snorri.

The settlers made little provision for the winter. The country was bountiful, and recalling perhaps that the Leif and Thorvald expeditions had experienced no food shortages in winter, they did not trouble to accumulate a store of provisions either for themselves or their livestock. As the season advanced it brought winter storms, the seas were too rough for the rowboats and the fishing suffered. The hunters found it impossible to kill enough game to feed the 160 people and for a time, the company had a difficult winter. They rejoiced when a dead whale floated in to shore. The cooks butchered and boiled it but they all fell sick from eating the meat and they threw what they had not eaten into the sea. Then, suddenly, the weather improved so that they could get out onto the sea and fish, and from that time there was enough food to take the edge off their hunger.

In the spring the provisioners went up the channel and found good hunting on land and fishing in the sea, and they were able to gather eggs in the breeding grounds of the birds. Food was no longer a source of worry and the company set about executing the plans they had made during the winter.

Thorhall the Hunter, and nine companions had decided to examine the coast that lay to the north of the camp, thinking the expedition might have passed by Leif the Lucky's camp while coursing south the previous year. It was an unfortunate decision for storms blew them eastward across the Atlantic and they were shipwrecked off Ireland. It was reported that they were beaten and enslaved, and that Thorhall lost his life there.

The Hop settlement

Thorfinn chose to explore in a southern direction. The saga tells that Thorfinn and Snorri journeyed "a long time" and reached a river flowing into a lake and hence to the sea. The river was navigable by ship only at full tide. They found wild wheat growing in the fields, pasture land for their cattle and grape vines where the land was hilly. The river teemed with fish that could be trapped by blocking their escape channels when the tide went out. They called the place Hop (Landlock Bay).

The story of this expedition, as told in *Eirik the Red's Saga*, gives conflicting accounts of the length of the adventure, and who and how many people accompanied Thorfinn. The saga relates[10] that

> It is in some men's reports that Bjarni and Freydis had remained behind there [at Straumfjord], and a hundred men with them...while Karlsefni and Snorri had traveled south with forty men, yet spent no longer...than a bare two months, and got back again that same summer.[11]

Elsewhere in the saga we are told that Thorfinn, Snorri and Bjarni went south with all "the rest of their company [that had not accompanied Thorhall the Hunter]" and that they "built themselves dwellings...[and] spent the winter there." According to this account, Eskimos arrived at the Hop camp in their skinboats one morning in the fall of that year. After some hesitation they came ashore—small men with broad faces and big eyes, and "ugly" hair on their heads—to look long and hard at the Norsemen and their activities before returning to the sea and moving off to the south. They came back in the spring with rich furs which they bartered for red cloth that they tied round their heads. They also wanted spears and swords but Thorfinn and Snorri forbade the sale of arms to the natives. It was the first recorded instance of fur trading between North American natives and Europeans. The trading was interrupted when the settlers' bull ran out of the forest bellowing loudly; the Eskimos were frightened, ran to their boats and paddled off to the south.

The Eskimos returned in great numbers three weeks later, clearly bent on fighting. Yelling loudly, they beached their craft and attacked, firing stone missiles from their war-slings. The Norsemen fled before the onslaught and when Freydis, the daughter of Erik the Red, saw this, she taunted her countrymen. She picked up the sword of a fallen Norseman, dead with a flat stone sticking out of his head and as the Eskimos rushed toward her, she bared her breasts and slapped them with the sword. The sight frightened the Eskimos. They gave up the chase, ran to their skinboats and paddled off in haste. Two of Thorfinn's men and a number of Eskimos were killed in the encounter.

On the way back to Straumfjord, the Norsemen came on five Eskimos asleep near the sea. They felt sure these men were a scouting party for the main body of Eskimos and therefore a threat—and so they killed them.

Where was Hop? The description of Hop with its river navigable only at high tide and teeming with easily-trapped salmon, of wheat and grapes growing wild, and abundant pastures for cattle is remarkably similar to the description of Leifsbudir. If Hop and Leifsbudir were one and the same, Thorfinn and Snorri must have journeyed south from a headquarters on the Labrador coast, and in that event the Straumfjord base camp was in Labrador.

According to Jones[12], Eskimo occupation along the east coast, in the year 1000, reached as far south as White Bay in northern Newfoundland; Algonquin Indians were dominant south of this prominent feature. If we accept Jones' limits for Eskimo and Indian habitation along the coast, the presence of Eskimos at Hop points to White Bay in northern Newfoundland as possibly the most southerly site of Hop. The exact locations of Straumfjord and Hop, and whether one of these encampments was identical with Leifsbudir, remain subjects for conjecture.

Retreat from North America

The experience of living at Straumfjord led the colonists to the conclusion that although this was a bountiful land and a desirable place to settle, it was a land where they would live with fear. In this world they would be constantly under threat from a hostile native population. The Norsemen had better weaponry and they were superior in physical size and therefore, they would have an advantage in hand to hand fighting. But they would always be outnumbered.

The Norsemen may have realized, too, that they would not be able to enjoy an acceptable standard of living without ongoing assistance from their Scandinavian base in Europe. Voyages of a year's duration from Iceland and Greenland to cut timber were profitable, but the likelihood that a permanent colony in this part of the world would become self-sufficient, much less profitable, was remote. European merchants would not finance indefinitely a settlement in North America unless there was a near-term prospect for earning a return on the investment.

In the face of these realities the Greenlanders decided to abandon the colony. No doubt the resolve was influenced by a new attitude among Scandinavian people. The drive to conquer and inhabit new countries had run its course; the westward thrust that had followed the Viking raids had lost its force.

Thorfinn could not leave Straumfjord without searching for Thorhall the Hunter, and his companions. Thorhall had been with Erik the Red for a long time—as a hunter in summer and a bailiff in winter—and Thorfinn was reluctant to return to Greenland without him. Accompanied by Thorvald, he set off with one ship and sailed up the coast. After they had been voyaging for some time, they entered Hamilton Inlet and dropped anchor. There, while they sat and ruminated about what a fine country this was, Thorvald was hit in the belly by an arrow shot by a lone native. The Norsemen gave chase but they could not catch the man. Thorvald pulled out the arrow saying, "There is fat round my belly."[13] He soon died of the wound.

Karlsefni found no trace of Thorhall who had been blown to Ireland and wrecked in the previous year. There would be only two ships—Karlsefni's and Grimolffson's—to carry the colonists and cargo back to Greenland. Karlsefni took the ship back to Straumfjord, intending to spend a third and last winter at the settlement.

It was not a happy winter for the settlers. The long absence from a normal social life began to tell and there was much unrest aggravated by the scarcity of women; it caused bitter quarreling between the married and unmarried men.

In the spring of 1016, they loaded the two ships with vines, grapes, wood and furs, and sailed north along the coast of Labrador. They made a pause at Markland and here Karlsefni's men surprised a group of natives—a grown man with a beard, two women and two young boys. The Norsemen captured the children and carried them off.

On the homeward voyage, Bjarni Grimolfsson encountered severe weather in the Labrador Sea and his ship and the small boat he was towing were carried southeastward toward Ireland. The sagas have it that the ship was worm-eaten and began to sink and it was decided to transfer to the towboat. She would hold only half their number and Bjarni proposed they draw lots for the places in her. As fate would have it, Bjarni was one of the fortunates but when he had transferred to the towboat, a young Icelander called out, begging him to change places with him.

"So be it," said Bjarni, "for I see you are greedy for life, and think it a hard thing to die."

They changed places and Bjarni perished in the worm-eaten ship with half the crew. The men in the towboat reached Ireland where they afterwards told the story.

Karlsefni, his wife and son Snorri, now three years old, and the two captured native boys successfully reached their home port in the other ship.

This ended the Norse attempt to colonize Newfoundland. Voyages to Vinland, but more particularly to Markland, in search of saleable cargo with the expectation of returning within a year, continued and even increased for a time. Eventually they became less frequent. Ships from Greenland, Iceland and Ireland only occasionally touched the shores of Newfoundland, sometimes by accident, sometimes for the purpose of loading wood and fruit, sometimes merely for replenishing water and food, and for repairs. The Scandinavians had made no lasting impression on North America or its natives, and as the voyages lessened in number, the imprint of their brief presence began to fade. The last known voyage occurred toward the middle of the fourteenth century but ships probably continued to reach North American shores, perhaps even to the time of Columbus.

The case for an Irish pre-Scandinavian colony in North America

Thorfinn Karlsefni moved to Iceland two years after he returned to Greenland from Straumfjord taking with him the two Eskimo boys he had captured in Labrador. The boys, now baptized in the Christian faith and living in his household, were learning to speak his language. When they could converse with the Norwegians, they related that

> A country lay on the other side [the south side of the Gulf of St. Lawrence]...opposite their own land, where men walked about in white clothes and whooped loudly, and carried poles and went about with flags.[14]

The Norse concluded that this "country" must be Hvitramannaland (which was called the "Country of the White Men" by some and "Ireland the Great" by others).[15] The reference has been used as evidence to propound the existence of a colony of Irish Christians, founded before the coming of Leif the Lucky, its members practicing their religious rites on the south side of the Gulf of St. Lawrence. Were these people the remnants of the Irish monks and hermits that had fled their homeland about 800 to escape the raiding Vikings, choosing to live in isolation on the east coast of Iceland? And when Norwegian settlers began streaming into that country a century later, had they assembled a fleet and fled again, their destination probably Greenland, a land west of Iceland their fishermen could hardly have escaped seeing from out at sea? The Canadian historian and archivist, Gustave Lanctot, has postulated that the weather did not favor the fleeing Irish and that:

> north winds and fogs drove the convoy off course for days and days.... The wanderers were borne overseas past Greenland's southernmost tip to the coast of Labrador where the imperious current carried them into the Strait of Belle Isle.
>
> They entered the Gulf of St. Lawrence and set foot on a small island.[16]

Lanctot speculated that the island may have been Brion Island (near the Magdalenes) where, several hundred years later, Jacques Cartier found wild wheat growing. It would offer an explanation for Thorvold's discovery "on an island in the west...[of] a wooden grain-holder"[17] when he explored the west coast of Newfoundland in 1005. Lanctot believes the facility was built by the Irish to store wild wheat harvested on the island.

Lanctot has concluded that the monks found they were too crowded on the island—that they set forth again and came ashore next on Cape Breton Island. The climate pleased them, the gulf had fish for the taking, there was fertile land for planting the seeds they had brought from Iceland and the local Indians (the Micmacs) seem disposed to allow them to live peacefully in their midst. They stayed, the first Europeans to settle in mainland North America. The probable time of the landings was about 900.

The remnants of the wooden grain-storage building found by Thorvald is only one of a number of reasons advanced by Lanctot, as evidence that the Irish reached Canada ahead of the Vikings. Icelandic sagas relate that an Icelander, Ari Masson, was driven off course and

> drifted to White Men's Land, which some people call Greater Ireland. It lies in the ocean to westward, near Vinland the Good, said to be a six day sail west from Ireland. Ari couldn't get away, and was baptized there. This story was first told by Hrafn

Limerick-Farer who spent a long time at Limerick in Ireland. Thorkel Gellison quoted some Icelanders who had heard Earl Thorfinn of Orkney say that Ari had been recognized in White Men's Land, and couldn't get away from there.[18]

Was the White Men's Land "which some people call[ed] Greater Ireland" an Irish settlement near Newfoundland, in the Gulf of St. Lawrence? Did Irish monks baptize Ari? Does the mention that Ari "had been recognized in White Men's Land" imply that seamen from Ireland and Iceland occasionally called at the colony and that it was still in existence early in the eleventh century, more than 125 years after its inception?

Births in the lay part of the largely clerical (and celibate) colony would not have been enough to prevent its population from declining. Refugees from Ireland might have sought shelter there and bolstered the numbers for a time. The distances were too great and the conditions too harsh to sustain the group indefinitely and eventually its numbers would have dwindled. The remnants of the colony, if there ever was one, may have been absorbed into the Micmac community.

Greenland abandoned

The Greenland colonies were not only among the most northerly outposts of European civilization, they were also for a time, the most remote attempt to carry on a Scandinavian way of life. The founding of the settlements was aided by a benign climatic phase in the north Atlantic region; the ninth through twelfth centuries were comparatively mild and much more favorable for colonization than they are at present. There is, for example, no mention in the Norse sagas, that voyagers to Greenland and Vinland were troubled by drift ice—a menace to sea travel in later centuries that would have made passage west from Iceland more hazardous and less frequent.

The conditions for the existence of the Scandinavian community were marginal; it could continue only if circumstances did not worsen. Unfortunately, western Europe became stormy after 1200; the climate grew progressively and decidedly colder for a period of two centuries and early in the fifteenth century, Europe was in the grip of the Little Ice Age. The change of climate was fatal for the Greenland colonies. The temperature of the sea fell and there was an immense increase in the ice which drifts down the east coast of Greenland and swings northwest around Cape Farewell. It choked the fjords, enclosing and isolating the settlements of the west coast. The glaciers advanced and as the ground became colder, the treeline grew lower and the harvests were diminished. The seals followed the ice south along Greenland's west coast and the Eskimos followed the seals.

The Eskimo was wonderfully adapted to the long winter. Mobile and able to shelter himself wherever it was necessary, he used the seal to feed and clothe himself. Seal meat had become a supplement of the Norseman's diet but in the main, he depended on his fields to raise livestock and foodstuff for himself. He found himself ill-equipped to survive when his European-style resources failed—when the quality of his farm land was reduced by the worsening climate—and he may have come into physical conflict with the Eskimo. The most northerly settlement—the so-called Western Settlement—at latitude 65°N on the west coast, steadily lost settlers as the farms became less productive.

Greenlanders experienced other problems. They had established a commerce with Norway, bartering what their rigorous environment could provide—fish and other sea animals, hides, furs, walrus tusks—for the manufactured goods only an advanced civilization could provide. Unfortunately, the products they could export were available more cheaply in Europe. Greenland was made a Norwegian possession in the thirteenth century and trade between the two countries became a state monopoly; royal consent was needed to buy and sell in Greenland and this was followed with a tax levied on all business done with Greenland. As a result, the voyages to Greenland became less profitable and they became fewer in number; eventually there was only one ship visit a year. Even worse, in the fourteenth century there were years when no ship arrived and Scandinavian goods became scarce. The last of these "official" ships returned to Norway in 1410.

The English continued to visit Greenland:

> We may conclude that an occasional ship was storm-driven to Greenland...and that resolute and high-handed English skippers in the fifteenth century sailed into Greenland waters for fish and sea-beasts, for honest trade where it offered, and for plunder where it lay to hand.[19]

The growing neglect of Greenland by Norway was not helped by the Black Death—the plague that ravaged Europe between 1347 and 1351. The population of western Europe did not regain the pre-1347 level until the beginning of the sixteenth century.

The result of all this was inevitable—for most practical purposes, Greenland was abandoned by the Norwegian government before the middle of the fourteenth century. Still, colonists lived on in Erik the Red's original settlement on the southwest coast, perhaps into the early years of the sixteenth century. Finally the settlement ceased to exist, extinguished by an increasing isolation from an indifferent world. The country returned to its original wild state.

The cod-banks off Iceland helped that country survive—Greenland had no such resource. The English had begun fishing the Icelandic banks in 1408–9[20] and their numbers had grown with the years. According to Jones:

> There was a swarming of English ships in Icelandic waters in the fifteenth century, a hundred a year from Bristol and other ports.... Their skippers and crews were hard men plying a hard trade in a hard age; they included among their number adventurers and (some) rascals, and abduction, robbery, ill-treatment, and murder were among the islanders' occasional hazards. If anything, matters grew worse when the Scots and Germans came seeking their cut of northern profit.... [Nevertheless] English trade with Iceland was indispensable to the Icelanders and helped them through a very bad time.[21]

A brisk trade, based in large part on the fish catch, developed between Iceland and the Azore Islands, Lisbon, Bristol and other ports in the British Isles. The trade assured that knowledge of the Scandinavian experience in North America and Greenland was not lost to the world. In Iceland it was kept alive by tales passed from one generation to the next and by a few historians who had collected and recorded the stories in the years between 1100 and 1250. When seamen from other nations visited the island, the stories enjoyed a wider audience and were carried to home ports in England, Portugal, France, Spain and other countries in Europe. It is not improbable that the more venturesome fishermen from these countries investigated the stories and discovered, and began frequenting, the cod banks off Newfoundland in the fifteenth century, before the first Cabot voyage. It is likely, when one takes into account the uneven quality of navigation and the prevalence of storms in the North Atlantic, that there were chance encounters with Greenland and North America, and that landings were made to obtain food, gather firewood and fill water casks. There are no records of such encounters.

Part Two

The Rediscovery of North America

Scandinavians had been drawn to America by the lure of rich pasture and farm land, and stands of tall timber. Four hundred years later, European thought again turned to other continents, but now the attraction was trade and it led to remarkable discoveries. The Portuguese initiated this second age of discovery early in the fifteenth century, beginning a program of exploring systematically southward, down the west coast of Africa which lay conveniently at hand. Other Europeans were after a bigger prize; they yearned to trade with Asian countries such as India, the Spice Islands and China. At this time there was no ocean route from Europe into the Pacific Ocean. Virtually all merchandise bound for Europe from Asia passed overland through the Muslim countries of the Middle East and their people were hostile to anything that threatened their role as middlemen in the trade between East and West. The solution evidently lay in finding a new and independent sea route to the Far East.

The Far East—particularly the southeastern flank of Asia, from China to India with its attendant islands (the Malay Archipelago)—and Africa were a source of exotic goods that began reaching the eastern shores of the Mediterranean long before the birth of Christ.[1] From Africa came ivory; negro slaves; gold, copper, tin, lead and iron; precious stones; frankincense and myrrh; animals such as bears and infant elephants for royal zoos, and oxen; hides; olive oil, wine and honey; various kinds of wood; ostrich feathers and eggs; panther skins and giraffe tails. From Asia came silk and calico; purple dye and indigo; rubies, lapis lazuli, diamonds and pearls; slaves; musk and perfume; ebony, sandalwood, teak and Indian cabinets; gold, silver, copper, iron, and cinnabar; dates, wine, and spices such as pepper, nutmeg, cinnamon, cloves and ginger.

Most of the items were luxury goods but spices were considered essential. They were in common use both because it was the fashion to eat highly spiced food and in a world lacking refrigeration, spices disguised the taste of tainted food.

3

Trade Routes Between East and West before the Voyages of Columbus and Cabot

From very early times, three waterways figured prominently in the transportation of goods from Africa and Asia to the eastern shores of the Mediterranean: the Persian Gulf in Asia, the Nile River in Africa, and the Red Sea between Africa and Asia.

European-bound shipping from China and the Spice Islands passed through the Strait of Malacca to the west coast of India where cargo was transferred to ships plying the Arabian Sea. Westward from India, ships followed the coast into the Persian Gulf or continued westward, into the Red Sea.

From early times the geographical position of the valley at the head of the Persian Gulf dictated that it should be an important crossroads for trade.

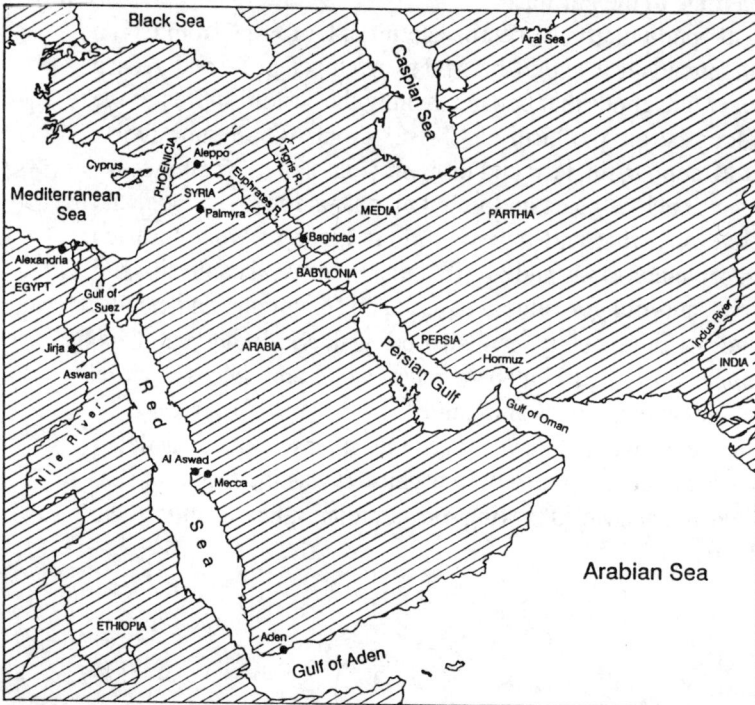

Figure 10. The Middle East of pre-Biblical times.

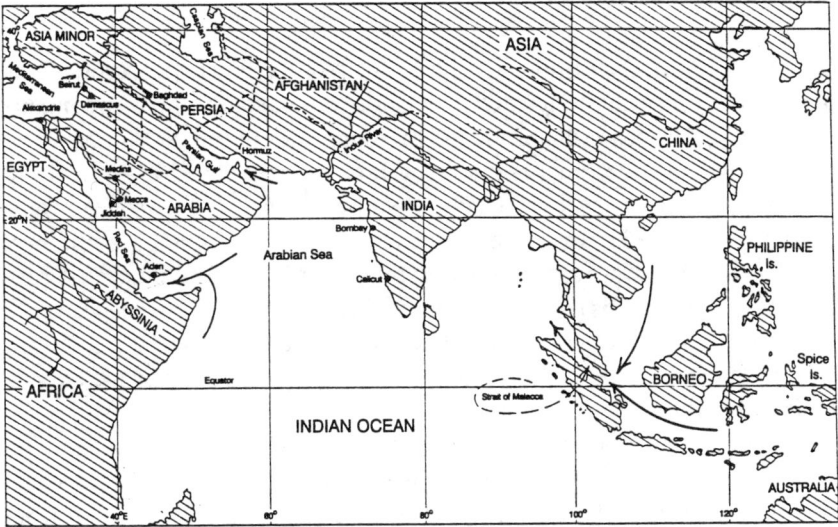

Figure 11. The principal sea and land routes from the Far East to Europe before Vasco da Gamas's voyage to India in 1497–8.

Here, in a fertile plain at the center of the known world, the ancient trade routes along the Euphrates and Tigris river valleys converged and caravan routes led to India, China and central Asia—to the Caspian Sea and central Russia—to Ephesus on the Aegean Sea—to Aleppo, Damascus and Seleucia (modern Antioch, Turkey) in Syria; Petra in Jordan; and other towns at and near the shores of the Mediterranean Sea—and to southern Arabia.

The Nile River, from its source east of Lake Tanganyika to its delta at the Mediterranean Sea, is more than 4000 miles (6400 km.) long. It played an important role throughout history as the main artery of Egypt, linking all parts of the country. In ancient times camel caravans from inner Africa reached the Nile near Jirja, where merchandise was loaded onto ships for the journey to the Mediterranean.

The Nile's basin is the dominant feature of northeastern Africa. The historian Herodotus observed that "Egypt was a land given to the Egyptians by the Nile."[1] He was referring to the annual flooding of the river which eroded soil and deposited it downstream and formed Egypt's cultivatable land. Its rich produce was in demand to feed people beyond Egypt. Beginning about 2000 B.C., successive rulers in the Middle East began designing changes to shipping routes to improve the delivery of the Nile valley produce to other parts of the Middle East.

The Red Sea is a slender ribbon of water strategically situated between Africa and Asia with an outlet into the Mediterranean Sea. Its Arabian (or eastern) shoreline is marked by a strip of low plains backed by ranges of barren hills which are interspersed with mountains that rise to a height of

45

6000 feet (1800 m.) and more. On the African (or western) side, desert plains in the north give way to elevated tablelands further south, and to mountains in Ethiopia. The sea is characterized by rough waters and an abundance of coral reefs and waterless deserts along both sides of its 1200-mile (1950 km.) length.[2] Al Aswad, twelve miles (twenty km.) south of the seventeenth-century port of Jidda, was one of the few ports on its inhospitable coastlines.

The Red Sea was important in Egyptian maritime commerce from very early times. Egyptians used it to reach the Arabian Sea in the twenty-seventh century B.C. and voyage southward down the coast of Africa and eastward alongside the southern coast of Arabia. They may have reached the Persian Gulf at this time.[3]

The Pharaoh Sesostris I (1971–1928 B.C.) had a freshwater canal dug from the Nile to the position of modern Suez on the Gulf of Suez. The canal was neglected and allowed to fall into disrepair. Necho II, pharaoh from 610 to 595 B.C., began its restoration, planning to enlarge it to enable ocean-going ships to reach the rich natural resources of the Nile valley. The distance from the river to the Sea was 1000 furlongs (125 mi. or 200 km.) but on account of the crookedness of the canal's course, its length was much greater. Necho gave up the project when an oracle told him foreigners would be the chief beneficiaries of the canal. According to Herodotus[4], 120,000 Egyptians lost their lives while working in the excavation.

The Persians began a campaign, in Necho's time, that in a mere twenty-five years won them an empire stretching from the Indus River in the east, to the Aral Sea in the north, to the Aegean and Mediterranean Seas in the west; it included Egypt. Darius I, king of the Persians between 522 and 486 B.C., repaired and completed Necho's canal; it was 150 feet (45 m.) wide and deep enough for merchant vessels.

The Persian Empire lasted a mere 150 years, overthrown by the Macedonian, Alexander the Great. Alexander intended to improve sea communications between Babylon, the capital of his empire, and the Red Sea and Darius' canal figured prominently in these plans. He died unexpectedly in 323 B.C. in the midst of these activities and the canal was allowed to fall into disrepair. About 250 B.C., Ptolemy II of Egypt had it reopened and he built a port near modern Suez to service it.

Mariners continued to hug the southern coastline of Asia, fearing the open sea. But sometime in the first century B.C., they came to understand the pattern of monsoons in the region and a direct sea route was developed across the Arabian Sea between the Gulf of Aden (the entrance to the Red Sea) and India. It increased the traffic; late in the century there were roughly 120 sailings annually from the Red Sea to India.

The rise of Islam

Mohammed, founder of Islam, was born in Mecca in A.D. 570. Few men have had as profound and enduring effect on mankind; his influence was religious, historical, political and social. Within eighty years of his death, the movement he started had taken control of a region that extended from India in the east to Spain in the west, and founded a new civilization. Today the faith and doctrine he handed down are observed by about a billion followers.

The tribal structure of Arab society was not much changed by the advent of Mohammed and the spread of his teachings. The restraints inherent in a central authority were contrary to the Arab way of life and were accepted only reluctantly. Despite this, Mohammed did succeed in persuading the majority of the tribes to accept a nominal adherence to Islam and to pay a tax. But at his death in 632 A.D., many tribes relinquished the faith, refused to pay the tax and renewed their independence. A number of rival prophets appeared and dissident tribes rose in revolt.

Abu Bakr (632–4), the first caliph, used much of his reign to wage war against these tribes and other tribes that had not accepted Mohammed, and he had considerable success in uniting Arabs as followers of the new faith. The spread of Islam had no effect on the warlike nature of the tribes, and Abu Bakr cast about for some activity to replace their habitual intertribal fighting. He decided to direct this energy against Arabia's neighbors. He chose Syria as his first target and in 634, he launched forces against its southern flank. He died before the campaign was completed.

Abu Bakr's warring adventures were continued by his successor, Omar I (634–44). He wrested Syria and Egypt from the Byzantine empire and destroyed what was left of the Persian empire. His forces reached India in 643, the year before he died.

The canal between the Nile and Red Sea had been abandoned again. Now, in the seventh century A.D., the Arab commander in Egypt, Amr ibn al-As, had it restored to make it possible for ships to load grain in the Nile valley and cross the Red Sea to Arabia. In 761–2, the caliph al-Mansur had the canal blocked in order to deny grain to Mecca where his uncle was in rebellion against him; it was never reopened despite the attempts of two caliphs in the years between 1135 and 1138.

The caliphs that followed Abu Bakr extended the Arab dominions until they stretched from the Indus River in the east to Morocco in the west. They gained control of Spain in 712 but lost it in 756.

From very early times, the countries ringing the eastern shores of the Mediterranean had been the link between Europe and Asia; the commerce and culture of two worlds had passed more or less freely through these countries. When the Arabs reached the Mediterranean, its shores became a frontier across which a militant force—the new Islamic faith—confronted Europe. The Red Sea and the Persian Gulf routes were no longer independent, competing for the shipment of goods between the Far East and Europe; both were in the hands of the Muslims and they used them for their own advantage to control the traffic and commerce between Europe and Asia.

As the Middle Eastern powers that controlled these water passages grew more combative in their efforts to exclude western traders, Europeans cast about for other ways to reach the sources of Oriental goods.

1488: Dias finds a sea route into the Indian Ocean

The region occupied by present-day Portugal endured centuries of strife—with the Muslims who invaded the region in 711; with the Holy See; and with Castile and León (which comprised most of modern Spain). The fighting subsided after Portugal's king, John I, arranged a truce with Castile in 1387; it was renewed at intervals until a peace was concluded in 1411.

The habits of war were not easily forgotten. To consume the energies of his more belligerent border men, John led a force, including his three sons, in a successful attack outside the limits of the Iberian Peninsula—against the port of Cueta in Africa, one of the "Pillars of Hercules" of Greek mythology. The location of Cueta, opposite Gibraltar, gave Portugal a military and trade presence in Africa at the gateway between the Mediterranean Sea and Atlantic Europe. Ceuta was noteworthy as the northern terminus of a caravan route over which moved gold, ivory and slaves for trade with the merchant ships that called there.

Henry, third son of John I, had distinguished himself in the fighting at Cueta; it earned him a knighthood on the field of battle and it may have been the spark that ignited a latent ambition to improve Portugal's stature as a world power. That ambition took several forms foremost among which was expansion into Africa.

The exploitation of Africa would come by sea. Situated on the southwest edge of Europe's seaboard, Portugal is positioned within easy reach of the west side of Africa—a vast coastline largely ignored by European traders. Flanked on two sides by the Atlantic Ocean which can be seen from every Portuguese summit, Portugal is by nature a maritime nation. Cape Roca, near the mouth of the Tagus River, is the most westerly point of mainland Europe where, as the poet Camões put it, "the land ends and the sea begins." Portuguese merchants and fishermen regularly sailed into the

North Atlantic—to England, Ireland, Iceland and possibly Greenland.

In 1420 Henry became Master of the century-old Order of Christ and he used its resources to equip a number of expeditions that thrust west into the Atlantic Ocean and south along the coast of Africa. A long-term objective of these probes lay in developing a route to the underside of Africa's bulge into the Atlantic. Here, inland, in the region of the headwaters of the Niger and Senegal Rivers, alluvial gold was mined and carried to the Gold Coast (modern Ghana) for shipment across the desert to the Mediterranean Sea. Already in the seventh century, a pattern of trade routes crossed the Sahara desert. Ghana was the center where gold from the western Sudan and salt from the Sahara desert were exchanged for exports from North Africa and kola nuts and slaves from tropical West Africa. The Portuguese strategy was to reach Ghana and divert this trade to Portugal by sea.

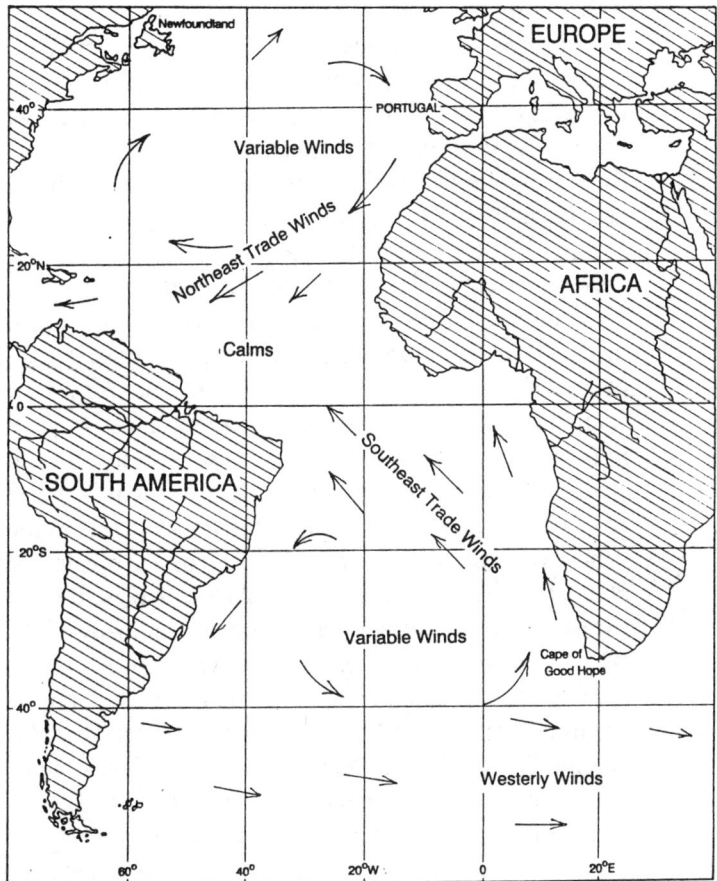

Figure 12. Prevailing winds in the Atlantic Ocean. The Portuguese used the trade winds and the width of the ocean to explore the coast of Africa and develop a route to the Cape of Good Hope and back to Portugal. (after Bartholomew: *The Comparative Atlas*, Meiklejohn & Holden, London, p. 7).

In the beginning, exploration of the west coast of Africa was hindered by ignorance of the pattern of prevailing winds. Above the equator, the trade winds favored sailing down the coast but tacking against these winds on the return voyage alongside the coast was so time-consuming as to be impractical. In time the Portuguese discovered that the winds of the Atlantic Ocean, north of the equator, execute a clockwise motion. Ships could catch favorable northeast winds for the voyage back to Portugal by moving well out to sea. It was one of the more important navigational discoveries of the time for it literally made the African voyages possible. And it forced Portugal to take a proprietary interest in the Atlantic Ocean to guarantee her mariners the freedom of the sea to sail their ships where the winds dictated.

In 1427, Henry's seamen came onto the Azores. These islands were well out into the Atlantic—almost a third of the way across the ocean at this latitude—and, like the Madeiras which they had reconnoitered in 1418, they were uninhabited.

Perhaps Henry's most significant achievement followed from the realization that he could improve the expertise of his seamen by promoting the use of scientific (as opposed to intuitive) navigation techniques. Some time after 1438, to further this concept, he built the Vila do Infante near Sagres (on Portugal's southwestern tip) and brought together skilled geographers and navigators. One of the tasks of the group was to teach Portuguese seamen to use the stars to navigate more efficiently and confidently, so that they need not fear losing sight of the land as they penetrated the unknown. The southern thrust of Portuguese expeditions presented an additional problem; as they approached the equator, Polaris (the North Star) barely cleared the horizon, seriously impairing its use as a navigational aid for finding latitude and the direction of north. It was imperative to discover stars in the southern skies that would be useful below the equator.

In the course of studying historical records, the Sagres group rediscovered some of the wisdom of the ancients lost to the world through the years. They came onto an account recorded by Herodotus in his History[5] about 450 B.C. of a project undertaken by Necho II of Egypt to discover the extent of Africa. Necho commissioned a company of Phoenicians about 600 B.C., to sail south through the Red Sea and down the coast of Africa with the object of circumnavigating the continent and returning to Egypt by way of Gibraltar and the Mediterranean Sea. Three years later, the Phoenicians entered the Mediterranean from the west and returned to Egypt.

Popular belief in Henry's time held that Africa was part of an Antarctic continent. The ancient account, if true, indicated that there must be an opening, somewhere to the south, that had enabled the Phoenicians to pass from the Indian Ocean into the Atlantic. It led to another reason for exploring

Africa's west coast—that of discovering the Phoenicians' track and pioneering a sea route, out of the Atlantic into the Indian Ocean, to the riches of Asia, free of Muslim control.

In 1444, an expedition landed on the Cape Verde Islands and by 1460, the year Henry died, the Portuguese had explored the coast of Africa to Sierra Leone, less than ten degrees of latitude north of the equator and a short distance from Ghana.

Henry is called "The Navigator" for the influence he had on the development of practical scientific navigation and for sponsoring voyages of discovery down the coast of Africa and into the Atlantic. His influence may be said to have had an even wider reach, providing the impetus for the maritime explorations that led Europeans to expand into Asia and North America in the sixteenth century.

The African voyages lagged after Henry's death—during the reign of Afonso V—but were renewed when John II succeeded to the Portuguese throne in 1481. To strengthen the Portuguese hold on the coast of Africa, John—young, energetic and ambitious—decided to build a fortress and trading post on the Gold Coast (Ghana). It was intended to discourage European "intruders" and to control the African natives. The result was São Jorge da Mina (St. George of the Mine), a garrisoned medieval-like castle, that protected Portuguese interests in the region for centuries.

John's expeditions crossed the equator and reached the mouth of the Congo River in 1482.

In August 1487, Bartholomew Dias sailed from Lisbon with three ships. The purpose of the voyage was to continue charting the coast of Africa but additional achievements were anticipated. The previous expedition had reached latitude 21°50'S (Cape Cross) and there was the expectation that on this voyage, Portuguese ships would finally round the continent.

And if he reached the east coast of Africa, Dias had instructions to search for the kingdom of the legendary Christian king-priest, Prester John, said to possess fabulous wealth and power. The legend rose after several European rulers including the Byzantine emperor: Manuel I, and the Holy Roman emperor: Frederick I, received letters in 1165 purportedly written by Prester John, claiming divine authority and inviting Manuel, who was addressed as an inferior, to visit his kingdom—"the three Indies." The kingdom was said to be a land of milk and honey, peace, truth and justice; where there was no vice, avarice, envy, strife or flattery. After the middle of the fourteenth century, when a search had failed to find the kingdom in India or Persia, it was generally identified with Ethiopia. John II of Portugal, like other European sovereigns, was anxious to court the favor of this fabulous king, if he existed, because a powerful Christian ally in Asia or

Africa would be a decided advantage in circumventing the Muslim policy of discouraging direct contact between western merchants and the eastern sources of goods.

Dias went ashore at Cabo da Volta, near Angra Pequena (latitude 27°S), and erected a cross to mark Portugal's claim of sovereignty over the region. He put out to sea again and after running southward for thirteen days without sight of land, he came about and steered north. On February 3, 1488 he intercepted the African coast at Mossel Bay, about 200 miles (320 km.) east of the Cape of Good Hope. He followed the coast eastward to the mouth of the Great Fish River (near Port Alfred) where the northeasterly trend of the coast became unmistakable. He had rounded the southern tip of Africa and reached its east coast. Dias wanted to continue up the coast but his officers and crew insisted he return to Portugal. He had to be satisfied with a partial victory but it was a momentous one. European mariners had finally broken free of the Atlantic and sailed into another ocean. The way to India by sea lay open.

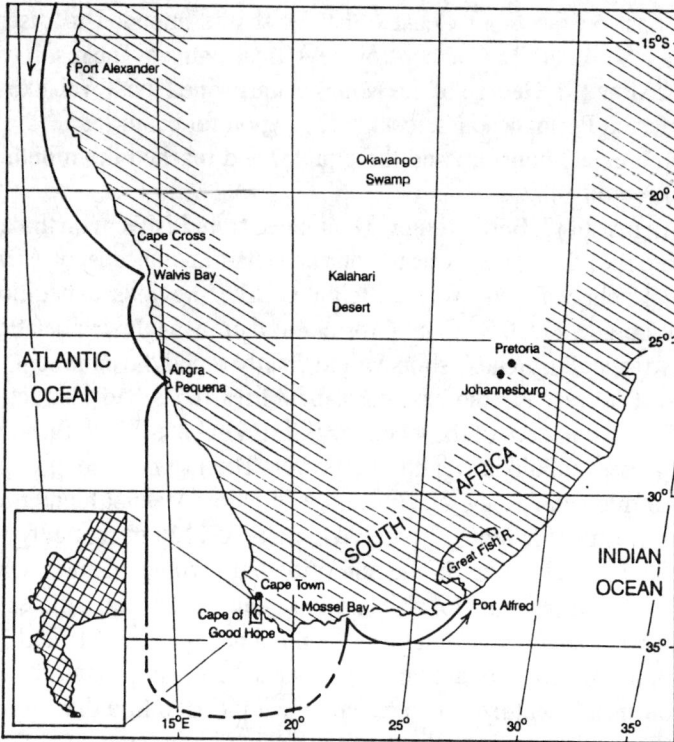

Figure 13. The voyage of Bartholmew Dias around the Cape of Good Hope and into the Indian Ocean in 1487–8.

4

The Voyages of Christopher Columbus
1492–1504

Columbus' early life

Christopher Columbus was born Cristoforo Colombo in 1451, in Genoa, into a Catholic family that had lived in Italy for at least three generations. His father and grandfather, respectively Domenico and Giovanni Colombo, were wool weavers.

Columbus worked at the family looms but all the while he must have felt the pull of the sea. The Genoese waterfront, crowded with ships from all parts of the Mediterranean, was a constantly changing scene that stirred the imagination and whetted the appetite for travel to distant lands. Genoa was the home port of a number of well-known navigators and the location of a company of mapmakers that supplied charts far and wide. Its shoreline was a hive of shipbuilding activity. Young boys turned naturally to the sea for their sport and at an early age sailed small craft in the Ligurian Sea, perhaps as far as Corsica.

At the age of twenty, Columbus left his family's trade for a life at sea and took part in several naval encounters in the Mediterranean aboard a Genoese ship. In these years he learned the elements of seamanship.

In 1476, he shipped as a deckhand on a Genoese merchantman, part of a convoy organized by Genoa to protect cargo headed for the English Channel. The convoy was attacked by a Franco-Portuguese fleet off Cape St. Vincent on the coast of Portugal. The battle raged all day and finally, Columbus' ship was set afire. He leaped into sea, caught hold of an oar and, although wounded, managed to swim the six miles (10 km.) to the Portuguese shore. He reached land near Sagres where Henry the Navigator, earlier in the century, had assembled the geographers and navigators who changed the way Portuguese mariners sailed the seas. He and other survivors of the battle were well treated by the Portuguese.

Columbus was illiterate—his native Genoese dialect was essentially a spoken language, only rarely written. Now, in Portugal, he educated himself, learning to read and write the more useful languages and studying mathematics and celestial navigation to augment the practical seamanship he had already acquired. Although Columbus later wrote proudly of his birthright, he never returned to live in Genoa and he wrote exclusively in Spanish. He represented himself successively as Colombo, Colomo, Colom and Colón; he never used the form "Columbus."

In 1477, a year after he landed in Portugal, Columbus shipped aboard a Portuguese vessel to Iceland. He went to sea again in the following year, this time as the captain of a Portuguese ship chartered to buy sugar in the Madeira Islands.

In 1479, Columbus, now twenty-eight years of age and qualified as a master mariner, married the daughter of the sea-going, hereditary captain of the island of Porto Santo, in the Madeiras. The couple moved to Porto Santo where his mother-in-law placed at his disposal, her husband's charts and journals. Columbus' son, Diego, was born in Porto Santo.

Living in the islands gave Columbus a wider experience with the Atlantic Ocean and he must have noted the evidence of another civilization beyond the western horizon, washed up onto the shores—huge pine logs derived from trees that did not grow in the world he knew, curiously carved wood, and bodies of men with unfamiliar features. He may have concluded as had other forward-thinking seamen of the day that contrary to the teaching of the ancients, man's knowledge of his earth was very limited and much remained to be discovered. It is not known when he conceived the idea of voyaging west across the Atlantic with the purpose of reaching the Indies on its far shore; the idea may have begun to germinate at this time.

In the years between 1481 and 1484, Columbus played some part in the early activities connected with King John II's citadel (St. George of the Mine) on the Gold Coast, either in the enterprise itself or on a trading expedition. The experience of voyaging down the African coast left an impression on Columbus as judged from later frequent written references to the region. The association with Portuguese navigators, then among the best in the world, improved his seamanship but he never attained the skill that enabled him to rely entirely on scientific navigational aids for guiding his ship to a destination. After the voyage to America he wrote: "In the carrying out of this enterprise of the Indies, neither reason nor mathematics nor maps were any use to me."

Columbus' concept for a voyage to the Indies

Back in Lisbon, Columbus read widely, convincing himself that it was feasible to reach the Far East by crossing the Atlantic. It was not a new idea.

It seems that Aristotle believed the distance was reasonably short; a note in Columbus' handwriting in the margin of one of his books states: "Aristotle [says] between the end of Spain and the beginning of India is a small sea navigable in a few days."[1] And in Columbus' time, the Florentine cosmographer, Paolo dal Pozzo Toscanelli, with whom Columbus corresponded, was an advocate of the voyage and encouraged Columbus with letters and a chart intended to prove that the sea distance was relatively short.

Europe did not lack for adventuresome and fearless seamen but Columbus had an almost unique objective. His contemporaries explored southward along the African shores or ventured westward into the Atlantic to find lost legendary islands or bases for commercial fishing, or voyaged to Iceland and perhaps Greenland and even Newfoundland. His destination was the Indies; he wanted to circumvent the Middle East nations that barred western travelers, by finding a new way to Asia and unlocking the riches of the Orient for European merchants.

Columbus' notion, that it was feasible to reach the Orient by sea from Portugal, was based on three concepts of which only the first was accurate and accepted by virtually all Western educated people of his time:

1) the earth was round,
2) the earth's surface was mainly land and consisted of one major mass (a belief that arose from the fact that the parts of the earth known to Western man—Europe, Asia and Africa—are virtually one land mass),
3) the "land distance" across this mass, from its western edge (the coast of Portugal), across Europe and Asia to its eastern edge (the coast of China), was 253 degrees of longitude. Therefore the "sea distance" from Portugal across the Atlantic Ocean to China, was only $360 - 253 = 107$ degrees of longitude.

Columbus reckoned the open-ocean distance was even shorter. The interval from the island of Japan to mainland China's east coast was reputed to be 30 degrees of longitude. Also, Columbus proposed to begin his voyage from the Canary Islands, 9 degrees of longitude west of Portugal. Thus, according to his calculations, the open-ocean part of the voyage would be $107 - 30 - 9 = 68$ degrees of longitude (a modern globe shows this is about the interval between the Canary Islands and Florida). At the latitude of the Canary Islands (28°N), 68 degrees of longitude is equivalent to 4150 miles (6680 km.), or about thirty days' sailing in Columbus' time.

Columbus made another error in converting degrees of longitude to miles. He took the size of the earth to be about 4/5 its actual size and thus he reckoned he should reach Japan's east coast in about twenty-four days.

The real "land distance" east from Portugal across Europe and Asia to

55

the coast of Korea is about 135 degrees of longitude. This leaves a "sea distance" for a voyage west, of 360 – 135 = 225 degrees of longitude and, unbeknown to European mariners, the continent of North America lay between Europe and Asia.

Financing the voyage

In 1484, Columbus obtained an audience with King John II of Portugal and appealed to him for financial backing to voyage to Japan. John was fully occupied with his African ventures; an expedition had reached the mouth of the Congo in 1482 and perhaps he thought he soon would have a more certain way of reaching the Orient. He referred the proposal to an advisory committee; it was rejected.

Columbus' wife had died and following the rejection of his proposal, there was nothing to hold him in Portugal. In midsummer, 1485, he and his six-year-old son Diego entered Spain at Palos, a little seaport in Andalusia, and began seeking an interview with Queen Isabella. He soon formed an association with a twenty-year old girl and she became his mistress (and bore him a son, Ferdinand, in 1488). Columbus got his audience with Isabella in May, 1486. She decided to have a commission of "learned men and mariners" examine the proposal. Columbus did not help his cause; he was vague about his plans—either he could not or would not clearly explain and defend them.

The commission's deliberations dragged on and early in 1488, Columbus wrote to John of Portugal, asking for another hearing. The king was in a state of euphoria; Bartholomew Dias was exploring the south end of Africa and visions of sending an expedition to India danced in his head. Nevertheless, he invited Columbus to appear before him but in December, 1488, before an audience could be arranged, Dias returned with news that he had rounded the southern tip of Africa. The way to the Indies by sea was open and the king had no further need for Columbus and his scheme to reach the Orient by sailing across the Atlantic.

Early in 1489 Columbus returned to Spain; he could still hope Isabella's commission would approve his proposal. Meanwhile, his brother Bartholomew went to England and France, looking in vain for support. Late in 1490, the commission reported unfavorably, saying (correctly) among other objections, that the sea distance to the Orient was much greater than Columbus supposed.

It seemed the end of his quest although Isabella had said he could apply again when the war with the Moors was finished. Columbus waited almost a year and then decided to join his brother in France. A friend, Father Juan

Pérez, forestalled the departure by persuading the Queen to invite Columbus to the court to once again discuss his plans for the voyage. She agreed and moreover, sent Columbus money to buy decent clothing and a mule to ride.

Late in 1491, Columbus appeared in the queen's court. A new commission seemed favorably inclined toward the voyage, perhaps sensing that that was what Isabella wanted to hear. But then her council rejected the proposal on the grounds that the cost was too high. Also, the rewards Columbus expected for undertaking the voyage had increased. Among other things, he demanded the rank of Admiral and a hereditary appointment as Governor and Viceroy of any lands that he might discover (it seems he thought he could easily force the people of Japan or China, where he expected to land, to give up their sovereignty), and that he and his heirs should receive ten percent of the value of the trade developed with these lands. He would not budge from these demands and in January, 1492, he left the court intending to journey to England or France in search of support. The keeper of the king's purse intervened, persuading Isabella to recall Columbus and grant his wishes, pointing out that Columbus' rewards were dependent upon him finding new lands.

There was still the matter of outfitting the expedition. Isabella solved that by fining the seaport of Palos two fully equipped caravels: the *Pinta*, length 69 feet (21 m.) and the *Niña*, length 55 feet (17 m.). Columbus chartered a Galician ship, length 85 feet (26 m.); she later became known as the *Santa Maria*. The ships were armed with enough artillery to repel boarders but they were not equipped as fighting ships.

Columbus' first voyage to America

Columbus left Spain from Palos a half hour before sunrise on August 3, 1492, with the three ships and a total crew of ninety; he was on board the *Santa Maria*. He passed through the Strait of Gibraltar and followed the coast of Africa southwest, heading for the Canary Islands (latitude 28°N) where he intended to begin the crossing. He expected to catch the trade winds which he knew blew from the east in the region of the Canaries. A westerly bearing in latitude 28°N—had he clung to it—would have carried him to a landfall on the coast of Florida. Inadvertently, he had chosen nearly the longest east-to-west distance across the North Atlantic Ocean. His charts showed the legendary island of Antilia lying on this course. He hoped to intercept it for it would be a convenient place to rest and take on supplies of fresh water and food.

He reached the Canary Islands on August 12 but the *Pinta* had suffered some damage on the way and she was delayed. On September 2, the three ships were anchored off Gomera, an island on the west side of the group, and began taking on water, bread, cheese and salted beef in preparation for the next leg. Columbus left the anchorage on September 6 and started on the historic voyage across the Atlantic. On September 9, they lost sight of Ferro, the westernmost island; the known world lay behind them.

In Columbus' day, a qualified pilot found the latitude of the ship's position (its distance north or south of the equator) by measuring the altitude of one or other of two celestial bodies—Polaris (the North Star) at night or the sun at local noon. He made the observations with a marine quadrant or astrolabe—crude instruments, accurate at best to a degree when used at sea on a pitching ship. There was no way of measuring the longitude (the ship's distance east or west of a north/south reference line).

Columbus was not proficient at using celestial observations to guide the ship. His journal shows that he navigated principally by "dead reckoning" by which is meant he plotted the course and position of the ship from three factors—direction, speed and time. The compass-bearing steered by the helmsman determined the direction of each "leg" of the course; the speed of the ship was estimated by eye; the length of each leg was calculated from the estimated speed of the ship and the time taken to complete the leg as measured with an hour glass.

Ten days after leaving Ferro, they reached the position, on Columbus' charts, of the legendary island of Antilia. There was no land, nor could they find the ocean-bottom with a deep-sea lead. The winds were variable here and this relieved some of the seamen who had begun to worry that they would not be able to return to Spain against the winds that had blown constantly at their backs.

Five days later, a seaman aboard the *Pinta* pointed into the setting sun and cried he could see land. Immediately everyone could see it and Columbus fell to his knees and gave thanks. He turned the fleet southwest to intercept it but in the morning the sea was still barren of land. The "land" had been a mirage or a bank of clouds.

By October 1, when they had been almost a month at sea, the men grew uneasy and mutinous; none of them had been this long out of sight of land. Each day, as the distance from home lengthened, the muttering grew more general—there was no land in this waste of water. The men talked of deposing the Admiral and turning for home. By October 6, according to Columbus' reckoning, they should have reached the Orient and even he became uneasy.

On October 7 they observed flocks of birds flying south-southwestward and it buoyed their spirits. Columbus was persuaded to abandon his westerly course and follow the birds. As it happened, it was the shortest route to the nearest land but, although they continued to see birds on this course by day and by the moonlit nights, several days passed with no sight of land. The mood of the men turned to despair and they began to talk of mutiny again. Finally, on October 11, Columbus promised to turn back if they did not find land in three days.

That day, running before a hard wind in a heavy sea, signs of land— floating branches with green leaves, and flowers—were so numerous that all hands were again sure that the Indies lay within reach and they were willing to go on. Columbus did not shorten sail at sunset but he instructed the watch to be alert so that they would not pile up on the shores he now knew lay close at hand. He offered rewards for the first sight of the land. About 10 p.m., they thought they saw a light flickering in the distance but it disappeared; it was probably a campfire.

The three ships drove on in the moonlight, racing through the night, the *Pinta* in the lead, the *Santa Maria* a half mile behind on her port side, the *Niña* on the other side. Two hours after midnight, on October 12, they heard the lookout on the *Pinta* cry: "Tierra, tierra"—he had found the land. They shortened sail and held their position until dawn when they saw an island

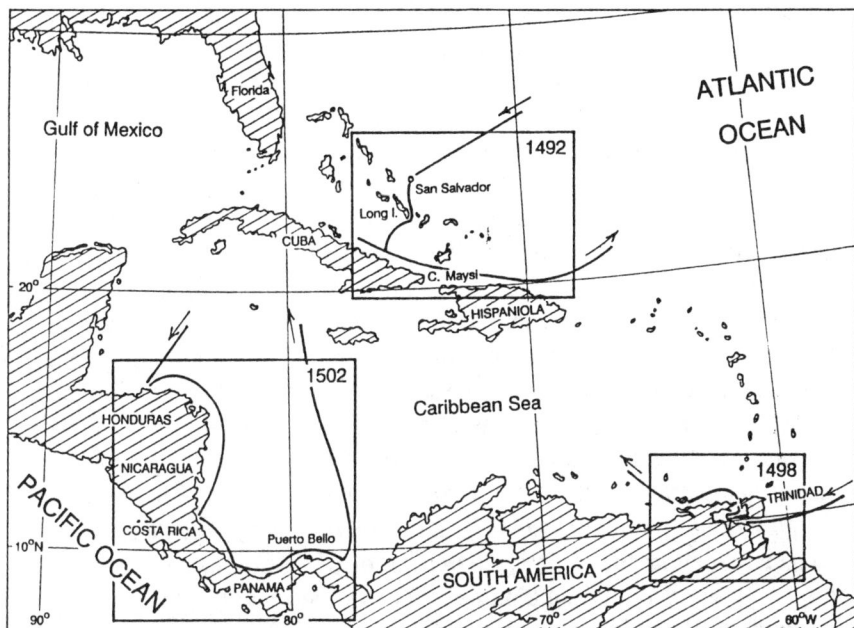

Figure 14. The site of Christopher Columbus' exploration of the Caribbean Sea. 1492—the discovery voyage; 1498—first brush with mainland America when he circled the island of Trinidad in South America; 1502—voyage alongside the coast of Central America.

before them. It was surrounded by a reef but they soon found an opening and entered a shallow bay ringed by a white coral beach. Columbus went ashore with his two captains and erected a royal standard, declaring the land now belonged to Spain; and he gave thanks to his God for guiding the fleet to its landfall. He named the island San Salvador (Holy Savior); it was one of the Bahamas which lie east and southeast of Florida.

Columbus explored San Salvador in the next two days. He met natives and in the belief he was in the Indies, he called them Indians. He was interested to see gold ornaments hanging from their noses. He would have to locate the source of this metal or at least obtain significant quantities of it as well as spices, to prove to his royal sponsors that he had found the Orient and that the voyage had been a success. The natives pointed out the directions of other islands to the south and west, assuring him that he would find much gold. But those islands—Long, Crooked and Fortune—proved to be much like San Salvador—covered with jungle and inhabited by friendly, naive, uninhibited people whose women freely gave their bodies. There was no evidence to suggest this was the wealthy, exotic Orient.

Columbus learned from the natives that there was a large land mass (Cuba) to the south. The plot of his course told him he should be in the vicinity of China but they encountered no Chinese junks on the way and when he went ashore, Columbus saw there were no golden dragons or temples. In response to inquiries, the people of the island intimated there was gold in the interior but he found none.

He followed the coast of Cuba eastward and on December 5 came to its most easterly point—Cape Maysi. Columbus took this to be the eastern extremity of mainland Asia just as Cape Roca, in Portugal, was the most westerly point of mainland Europe. He considered that it should be possible to walk west from Cape Maysi around the earth to Cape Roca.

Columbus continued eastward from Cuba. On the island of Hispaniola, the natives wore more and heavier gold ornaments suggesting to the Spaniards, that they were nearing the source of supply. An expedition found women in the interior panning the rivers and Columbus himself saw large nuggets of the precious metal. It was the good news he was hoping to carry back to Spain and he was certain now, that he had found the Indies.

On Christmas day at midnight, after a particularly enjoyable evening on Hispaniola with the natives, the expedition suffered a loss when the bow of the *Santa Maria* grounded on a coral reef as she swung at anchor. Soon a ground swell drove her so high onto the reef they could not get her off. Her bottom was holed, the hull began to fill with water and Columbus had to abandon her. He decided it was a message from God directing him to found a settlement. He used timbers from the *Santa Maria* to erect a structure and he fortified it with her guns. He decided to leave twenty-one willing Spaniards to man the fort. He instructed them to explore the country with the purpose of finding a good location for a permanent settlement where they could trade with the natives for the gold they panned in the rivers. He told them to treat the natives kindly and fairly.

The *Niña* and *Pinta* cleared Samaná Bay, near the eastern end of the island, before daybreak on January 18, 1493, starting the long voyage back to Spain. It proved to be a difficult passage. They were bedeviled by contrary winds and by gales. Columbus, afraid that they would all perish and news of his discovery would be lost, wrote an abstract of the voyage, wrapped it in waxed cloth, placed it in a cask and threw it overboard. Faked versions of the Admiral's "Secrete Log Boke" are still being offered to credulous collectors.[2] The ships became separated south of the Azores and never did regain contact.

Columbus reached Portugal on March 4. The *Niña* was so badly battered he put into Lisbon for repairs although his home port was little more than a day's sail away. While the work on his ship was in progress, he had an audience with John II who had refused to finance the voyage. Columbus left Lisbon on March 13, rounded Cape St. Vincent the next morning and anchored off Palos on March 15. The *Pinta* arrived on the same day.

The Treaty of Tordesillas

Columbus' voyage caused a territorial conflict between Portugal and Spain. Spain claimed the Atlantic waters east of Columbus' new world. Portugal countered that her discovery of islands in the Atlantic gave her jurisdiction over the Atlantic west of Africa. Pope Alexander VI proposed, in 1493, to divide the ocean with a line of demarcation—Spain would have exclusive rights west of a north/south line drawn 100 leagues west of the Cape Verde Islands; Portugal would confine its activities to the ocean and lands that lay east of the line.

John II of Portugal protested that this position for the line would hinder his exploration of the west coast of Africa. His ships needed more ocean space to maneuver and catch the trade winds that bore them northeastward back to Portugal. The two nations met at Tordesillas, Spain, in 1494 and agreed by treaty to abide by the pope's resolution except that the line would be positioned 370 leagues west of the Cape Verde Islands. The pope agreed to this change in January, 1506.

The league unit used to designate the position of the line in the Treaty of Tordesillas was, presumably, the marine league which is equivalent to three nautical miles. The length of a nautical mile is based on the length of a minute of arc of a great circle of the earth and it differs because the earth is not a perfect sphere. More significantly, there was no general agreement about the circumference of the earth in Columbus' time. The distance of 370 leagues could not be accurately defined. The modern British nautical mile is taken as equivalent to 6080 feet. With this unit as base, we calculate that 370 leagues is equivalent to $370 \times 3 \times (6000/5280) = 1261$ statute (5280-foot) miles. It was found later, that this positioned the Line of Tordesillas at about 45°W longitude. The 45°W meridian passes through the eastern bulge of South America, from Santos north to near the mouth of the Amazon River. Thus the 1494 version of the line gave Portugal a foothold in South America when all she had bargained for was sufficient ocean space to conduct her explorations of Africa and the islands in the Atlantic that remained to be discovered.

Columbus' other voyages to America

Columbus made three more voyages across the Atlantic between 1493 and 1504. On the second voyage, while cruising along the south coast of Cuba, he conceived the notion that he was half way round the world and in the vicinity of the Malaya Peninsula. He thought he was near enough to the Cape of Good Hope to consider returning to Spain by circumnavigating the earth, not knowing that the Americas blocked the way. Fortunately he abandoned the idea. Back in Spain, few people believed his claim that he had been near China. Word got around that he was a poor administrator. His reputation suffered and he came to be regarded as an impractical dreamer.

There was talk in Spain that Henry VII of England had engaged John Cabot to find a high-latitude short route to China and this may have helped Columbus find backing for a third voyage to the Indies in 1498. On this voyage he came onto the island of Trinidad, which shelters the Gulf of Paria on its western side, and sailed around it without realizing he had reached the continent of South America. After he left the region and sailed northward to Cuba (which he still considered to be mainland Asia) he realized that the fresh-water currents and "seas" (lagoons) in and around the gulf had to result from the presence of large rivers. This in turn could only mean that he had been sailing alongside a "very great continent."

Columbus' reputation in Spain continued to decline and finally Ferdinand and Isabella sent a royal commissioner to Hispaniola to take stock. The upshot was that Columbus was put in irons and taken aboard a ship bound for Spain. Dismayed at this treatment, he refused the offer to have his irons removed on the homeward voyage, choosing to leave the ship still fettered when it docked in Spain. Their Majesties were shocked at the news and ordered his release. He was given a royal audience but he had to wait almost a year to hear that he had been replaced as governor in his "Other World."

The royal couple authorized a fourth voyage. Its main purpose was to search for a strait between Cuba (which Columbus still assumed to be an extremity of China) and the continent (South America) he had discovered during the third voyage in 1498. The coast of the Gulf of Mexico and Central America had not yet been explored. It was here Columbus expected to find the strait (Strait of Anian) that Marco Polo had supposedly used late in the thirteenth century, to enter the Indian Ocean from China. His fleet reached Honduras late in July, 1502, and idled southeastward, searching the coast of Central America for signs of the strait and a likely location for a post where they could acquire the gold that the Indians wore as ornaments.

They passed alongside Nicaragua and Costa Rica, and early in October they entered the great Chiriqui lagoon in Panama. They spent ten days along its shore, trading with the Indians. Columbus did not have an interpreter and could not properly converse with the natives. Still, he learned that there was another sea (the Pacific Ocean) to the west, and that the way was barred by a narrow range of high mountains.

On November 2 they entered the harbor of Puerto Bello; it later became the Atlantic end of the Spanish mule track between the two oceans. It was a good center for the proposed trading post but the Indians were hostile and Columbus moved on. Now the winds turned against him and it began to rain and he returned to Puerto Bello to wait out the weather. The fleet rode at anchor at Cristóbal, in the present Panama Canal Zone, between Christmas and New Year. Had he taken the opportunity to go up the Chagres River to its headwaters, he would have been within a dozen miles (20 km.) of the Pacific Ocean and a solution to the geographic problem that vexed him.

Columbus returned to Spain in 1504. It had not been a good voyage; nature, the natives, lack of provisions, his men and Spanish officials had all conspired, it seemed, to frustrate and humiliate him. He was sick in mind and body and it was almost a year before he was strong enough to plead with Ferdinand (Isabella had died a few months after his return to Spain) to restore him to his former power and prestige in the Indies. It was not to be; Columbus was judged not fit to govern.

Columbus' health worsened and he died on May 20, 1506. His remains were placed in a monastery in Seville, Spain but they were exhumed in 1542 and taken to the island of Hispaniola where the great admiral was finally laid to rest.

He was a complex man—"a practical navigator...with an uncanny ability to feel his way repeatedly to a given land fall"[3] but who could not reliably determine his latitude from a measurement of Polaris. He was driven by a vivid imagination about lands to be discovered beyond the western ocean; secretive and vague about his plans yet certain about the honors and wealth he wanted as rewards for success. He was a poor administrator, unable to work with people whether Spanish or native American, yet able to impress a valuable few who repeatedly interceded for him with the Spanish court. Seemingly unable to assess the realities of his discoveries, he died an unhappy man feeling himself humiliated although the honors accorded to him after his first voyage stunned the royal court.

5

The Portuguese Pioneer a Sea Route to India
1497–98

In 1487, in the year that Dias left Lisbon on the voyage that brought him into the Indian Ocean, John II called upon two Portuguese travelers— Pedro da Covilhão and Alfonso de Paiva—to undertake a two-fold mission for him. Firstly, he wanted them to discover the source of the spices that were carried "through the countries of the Moors" to Venice which was the principal distribution point in Europe for African and Asian merchandise. The object of this investigation was to determine if the spices could be conveyed from their source directly to Portugal, thereby transferring the distribution center from Venice to Lisbon. Secondly, John wanted the men to learn the whereabouts of the legendary Christian kingdom of Prester John. The growth of Islam and its hostility toward Europeans wishing to engage in the trade controlled by the Muslims made it desirable to ascertain if a powerful Christian kingdom and possible ally, existed in Africa or Asia. John had already instructed Dias to search the southeastern seaboard of Africa for the mysterious kingdom; Covilhão and Paiva were to probe Asia and the northeast section of Africa with the same purpose.

The two men journeyed by way of the Mediterranean to Cairo where they joined a caravan of Moors traveling south along the west side of the Red Sea. Paiva entered Ethiopia where he disappeared and was not heard of again. Covilhão crossed to Aden and took ship for India. He reached Calicut, at that time the busiest trade center in southern India, and visited Goa further to the north, hunting unsuccessfully for information about the kingdom of Prester John. On the return voyage west he stopped at Hormuz, the important center of commerce at the entrance to the Persian Gulf, and he journeyed some distance south along Africa's east coast before reaching Cairo. Here he met two of John's emissaries and gave them a detailed account of his travels. The report proved valuable, later, in planning Vasco da Gama's expedition to India.

Covilhão then visited the port of Al Aswad, on the Red Sea's east coast, and he may have gone inland to Mecca and joined a caravan to Medina.

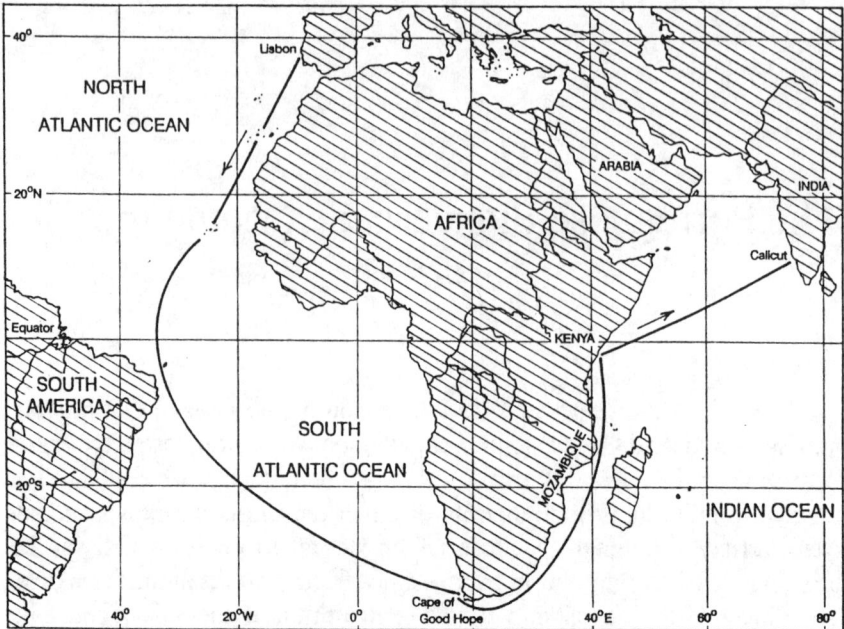

Figure 15. Vasco da Gama's voyage from Portugal to India in 1497–8.

Eventually (about 1490) he reached Ethiopia where he was welcomed as a person of wide knowledge, deserving respect. The king gave him lands and honored him but he would not let him leave the country. Covilhão apparently accepted his fate for he settled down, married an Ethiopian and became a valuable source of information about the country for visiting westerners.

The impact of Dias' achievement, in 1488, of rounding Africa and entering the Indian Ocean was overshadowed in 1493, by Christopher Columbus' return to Spain with the claim that he had reached the Indies by sailing west across the Atlantic. It may have made John II of Portugal pause for a time, to consider the possible merits of a longer and more difficult route around the south end of Africa to reach those same Indies. However, Columbus had found no spices, discovered no exotic cities and had seen no Orientals. John went ahead with his plans, ordering that an expedition be readied to make the voyage to India.

The expedition, consisting of four vessels and commanded by Vasco da Gama, sailed from Lisbon on July 8, 1497, in the year that Columbus was preparing to make his third voyage. It rounded the Cape of Good Hope on November 22. Da Gama paused to break up his storeship and then he moved northwestward up the coast. The fleet of three ships reached Mozambique on March 2, 1498, where da Gama discovered that the local people were Muslims and that they traded with Arab merchants. Four Arab vessels loaded with gold and silver, jewels and spices were in port at the time. This was more promising than anything Columbus had found on his voyage.

Da Gama continued up the coast, guided by a native pilot, and arrived at Malindi, Kenya on April 14. He was told that the expedition should leave the coast of Africa here and set a course for India across the Indian Ocean. He located a pilot who knew the route and began the final leg of the voyage. After twenty-three days at sea, the fleet sighted the Western Ghats Mountains along India's west coast; it reached Calicut on May 20, 1498.

Da Gama left India in August, 1498, heading for Kenya across the Indian Ocean, carrying Oriental merchandise—proof that the voyage to the fabled Indies had been a success. The return voyage proved difficult. Contrary winds lengthened the time to cross the Indian Ocean to three months and many of his seamen sickened and died of scurvy before they reached Africa. At Malindi, he burned one of his ships for want of enough seamen to man her. The remaining two ships rounded Africa together on March 20, 1499 but a month later, off the west coast, they became separated in a storm. Da Gama reached Lisbon on September 9, 1499, almost a year after he left India.

In the space of five years, European mariners had crossed two oceans and initiated an age of discovery.

Within ten years of da Gama's return, the Portuguese had a strategy in place for controlling the shipment of merchandise from Asia and Africa to Europe. The plan called for regulating the passage of ships from the Far East through the Strait of Malacca, and commanding the entrances to the Persian Gulf and the Red Sea from military bases at Hormuz and Aden. Strategically situated fortified positions on the coasts of Africa and Asia would harass the shipping of other European nations. The intent was to force the trade between Europe and the Indies to go around Africa—in Portuguese ships. Lisbon would be the terminus of the sea route from the East, replacing Venice as the European center for the distribution of eastern merchandise.

At this time Venetians controlled the transport of Oriental goods from ports of entry on the Mediterranean to Venice. Early in the fifteenth century, Venice had in use for this trade, 300 large transport ships, 3000 smaller vessels and 45 galleys, manned by 36,000 seamen.[1] With the discovery of the direct sea route to India around Africa, the Red Sea lost much of its importance as a shipping lane and the Mediterranean became a backwater of world trade and traffic. The role of middleman between East and West played by countries that lined the eastern shores of the sea was greatly diminished.

It is interesting to note that the Red Sea regained its prominence four centuries after da Gama's voyage—in 1869—with the completion of the Suez Canal. With that event Necho II's vision of a shipping connection between the Red and Mediterranean Seas finally became an established fact. The Suez significantly shortened the shipping distance between Europe and the Far East and resulted in making the Red Sea one the world's great shipping lanes.

6

John Cabot—Voyage to North America
1497

John Cabot is generally credited with being the first European to reach mainland North America after the Vikings abandoned it. Little is known about the life of this man; the location of his landfall and even the details of his voyage to America are a subject for disagreement among historians.

There is reason to believe he was born Johan Cabot Montecalunya1 in Genoa, about 1451—the year of Columbus' birth. The two explorers may have known each other as boys. Cabot's father moved the family to Venice when the boy was ten years old. John was married here and in 1476, after residing in the city for fifteen years, he became a Venetian—a citizen of Venice.

In Venice, a trade center and a base for navigators and mapmakers, Cabot had an opportunity to observe the pattern of trade that was the lifeblood of the city. He came in contact with sailors and traders who shipped in from all parts of the Mediterranean. Like many other young men of Venice, he went to sea, gaining practical experience as a sailor and learning some of the navigational methods of the day.

In his early adult years (in the 1470s), Cabot traveled widely and in the process he reached the ancient city of Mecca (Makkah), the locus of ancient caravan routes that led south to Aden on the Arabian Sea, north to seaports on the eastern shores of the Mediterranean Sea, and northeast across the desert to the Persian Gulf. At this time Mecca was the greatest market in the world for products of the Far East.

Cabot saw firsthand the difficulties experienced by Europeans who wished to trade in the Orient. The Islamic nations controlled the caravan routes and to protect the profits of their part as middlemen in the trade, they discouraged Europeans from traveling to the Orient. In the thirteenth, fourteenth and fifteenth centuries, only a few Europeans had dared to reach the Far East by passing to the north of the Middle Eastern countries through the Black Sea, or to the south through Egypt and Abyssinia into the Arabian Sea.

When Cabot inquired at Mecca about the source of spices, he was told that they were carried by successive caravans from remote regions through several distant countries. He concluded that the source was in the northeastern part of Asia.[2]

These were the years when Columbus was beginning to consider the merits of crossing the Atlantic to reach the Orient. It is not known when Cabot conceived the similar idea of finding a sea route to the source of the spices. It seems certain he was influenced by the antagonism he witnessed toward western traders in Mecca. Like Columbus and perhaps a few other thoughtful European navigators of his day, Cabot came to the conclusion that because the earth was round, it should be possible to reach the Orient by sailing westward around the earth. He concluded that the voyage across the Atlantic to the source of the spices in northeast Asia would be comparatively short.

Islamic control of the sea trade between East and West was nearing its end. Portuguese mariners had been slowly feeling their way south along the west coast of Africa in the second half of the fifteenth century. Finally, in 1488, ten or fifteen years after Cabot visited Mecca, Bartholomew Dias rounded the Cape of Good Hope and pioneered a passage that Vasco da Gama used in 1497 to reach India—five years after Columbus attempted to attain the same objective by sailing in the opposite direction. Thereafter, European maritime nations would be competing with each other for control of the spice trade.

Cabot moved his family to England about 1485 and settled them in London. It is not clear why he chose to live in England. If he had already envisaged a voyage of exploration across the Atlantic, England offered advantages over Portugal and Spain. For one, English entrepreneurs, particularly the merchants of Bristol, had for at least the past five years been financing exploratory expeditions into the Atlantic. Also, because east-to-west distances around the earth decrease polewards, the voyage from the more northerly shores of England across earth's expanse of ocean to northeast Asia, ought to be shorter than say, from Spain or Portugal. The advantage of a shorter distance carried a penalty; it meant braving the stormy North Atlantic.

Cabot searches for financial support

There is evidence to believe that Cabot obtained employment with an English engineering firm and lived in Valencia, Spain, as the agent of that firm from 1490 to 1493. During this time he submitted a plan to King Ferdinand for improving the city's harbor facilities. The plan was favorably received by the king but the project fell through when the city council refused to appropriate the funds. He was still in Spain when Columbus returned in 1493 and it is not unlikely that he met and talked with the discoverer of the West Indies.

Columbus' success probably acted as a spur for Cabot, for he visited Seville and Lisbon in the next two years "seeking to obtain persons to aid him"[3] financially, for a voyage of discovery into the Atlantic Ocean. He was not successful and he returned to England in 1495. A letter dated March 28, 1496, from Ferdinand and Isabella of Spain to Gonzales de Puebla, their ambassador in England, indicates that the royal couple was not impressed with Cabot or his scheme—that they thought Cabot was merely a tool of the King of France:

> In regard to what you say of the arrival there of one like Columbus for the purpose of inducing the king of England to enter upon another undertaking like that to the Indies, without prejudice to Spain or to Portugal.... We are of opinion that this is a scheme of the French king's to persuade the king of England to undertake this so that he will give up other affairs.[4]

The growth of trade following the Norman conquest had made Bristol the most important seaport in England after London. Bristol had become a manufacturing town as well as a port and now, late in the fifteenth century, it was a distribution center for both overseas and inland merchandise. The town was prosperous and its merchants were used to risking money to sponsor adventurers. They had backed the search for islands in the Atlantic Ocean when English fishermen had been excluded from the Icelandic cod-fishing banks about 1478. The English fishery was in need of lands, in or on the other side of the Atlantic, that could be used as fishing stations. The merchants had gone even further afield and sponsored voyages into the eastern Mediterranean in expectations of entering the spice trade. Thus Bristol was an obvious place for Cabot to solicit interest in a westward voyage to the source of spices and soon after his return to England he journeyed to the town. Apparently he was welcomed by the merchants and offered assistance in petitioning the king for letters-patent to make the voyage.

Henry VII learned of Cabot's proposition in the winter of 1495–6 when he and his court visited Bristol. He had passed up an opportunity to sponsor Columbus, another Genoese, and now Columbus had returned from across the Atlantic with the claim that he had reached the Indies. There is nothing in Cabot's scantily-known history to indicate that he had acquired the experience to command an expedition and guide a ship across an unknown ocean but Henry was not about to miss out a second time. When Cabot petitioned[5] in March, 1496 for permission to undertake a voyage of discovery, Henry granted letters-patent to Cabot and his three sons—Lewis, Sebastian and Sancio. They were authorized to equip, at their own cost, as many as five ships of any size and carry any number of men, and undertake a voyage of discovery to search for lands "unknown to all Christians."[6] Having obtained his charter, Cabot approached the merchants for financial assistance. Although his ultimate destination was the Orient, he may have held out the prospect of finding islands on the way—islands they could use as independent bases for their fishing operations. Cabot probably envisaged the islands as advance depots for his voyage to the Orient—to shorten the time the ships would be out of contact with land.

In spite of their professed interest in exploring the Atlantic, Cabot was able to persuade the merchants to outfit only one ship. The *Matthew*, a ship "of fifty toneles," carried "twenty men and food for seven or eight months."[7] She measured "60 to 70 feet (about 20 m.) overall, [had] a beam of 18 to 20 feet (6 m.), and a draft of from 6 to 9 feet (2–2.5 m.)."[8] She was about the size of Columbus' intermediate-sized ship, the *Pinta*. The historian, Jackson, has estimated that, "given a moderate sea and wind ranging from right astern to abeam" a speed of "six to seven knots would be a realistic estimate of her capabilities."[9]

Cabot's voyage to America

If Cabot or any of his men kept journals of the voyage to North America, they have not survived or they remain to be found. Until recently, our total knowledge of the historic voyage to America had been deduced from a few government documents recording the granting of the letters-patent[10] and the reward of a pension[11] to Cabot, and three letters by foreign agents residing in England at the time of the voyage. One of the letters was written by Lorenzo Pasqualigo[12] to his brothers in Venice on August 23, 1497. The other two, dated respectively August 24[13] and December 24[14], 1497 were sent by Raimondo di Soncino to the Duke of Milan and were based on a talk he had with Cabot after the voyage. The two men were posted in England to observe and report events; they were educated and literate, and able to converse with Cabot in his native language. All this suggests that the information in the letters was as accurate as Cabot knew it to be.

A new document[15] became available in 1956, when Dr. Louis Vigneras published a letter which he had discovered in the archives at Simancas, Spain; it has enabled historians and geographers to embellish the account of Cabot's voyage and improve its accuracy. The letter, written in Spanish, is addressed to the "Almirante Mayor," a title identified with Christopher Columbus in a number of documents of the day, and is signed "Johan Day." It is not dated but its contents—describing a successful voyage from Bristol to the "Island of Seven Cities" by an unnamed explorer and mentioning plans for "exploring the said land more thoroughly next year"—clearly signify that it is concerned with the Cabot voyage and was prepared within a few months of Cabot's return. The Day letter lacks the feeling of intimacy with Cabot of the other two communications but does give the impression it was written by a well-educated, knowledgeable observer. Despite this fresh document, most of the details of the voyage—the exact dates of the voyage, its course and the precise location of Cabot's landfall—are still subjects for controversy and conjecture.

When did Cabot make his voyage?

The Pasqualigo letter, dated August 23, 1497, fixes 1497 as the year of Cabot's voyage: "some months ago his majesty [Henry VII of England] sent out a Venetian...[who] has returned safe, and has found two new very Large and fertile islands." Pasqualigo added that "he has been three months on the voyage; and this is certain."

The only definite statement that refers to the start of Cabot's voyage is found in the Day letter; it relates that Cabot "left England toward the end of May."[16]

Cabot must have returned by August 10 because the list of Privy Purse Expenses of Henry VII shows for that date, in 1497, the grant of a pension "to hym that founde the new Isle."[17]

If we choose, say, May 20 as the date of departure and August 7 as the day Cabot returned to Bristol, the time for the entire voyage calculates out to a scant seventy-nine days. This is somewhat short of the three months stated by Pasqualigo to have been the length of the voyage and, as we shall see, little enough time to accomplish all that is claimed for the voyage. It suggests that Cabot left England somewhat earlier than May 20.

Cabot's point of departure from Ireland

There is no general agreement on Cabot's point of departure into the Atlantic. We know he "set out from Bristol,"[18] crossed St. George's Channel to Ireland and skirted its southern coast. The Day letter states that "the cape [in North America] nearest to Ireland is 1800 miles west of Dursey Head."[19] Some analysts of the voyage have interpreted this to mean that

Cabot started across the Atlantic from Dursey Head. It is on the southwestern tip of Ireland, in the same latitude as Bristol (51.5°N) and therefore, a natural point of departure.

The second Soncino letter seems to indicate that Cabot left Ireland in a higher latitude for it relates that "having passed Ireland...[Cabot] then shaped a northerly course."[20] An initial northerly leg of the voyage, alongside Ireland's western shoreline, could have had a number of logical purposes[21]:

1) Martin Behaim and other cosmographers of Cabot's time held that the archipelago which Columbus had encountered in 1492, extended northward to about latitude 54°N and barred the way to the Orient. Cabot may have planned his course to skirt the archipelago on the north.

2) a crossing in a northerly latitude would be less likely to cause conflict with Spain; she claimed that the Treaty of Tordesillas gave her exclusive rights to all the "heathen" lands west of longitude 46°W.

Achill Head, in latitude 54°N, is a logical point of departure from Ireland's northwest coast[22] into the Atlantic. Dursey Head and Achill Head are in the same longitude.

The outward voyage

There are two comments in the letters about the outward voyage. Soncino says that after leaving Ireland, Cabot "began to navigate to the eastern parts, leaving (during several days) the North Star to the right; and having wandered about considerably, at length fell in with terra ferma."[23] The phrase "having wandered about considerably" leaves the impression that Cabot did not attempt to maintain a strictly westerly bearing for the entire voyage.

The inference, that Cabot altered course on occasion, is supported by the comment in the Day letter that he "must have been on the way for 35 days before sighting land."[24] Cabot was running before a wind from the "east north-east and the sea was calm"[25] and he should have reached North America from the coast of Ireland in under twenty days had he held a steady westing course. It follows then, that Cabot did not necessarily land in the latitude of his point of departure from Ireland (Dursey Head = 51.5°N or Achill Head = 54°N). He may have investigated leads or hunches, thereby lengthening the duration of the voyage and influencing the location of his eventual landfall.

The Day letter states that "the cape [in America] nearest to Ireland is 1800 miles west of Dursey Head." The mile in Cabot's time was equivalent to 5000 feet and thus the Day ocean-distance from Dursey Head to the new land works out to 1800 x (5000/5280) or roughly 1700 statute miles (2700 km.).

Pasqualigo reported: "That Venetian...says he has discovered mainland 700 leagues away."[26] This evidently referred to the shortest distance from Bristol to America. If we assume that Cabot gave the distance in English leagues (one league is roughly three 5000-foot miles), the distance is approximately 700 x 3 x (5000/5280) or 2000 statute miles. Subtracting the distance from Bristol to Dursey Head, (2000 minus 350), leaves 1650 statute miles for the distance from Dursey Head to America. This compares well with the 1700-mile value derived from the Day letter.

When the two distance values—1700 and 1650 statute miles—are compared with actual distances, they are seen to fall well short of the distances across the Atlantic Ocean in latitudes 54 and 51.5°N:

APPROXIMATE DISTANCES (in statute miles)

Achill Head to Labrador along latitude 54°N	1850
Dursey Head to Newfoundland along latitude 51.5°N	1950
Dursey Head to Cape Breton	2250

The comparison calls into question the accuracy with which Cabot plotted his course. Although the distance from Achill Head is in best agreement with Cabot's distances, we are obliged to conclude that the data are not good enough to point with certainty to a particular point of departure from Ireland or to his landfall in North America. Still, the comparison does allow us to conclude with reasonable assurance, that Cabot did not make his landfall on Cape Breton Island as has been suggested by some historians.

If the generally westward direction of Cabot's outward voyage from Ireland carried him to the coast of America between latitudes 54 and 51.5°N, he made landfall somewhere between Hamilton Inlet on the Labrador coast and the northern tip of Newfoundland.

The coasting voyage

Day says that Cabot "landed on only one spot of the mainland, near the place where land was first sighted."[27] Cabot went through the usual ritual of taking possession of his discovery for the English king and he erected a cross and hoisted the banners of England and the Evangelist St. Mark (the

75

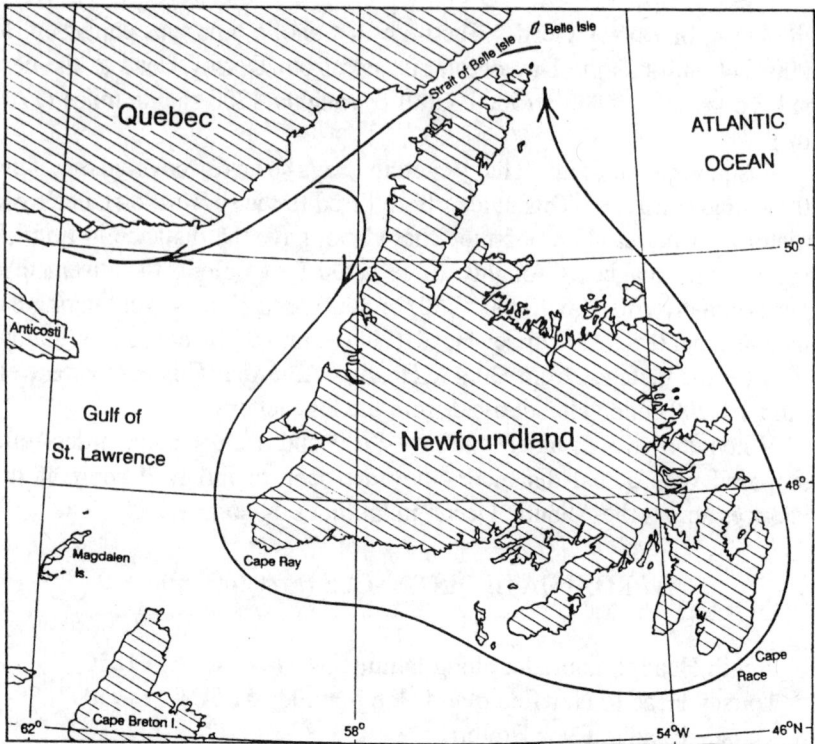

Figure 16. The probable course of John Cabot's "coasting voyage" in 1497.

symbol of the Venetian spirit) to mark the occasion.[28]

The landing site was well wooded with trees that reached to a height that made them suitable for masts and in places they found pasture land in which the grass grew in profusion. They discovered signs of human activity—carved and painted sticks, the remains of a campfire, snares, a needle for making nets, and signs cut into trees—but they saw no humans. Cabot collected some of the objects to take back to England. His men found a trail leading inland but because the Englishmen were few in number, they feared to explore it for more than the length of a crossbow shot.

Pasqualigo reported that having reembarked, Cabot "coasted for 300 leagues"[29] and Day related that Cabot "spent about one month discovering the coast."[30] What coast did Cabot explore? The Soncino letter tells us, in part, that after he left his landfall, Cabot took the ship "towards the east"[31] [that is westward, toward the Far East]. The reference offers a clue to his activities during the next month.

The description of Cabot's landing as a well-wooded region interspersed with rich grass pasture land is reminiscent of the Viking description of Leifsbudir, on the northern tip of Newfoundland. If Cabot's first sight of America was not in the vicinity of the Strait of Belle Isle (latitude 52°N), he probably saw the strait while searching the coast for a suitable place to land, and he marked it as the way to get past the land barrier and continue his westward journey. His destination was the Orient—specifically, the island of Cipango (Japan). It would have been obvious to him that his landfall was not the exotic, sophisticated Far East from which came spices, jewels and silk. Cipango must lie still further west. The opening into the strait beckoned and when Cabot left the site of his one and only landing, he probably entered it and sailed into the Gulf of St. Lawrence—"towards the east." We can assume he moved the *Matthew* alongside the north shore of the gulf which trends first southwest, then westward.

Cabot saw nothing that led him to believe he was nearing Cipango. The wooded coastline of the gulf (the south shore of Quebec) was empty of cities or any other signs of human habitation and stretched endlessly westward. Presently he decided to come about; he would leave the voyage to Cipango for another time. At some point on the return to the Strait of Belle Isle, he crossed the Gulf of St. Lawrence to Newfoundland and sailed southward along its western side.[32] He rounded Cape Ray and followed the shoreline eastward to Cape Race. Here the trend of the coast changed abruptly to north and he concluded he had sailed around an island; he thought it must be the legendary Island of Seven Cities. He determined the latitude of Cape Race and decided he was approximately opposite the Gironde River in France (he was actually a degree of latitude north of the river). Then he sailed northward—up the east side of Newfoundland—and reached its north-eastern tip where he had begun the "coasting" voyage into the Strait of Belle Isle. A month had passed. According to the plot of his course, he was now 1800 miles directly west of Dursey Head (latitude 51.5°N) in Ireland.

The homeward voyage and afterwards

Cabot began his homeward voyage from the cape which "is 1800 miles west of Dursey Head." An easting course from this point would have landed him in Bristol harbor. Day[33] tells us that his "sailors confused him [during the voyage], saying he was heading too far north" and they influenced him to alter the course. As a consequence, after fifteen days at sea "with the wind behind them," they passed to the south of England and landed on mainland Europe, in Brittany in latitude 49°N. From there Cabot "came to Bristol, and he went to see the King to report."

We can estimate the duration of the voyage by assuming times required to complete its various components, as follows:

outward voyage	35 days
time spent at landing site	3
time spent cruising the discovered coastline	30
voyage to Brittany	15
Brittany to Bristol	3
	86 days

The total of eighty-six days agrees well with Paqualigo's statement that Cabot was "three months on the voyage." Assuming he reached Bristol on August 7, the eighty-six-day total favors a departure day in the second week of May rather than "toward the end of May" as reported by Day.

Soncino stated in his letter to the Duke of Milan that Cabot's crew

> say that the [newly-discovered] land is excellent and [the air] temperate, and they think that Brazil wood and silks grow there; and they affirm that the sea is covered with fish which are caught not merely with nets but with baskets, a stone being attached to make the basket sink in the water...they say they will fetch so many fish that this kingdom will have no more need of Iceland, from which country there comes a very great store of fish which are called stock-fish.[34]

Cabot held out tantalizing prospects. It was reported he had

> set his mind on something greater; for he expects to go from that place already occupied, constantly hugging the shore [presumably the north shore of the Gulf of St. Lawrence and the St. Lawrence River], further towards the east until he is opposite an island called by him Cipango, situated in the equioctial region, where he thinks grow all the spices of the world and also the precious stones.[35]

It was what the Bristol merchants wanted to hear and it helped earn Cabot a payment from the king, of 10 pounds toward an annual pension of twenty pounds sterling.[36] Henry was very much taken with Cabot:

> ...his majesty here, who is wise and not lavish, likewise puts some faith in him; for since his return he makes him a very fair allowance.... And it is said that in the spring his majesty aforesaid will fit out some ships, and besides will give him all the malefactors, and they will proceed to that country to form a colony, by means of which they hope to establish a greater depot for spices in London than there is in Alexandria. And the chief men

in the enterprise belong to Bristol, great sailors, who now that they know where to go, say that it is not more than fifteen days' voyage thither, nor do they ever have storms after leaving Ireland.[37]

Pasqualigo related that

> The king has promised him [Cabot] for the spring ten armed ships as he desires...and has given him money that he may have a good time until then, and he is with his Venetian wife and his sons at Bristol...he is called the Great Admiral and vast honour is paid to him and he goes dressed in silk, and these English run after him like mad, and indeed he can enlist as many of them as he pleases, and a number of our rogues as well.[38]

The argument for a pre-Columbus English discovery of America

The Day letter to the "Almirante Mayor" includes a passage which raises the possibility that one of the expeditions financed by merchants of Bristol to find the legendary islands in the Atlantic, happened on North America before Columbus and Cabot made their historic voyages. The translation of the passage reads:

> It is considered certain that the cape of the said land [which is 1800 miles west of Dursey Head] was found and discovered in the past by the men from Bristol who found "Brasil" as your Lordship knows. It was called the Island of Brasil, and it is assumed and believed to be the mainland that the men from Bristol found.[39]

The Day letter is not the only known reference to a possible English discovery of America predating the Columbus voyage. Sir Francis Bacon noted[40] (more than a hundred years after the event) in his history of Henry VII:

> And there had beene before that time [1492] a discouerie of some Lands, which they tooke to be Islands, and were indeed the Continent of America, towards the Northwest.

Bacon intimated that Columbus knew land had been discovered between Europe and Asia but did not admit of the knowledge:

And it may be that some Relation of this nature comming afterwards to the knowledge of COLUMBUS, and by him suppressed, (desirous rather to make his Enterprise the Child of his Science and Fortune, than the Follower of a former Discouerie) did giue him better assurance, that all was not at Sea, from the west of Europe and Africke vnto Asia.[40]

Bristol merchants had begun sending ships west into the Atlantic and south off the coast of Africa, specifically to search for the elusive islands known as Brazil and Seven Cities, at least twelve years before Columbus reached the Indies. Pedro de Ayala, the Spanish ambassador to England, knew of the activities. He remarked to Ferdinand and Isabella in a dispatch dated 1498:

> For the last seven years the people of Bristol have equipped two, three [and] four caravels to go in search of the island of Brazil and the Seven Cities.[41]

A reference to a specific, albeit unsuccessful, voyage states:

> On the 15th of July, 1480, a ship of...80 ton, sailed from the roadstead of the Port of Bristol to seek the Island of Brasylle in the Atlantic west of Ireland...with Lloyd, the most scientific mariner in all England, as master; news was received in Bristol on Sept. 18th that she had sailed...without finding the island, and had been driven by storms into...Ireland.[42]

Also in 1480, Thomas Croft, a collector of customs for Bristol, and three Bristol merchants obtained a license to trade for three years wherever they might choose. The records[43] of the Commission of the Exchequer for 1483, show that the *George* and the *Trinity*, ships partly owned and victualed by Croft, left Bristol on July 6 of the following year (1481) "to serch and fynd a certaine Ile callid the Ile of Brasile." The ships' cargo included forty bushels of salt, "not by cause of merchaundise [that is, not for trade]" but presumably for salting fish. It suggests the owners were confident they knew the location of the island and planned to use it immediately as a base for fishing. There is no known record of the results of this voyage.

If one of the Bristol-sponsored expeditions resulted in a landing in North America, it probably occurred about the time of these voyages.

It is reasonable to question why a discovery of America, if made by merchants from Bristol about 1480, should receive no publicity. The history of fishing off Newfoundland as it is known from early in the sixteenth century, demonstrates that the fishermen were uncommunicative, even secretive, about their activities. They came from several countries—England, France, Portugal and perhaps Spain. What they had in common was a preoccupation with the fishing. Their involvement with the shores bordering the fishing grounds was minor and consequential; they used the land for drying the fish, for relief from the confines of the ships, for replenishing supplies of wood and fresh water, and for repairing ships and gear. They had no interest in the interior.

If Newfoundland was discovered from Bristol in the early 1480's, it happened in the course of prosecuting a private commercial venture. Good business sense would dictate that the discovery of rich fishing grounds should be kept secret from competitors, whether they were countrymen or foreigners. In contrast, Cabot talked about his plan to voyage to the Orient to anyone who might invest in the enterprise. His aims became widely known and when he returned from America, he readily acquainted the world with the results of the voyage; the funding of future expeditions depended on publicizing his successes.

Cabot's second voyage

In February 1498, Henry VII granted Cabot letters-patent for a second voyage with authority to outfit six ships and sail "to the londe and Iles of late founde by the seid John in oure name and by our commaundemente"[44] and, "constantly hugging the shore, [go] further towards the east until he is opposite an island called by him Cipango."[45] Cabot had entered the Strait of Belle Isle on the first voyage and sailed some distance westward along Quebec's south shore before turning back. The objective of this voyage was to return to where he had left off and continue westward until he reached Japan.

The only sure reference to the voyage is found in a dispatch dated July 25, 1498, to Ferdinand and Isabella of Spain from Pedro de Ayala, their ambassador in London:

> I think Your Highnesses have already heard how the king of England has equipped a fleet to explore certain islands or mainland which...certain persons who set out last year from Bristol...have discovered.[46]

Ayala added that Cabot had been in Seville and Lisbon, attempting to recruit experienced seamen (presumably seamen who had shipped with Columbus and/or da Gama) and that

The fleet he prepared, which consisted of five vessels, was provisioned for a year. News has come that one of these...has made land in Ireland in a great storm with the ship badly damaged. The Genoese kept on his way.

The literature is devoid of any account that can be attributed with certainty to Cabot's activities following the storm that sent one ship back to Ireland. This total absence of knowledge of the voyage after the fleet left Ireland led to the speculation that the expedition was lost at sea. The register[47] of the Collector of Customs & Subsidies for the port of Bristol, dated September 29, 1499, records annuity payments to Cabot of 20 pounds for the years 1497 and 1498, implying that he did return from the second voyage. Even more, there is reason to believe that Cabot was master of a ship that sailed to Greenland as part of a Portuguese-English expedition three years later—in 1501.

7

Cabot to Cartier
1499–1534

John Fernandes rediscovers Greenland

The Portuguese exploration of the South Atlantic Ocean and the west coast of Africa, begun before the middle of the fifteenth century under the stimulus of Henry the Navigator, had culminated in Bartholomew Dias' achievement of rounding Africa in 1488. Hitherto European mariners had been confined to the Atlantic Ocean; Dias had broken free of the Atlantic and sailed into another ocean. A decade later, countryman Vasco da Gama completed the work of Dias when he opened a sea route to India. It was free of Muslim control and it changed the pattern of world trade. Lisbon became the new Venice—a European center for the distribution of Asian and African goods. In the space of half a century, Portugal had surged to the rank of a world sea power.

The main focus of Portuguese sea activity in the Atlantic had become the region between Africa and South America but Portugal's mariners, among the most venturesome of the day, did not relinquish interest in the North Atlantic. They had begun probing westward into the North Atlantic before Columbus' first voyage and they renewed these activities when word of Cabot's discovery of new land began circulating throughout Europe. The principal object of the Portuguese voyages was not to find a way to the Orient; their route to the Far East was south, around Africa and across the Indian Ocean. Nor, like the Bristol merchants, were they searching for islands that could serve as stations for fishing fleets. The Portuguese who undertook these voyages of discovery did so to improve their social rank and financial well-being. They sailed, at their own expense, under letters-patent granted by the king of Portugal. The reward for a discovery of new land was:

> the captaincy of whatever Island or Islands inhabited or uninhab-
> ited that he may discover and newly find, together with such

revenues, honors, profits and privileges as we have granted to
the Captaincies of our islands of Madeira and the rest.[1]

John Fernandes, a seaman and landowner (a so-called lavrador) from
Terceira, an island of the Azores, was such an entrepreneur. The king,
Manuel I, granted him letters-patent on October 28, 1499, "to go in search
of and discover (or explore) certain islands of our sphere of influence at his
own expense."[2] The document made no reference to previous discoveries
and this has been taken by historians to imply that Fernandes had not yet
discovered any islands.

The letters-patent made no mention of where Fernandes might search
except that it should be in "our sphere of influence"—that is, presumably,
east of the Line of Tordesillas. The inclusion of the phrase may have been
intended to remind Henry VII of England, who was authorizing voyages
into the Atlantic, that Spain and Portugal claimed all lands in and beyond
the Atlantic.

A royal Portuguese proclamation published ten years later (in 1509),
was more specific about the area of Fernandes' search; it referred to his
voyage as "the expedition sent to discover in the northern parts"[3]—that is,
in the North Atlantic.

Fernandes left Portugal, probably from the Azores, accompanied by a
fellow islander, Pedro de Barcelos. Since the letters-patent were issued late
in 1499, it is likely that the year was 1500. They steered in a northwesterly
direction and eventually sighted land but, apparently, they did not go ashore.

Historians have deduced from the examination of a number of maps
produced between 1502 and 1529, that the landfall was Greenland. On the
Cantino map of 1502, for example, the legend applied to land that is
recognizable as Greenland, states:

> This land was discovered by license of the most excellent prince
> D. Manuel of Portugal, and is believed to be the peninsula of
> Asia. Those who discovered it went not ashore but viewed it and
> saw nothing but very rugged mountains.[4]

Fernandes and Barcelos did not return to Portugal but voyaged to Bristol
where they began arranging a joint Portuguese-English expedition. In the
spring of 1501, Henry granted letters-patent to a syndicate headed by three
Bristol merchants and three gentlemen from the Azores including John
Fernandes, authorizing them:

> to sail and transport themselves to all parts, regions, and territo-

ries of the eastern, western, southern, arctic and northern seas...[to search for lands occupied by]" heathens and infidels, in whatever part of the world they may lie, which before this time were and at present are unknown to all Christians...and to enter and seize...in our name...and occupy, possess and subdue these.[5]

Although the terms of the letters-patent gave the expedition the freedom to range widely, the explorers returned to Greenland and they renamed the island in honor of John Fernandes:

> Land of the Labrador, which was discovered by the English of
> the town of Bristol. They gave it that name because he who gave
> the directions was a lavrador of the Azores.[6]

The use of the name Labrador for Greenland has made some of the early literature on this period difficult to interpret because the name was later also used for the northeast coast of mainland North America. Later, of course, the name Labrador was reserved for the mainland and Greenland was again known by the name given to it by its Norse discoverer, Erik the Red.

A statement about Greenland, prepared in 1541 by Alonso de Santa Cruz for the benefit of the king of Spain, indicates that John Cabot accompanied the Portuguese-English expedition, probably in the capacity of captain. The relevant part of the passage relates that:

> It was called Labrador's land because a husbandman (Labrador)
> from the Azores gave tidings and information about it to the king
> of England at the time he sent Antonio Gaboto [John Cabot], the
> English pilot and the father of Sebastian Goboto, who was your
> Majesty's Pilot Major, to discover it.[7]

The probable participation of John Cabot in the 1501 expedition to Greenland is supported by an anonymous account in the *Cronicon regum Anglie*.[8] It tells that "a Straunger venisian, which by a caart made hym self expert in knowyng of the world, caused the kyng [Henry VII] to manne a ship" in 1501–02. The "venisian" [Venetian] was probably John Cabot.

The expedition evidently landed on Greenland before returning to England for the account goes on to say:

> This yere three men were brought out of an Iland founde by
> merchauntes of Bristow forre beyonde Irelond, the which were
> clothed in Beestes skynnes and ete raw fflessh, and rude in their
> demeanure as Beestes.

It is speculated that both Cabot and Fernandes died during this voyage. The name of Fernandes is conspicuous by its absence from a letters-patent granted in the following year, for a second Portuguese-English expedition and nothing more is heard of John Cabot. This latter expedition is presumed to have sailed in 1503 and centered its activities around Greenland although the list[9] of Privy Purse Expenses of Henry VII refers to the site of the expedition's work as "Newfounde Launde."

Gasper Cortereal rediscovers Labrador

Gasper Cortereal, like Fernandes a resident of the island of Terceira and a nobleman of Manuel's court, was another Portuguese interested in finding new lands and governing them for profit and prestige. He was an experienced explorer, having

> made efforts in the past, on his own account and at his own
> expense, with ships and men, to search out, discover and find by
> dint of much labour and expenditure of his wealth and at a risk
> of his life, some islands and a mainland.[10]

He petitioned the king for leave to renew the search and in recognition of his past efforts, Manuel granted his wish on May 12, 1500 and promised him "by right and heredity for ever, the governorship of any islands or mainland he may thus discover or find afresh."[11]

Cortereal left the port of Lisbon "at the beginning of spring, year 1500" with one or two ships and "a good compliment of people." Little is known about the voyage. Apparently he set a west-northwesterly course, intending to explore "the north side," presumably the North Atlantic Ocean. Eventually he reached a land "that was very cool and with big trees" which influenced him to call it Terra Verde. Cortereal found the inhabitants to be "barbarous and wild." He explored a "good part" of the coast and returned to Lisbon in the autumn of the same year.[12]

One report describes Cortereal's landfall as lying south of 50°N and this, together with the description of Terra Verde, leads to the assumption that he landed on the southeast coast of Newfoundland, the island that Cabot had circled in 1497. Newfoundland is west of the Line of Tordesillas; Cortereal either did not know he had crossed the line into the Spanish sphere of influence or he did not care. The voyage accomplished little beyond encouraging Portuguese fishermen to visit the cod banks of Newfoundland. Fishermen from England were already harvesting these waters.

Late in April, 1501, Cortereal began taking on provisions for a second voyage. His destination was again "the northern parts"[13] with the purpose "of finding out if it were possible to discover in that region any [new] lands or islands."[14] He left Lisbon on May 15 accompanied by his brother Michael with a fleet of three[15] well-equipped ships.

The description of this voyage is based mainly on a report[16] dated October 17, 1501, prepared for the Duke of Ferrara by Albert Cantino about a week after the return of one of the ships. The report relates that Cortereal set a course to the north and held it for four months without once sighting land. In the fifth month, the expedition encountered icebergs and being short of fresh water, Cortereal had his men approach them in their boats and they took all they wanted of the packed snow. They moved north again but after two days they reached a frozen sea. They were forced to change course and now they steered northwest and west. They enjoyed fine weather and were able to hold that bearing for three months, and on the first day of the fourth month they beheld "a very large country." As they closed in and followed the coast, they observed numerous large rivers flowing into the sea and they were able to ascend one for a distance of a league. They landed and discovered an abundance of "luscious and varied fruits, and trees and pines of such measureless height and girth, that they would be too big as a mast for the largest ship that sails the sea."[17] They found that the natives lived by fishing and hunting wild animals including a large, long-haired "deer."

Cortereal sent two of the three ships back to Lisbon with more than fifty captive natives. He decided to prolong his voyage and make his way "far enough along that coast to be able to learn whether it is an island or yet mainland."[18] The two ships reached Lisbon in October, 1501. They had been away less than five months—not long enough to account for the eight or more months of sailing time described in Cantino's report and this casts doubt on the authenticity of his description of the voyage. Cortereal was never heard from again.

A letter[19] by Pietro Pasqualigo dated October 18, 1501, describing the return of the first of Cortereal's ships, adds something to the information gleaned from the Cantino report. According to Pasqualigo, the crew said they had ranged a coastline for a distance of more than 600 miles (950 km.) and this, together with the presence of many exceedingly large rivers emptying into the sea, had led them to the opinion that they had reached a vast mainland. They were convinced that it was joined to "another land which was discovered last year in the north by other caravels belonging to this king [likely the Fernandes expedition of 1500 to Greenland]" and that it extended south to include the West Indies (discovered by Columbus) and Brazil (recently found by Portuguese explorers).

The talk of a vast mainland stretching unbroken from the frozen north

to the Portuguese possessions below the equator, inhabited not by sophisticated Orientals but by "barbarous and wild" natives, must have discouraged
anyone who clung to the hope that Columbus' original aim of finding a
water passage to Asia would yet be realized.

What was the locale of Cortereal's explorations? His generally north to
northwesterly course probably carried the fleet into the Labrador Sea,
between Greenland and Labrador. When its northward progress was halted
by packice, Cortereal steered westerly which brought them in sight of "a
very large country," presumably Labrador. The claim that they found an
"abundance of most luscious and varied fruits, and trees and pines
of...measureless height and girth" is not believable as a description of the
coastal region of northern Labrador. Discounting the rhetoric in Cantino's
report, it is reasonable to conclude that Cortereal made his landfall in the
vicinity of 55°N—near Hamilton Inlet—and then sailed south some "600
miles" (8 or 9 degrees of latitude) alongside the coast of Labrador and
Newfoundland. He may have been the first European after Cabot, to see the
coast of Labrador.

In May 1502, seven months after the two ships of the 1501 expedition
had reached port, there was still no word of Gasper Cortereal. He was long
overdue. His brother, Michael, left Lisbon with three ships to search for him
along the coast of the "large country." None of the three ships returned to
Portugal and although King Manuel sent two ships in the following year to
hunt for the Cortereals, no trace of the two fleets or the brothers was ever
found.

Sebastian Cabot's plan to found a colony in America

In the space of five years—from 1497 to 1502—the coasts of Newfoundland, Labrador, Greenland, and perhaps Nova Scotia had been visited
in that order by Europeans. They brought back accounts of fertile land,
immense forests and a pleasant summer climate, but they had discovered
that the New World was nevertheless a savage land. It was very cold in
winter. The coastline of Labrador was beset with pack ice that persisted into
July. Even in early summer the seas adjacent to Labrador and Newfoundland
were infested with drifting icebergs that could rip and crush the hulls of
ships. It made night sailing risky for half the year.

Still, the report following John Cabot's first voyage (1497), that the seas
were so full of cod, the fish could be caught with a weighted basket had
been tested and found to be no great exaggeration. The fishing grounds off
Newfoundland and Nova Scotia proved an irresistible lure that soon drew
privately funded voyages across the Atlantic from England and various

European seaports. Commercial fishing in this region, and the use of the adjacent shores for drying the fish, was commonplace by the English and Portuguese by 1502. Bretons (inhabitants of Brittany in France) learned about the bountiful fishing grounds from the Portuguese and began fishing there in 1504; they were soon followed by Normans. By October 1506, Portuguese fishermen were numerous enough on the cod banks to make it worthwhile for the king of Portugal to proclaim a tax on their catches.[20]

By the middle of the second decade of the sixteenth century, commercial fishermen had established routes for crossing the Atlantic, the better fishing grounds were well known and fishermen had made their selection of shoreline for drying their fish and laying up ships when repairs were needed. And some of them had begun following the practice of explorers elsewhere, of seizing natives and carrying them off to Europe for one purpose or another. Transatlantic voyaging had become almost routine by the end of the second decade. Unfortunately for the historical record, the fishermen were generally illiterate and they added little of their experience and knowledge to the written word of the times.

Official governmental interest in backing voyages of discovery lagged. The principal goal of ventures sponsored by Henry VII of England had been a northern sea passage to the Orient and the voyages had not yielded this prize. All the evidence indicated that the search for a northwest passage was a hopeless task. It seemed that the way through the arctic waters, if there was a passage, was barred by a frozen sea for the greater part of each year.

Still, would-be explorers had not all passed from the scene. One was Sebastian, son of John Cabot; he still dreamed of finding a northern water passage to the Orient. It seems Sebastian

> persuaded the king of England, Henry VII, that he could easily travel from there [Cortereal's Terra Verde = Newfoundland] to the country of Cathay, towards the North, and thus find spices and other things by this way, in the same way that the king of Portugal from the Indies; at the same time he proposed to go to Peru and America in order to people the land with new inhabitants, and to establish there a new England.[21]

It was an ambitious proposal to found a settlement in America as part of an expedition to reach China over an unknown northwest sea route. According to a number of early chroniclers, Sebastian did undertake a voyage to America but the accounts are contradictory and there remain basic questions—when was the voyage made, did he or did King Henry finance the voyage, what was his route and what part of America did he reach?

Historians are generally agreed that a voyage was made sometime between 1507 and 1509 with two ships, carrying 300 people of whom a number were the intended settlers. It is reported that Cabot sailed toward the north, searching for an opening to the west. According to one account, he reached a latitude of 67.5°N (about the middle of Baffin Island) before "he was stopped by the cold and by the thick ice of the Northern Sea, and was forced to turn back without reaching his goal."[22] Thereafter he sailed southward, down the east coast of North America still searching for an opening to the west, to latitude 38°N (Chesapeake Bay) or perhaps 25°N (Florida), before turning for home. The voyage accomplished nothing and the fate of the prospective settlers is not known; one reference has it that he put them "on a land to the North of Ireland, where the cold caused the death of almost all."[23]

Sebastian reached England with the intention of persuading the king to let him "return to that undertaking when the sea was not frozen."[24] He found the king had died and his son (Henry VIII) little interested in supporting the venture. Sebastian lived to become Pilot Major of Spain.

John Fagundes establishes a Portuguese colony on Cape Breton

John Alvares Fagundes, like Gasper Cortereal, was a nobleman of the Portuguese court who offered to search for new lands in return for a governor-ship of whatever he might discover. What is particularly noteworthy about Fagundes is that he, like Sebastian Cabot, planned to establish a colony on the newly found lands. Some time before 1521, he sought and obtained letters-patents from King Manuel. His charter stipulated that he must avoid Brazil and confine his activities to the northern parts of the continent.[25]

From a consideration of the place names on a number of maps dated about this time, the Canadian archivist, Hoffman[26,] has deduced that the region of Fagundes' first attempt at a settlement was along the southeastern coast of Newfoundland. Later, his people moved to the mainland—to Cape Breton in Nova Scotia. The evidence for this is taken from an old genealogical manuscript that reads in part:

> Joam Alvarez Fagundes discovered Terra Nova, or the country now called Cabo Bretão [Cape Breton], which the king granted to him, and where he established cod fisheries, which became a large source of profit to Portugal.

This is the first known reference to a settlement on the mainland of Canada in the post-Viking period of history.

A manuscript dated 1570, may refer to the same settlement. It relates that between 1520 and 1525

> certain noblemen of Vianna [a town in northern Portugal] associated themselves together and in view of the information in their possession regarding the Codfish-land of Newfoundland determined to settle some part thereof, as in truth they did in a ship and a caravel, but finding the region to which they were bound, very cold, they sailed along the coast from east to west [that is, along the south coast of Newfoundland] until they reached that running northeast and southwest, and there they settled. And as they had lost their ships, nothing further was heard from them, save from the Basques who continue to visit that coast in search of the many articles to be obtained there, who bring out word of them and state that they (the settlers) asked them to let us know how they were, and to take out priests; for the natives are submissive and the soil very fertile and good, as I have been more fully informed, and is well known to those who sail thither. This is at cape Breton, at the beginning of the coast that runs north, in a beautiful bay, where there are many people and goods of much value and many nuts, chestnuts, grapes and other fruits, whereby it is clear the soil is rich.[27]

Apparently the Indians did not remain submissive; a report dated 1559, relates that

> the Portuguese sought to settle the land which lies the lowest [Cape Breton and mainland Nova Scotia] but the natives of the country put an end to the attempt and killed all of those who came there.[28]

The manuscript does not definitely connect this settlement with Fagundes but it is evidence that the Portuguese made one and perhaps two serious attempts—around 1520—to colonize southern Newfoundland and Cape Breton.

The name "Cape Breton" probably dates from soon after 1504 when Bretons began fishing in the Gulf of St. Lawrence and using the beaches of Nova Scotia to dry their catches. The name—for example, "tierra de los bretones"[29] and "c. de bretones"[30]—was used on maps as early as 1527.

Estevan Gomez leads a Spanish expedition to northern America

In the years following Columbus' discovery voyage, Spanish navigators searched the Atlantic in the region of his landfall for a way into the Pacific. They failed and it became evident there was no passage through the middle of the Americas; the closest approach to the Pacific was by mule train across the Isthmus of Panama.

The year 1522 brought to Europe the startling news that two Portuguese—Ferdinand Magellan, a mariner, and Rui Faleiro, a cosmographer, had succeeded in finding a way into the other ocean. They had penetrated

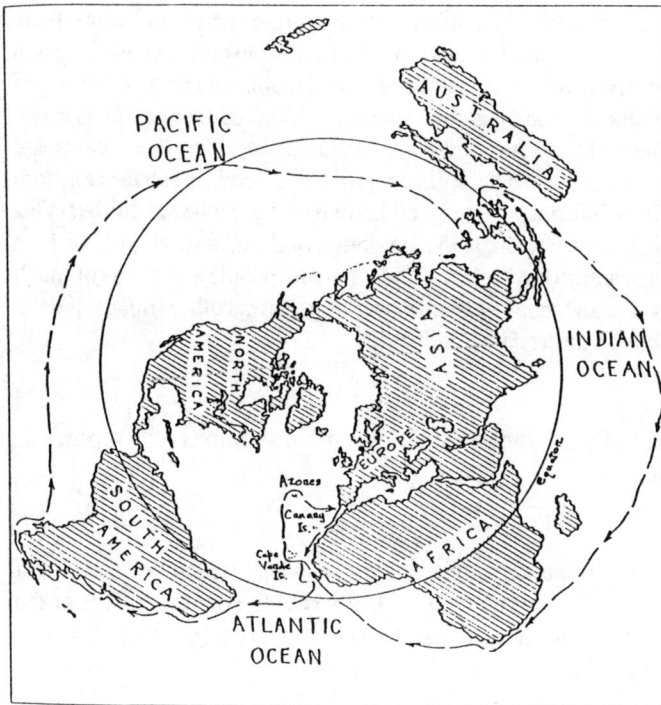

Figure 17. The track of Ferdinand Magellan's ship Victoria, 1519–22
(from Nuffield: *The Pacific Northwest*, 1990, fig. 5, p. 25).

the American land mass far to the south, entered the Pacific Ocean and crossed it from east to west.

Magellan had persuaded Charles I of Spain to sponsor the voyage—to find an independent sea route to the Spice Islands and prove that the islands lay on the Spanish side of the Line of Tordesillas (46°W) if it were continued around the earth (where it became 134°E). Magellan left Spain on September 20, 1519 and in October began probing the eastern coast of South American, searching for an opening, working southward. A year later, on October 21, 1520 in latitude 52°S, he entered the strait that was to bear his name and emerged into the "Sea of the South" (the Pacific Ocean) on November 28.

Magellan reached the Philippines in March, 1521 with three ships. It was the end of the voyage for him. He was killed in April, fighting with the natives. Only two of his ships survived the voyage to the Spice Islands and only one, the *Vittoria*, cleared the Islands, rounded the Cape of Good Hope and re-entered the Atlantic Ocean. The ship, leaking but loaded with spices, came into port in Spain on September 7, 1522.

The voyage was the first circumnavigation of the globe and it gave man a better understanding of the geography of the earth. It showed that there was more ocean than exposed land on its surface, thereby proving wrong a popular belief of the day. The voyage revealed that the Orient was a great distance west of Europe—much greater than Columbus had thought.

For merchant seamen, the greatest achievement of Magellan's voyage lay in the discovery of another way out of the Atlantic Ocean—this one westward, into the Pacific Ocean. The voyage revived a flagging interest in finding a northwest passage. Men reasoned that if there was a sea passage around the south end of the American land mass, there ought to be a way around its north end.

Spain had not concerned herself with attempts to explore the northeast coast of North America. But Magellan's discovery of the Southwest Passage was to cause Charles I to turn his thoughts to the north. Magellan's strait gave Spain access to the western side of South America but the route to Asia across the enormous expanse of the Pacific Ocean did not appear to be a practical way to reach the Spice Islands from Europe. Charles knew, of course, of the unsuccessful English and Portuguese efforts to find a north-west passage. But Spain like Portugal, had been notably more successful than most European nations at maritime exploration and building an over-seas empire. Could that success be duplicated in the "northern parts?"

Charles had no way of knowing, in his time, that the North Polar Sea does not lend itself to easy passage. The islands of North America, Asia and Europe extend north of latitude 80°, leaving only a relatively small patch of the earth's northern surface for ocean, and this ocean is always partly covered with sea ice. The configuration of land and sea is different in the southern hemisphere. There is little exposed land between latitude 40°S and the Antarctic Circle; this region of the earth is a vast expanse of open water where the Atlantic, Pacific and Indian Oceans coalesce to form the Antarctic Ocean. As a consequence, the sea lanes around the southern end of Africa

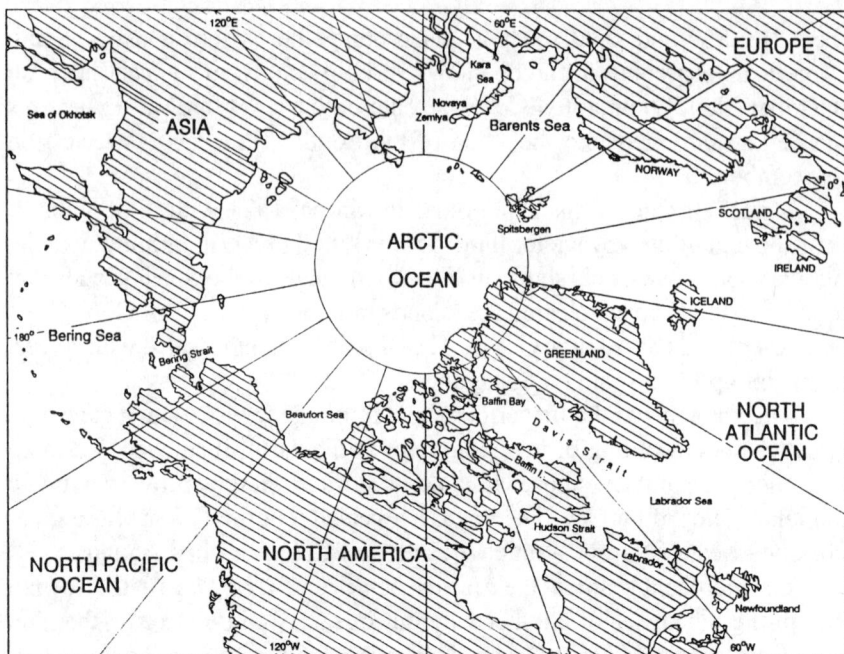

Figure 18. The Arctic Ocean—the "Frozen Sea"—barrier to passage
from the North Atlantic to the North Pacific Ocean.

and South America were discovered by Dias and Magellan soon after
Europeans began searching this region of the earth for ways out of the
Atlantic. By contrast, the first one-season crossing of the Northeast Passage
was accomplished in 1932—by icebreaker—and it was 1944 before the
Northwest Passage was negotiated in one season.

Late in March, 1523, Charles appointed Estevan Gomez, a skilled
Portuguese navigator, to captain an expedition into the northern seas, "to
go and discover Eastern Cathay...as far as our Molucca islands."[31] He
cautioned Gomez to avoid entering "the limits of the sphere of influence of
the Most Serene king of Portugal."

Charles ordered that a caravel of about fifty tons' burden be constructed
"and a departure be made with all speed"[32] and "that 200 ducats be paid to
[Gomez]...that he may make his preparations and set about fitting out the
said caravel."[33] The caravel was finished in 1524, and armed and furnished
with enough provisions for one year.

If Gomez ever submitted a report of his voyage to the king, it has been
lost; our knowledge of his contact with the northeast coast of America rests
mainly on the accounts of the historians of his day. It seems he sailed from
Spain, probably in the year 1524, maintaining a latitude of 40–41°N, and

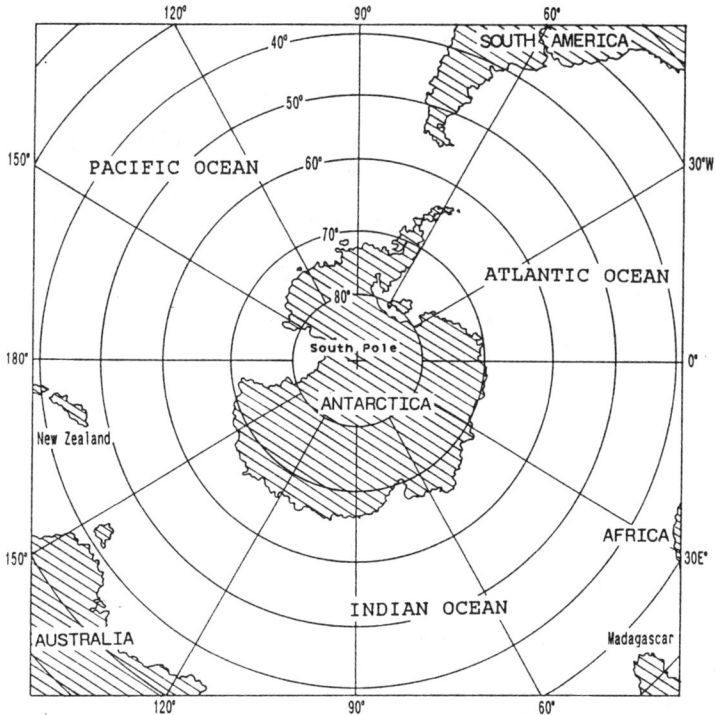

Figure 19. The Antarctic Ocean or south polar sea, an
expanse of water between 40° and 65°S where the Atlantic,
Pacific and Indian Oceans coalesce.

intercepted North America in the vicinity of Cape Cod. He turned up the coast and sailed some distance to the north. Thereafter he drove down the coast to Spanish America, past Florida and crossed to Cuba. He anchored in the port of Santiago to rest before starting back across the Atlantic. The voyage occupied about ten months.

The most detailed and revealing description of the northern leg of the voyage is found in an account by Alonso de Santa Cruz, written in 1541 and first made available for study by modern historians in 1918. The account relates that in coursing northward from Cape Cod, Gomez came on to "a very wide, deep river...[and] sailed for some distance up this river, thinking it was the strait of which he was in search."[34] The size and extent of the river convinced him that he was adjacent to a large continent. It was probably the Penobscot River in Maine. In describing the region south and west of St. Mary's Bay, on the southeast coast of Newfoundland, Santa Cruz states:

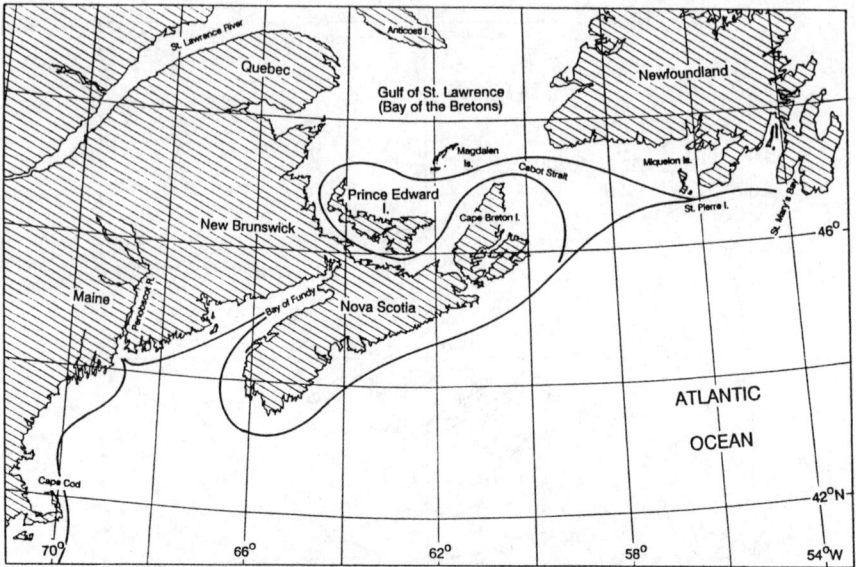

Figure 20. The track of Estevan Gomez's voyage into the Gulf of St. Lawrence in 1523 as deduced from the account of Alonso de Cruz: *Islario general de todas las islas del mundo* (1541).

Beyond the islands of the 11,000 Virgins [the St. Pierre and Miquelon Islands] the sea forms a very large bay called the bay of the Bretons [the Gulf of St. Lawrence], on account of the arrival each year in this bay and off this coast of the said Bretons for fish....

Beyond the said bay and further to the west near a cape named Cape Breton lies an island named St. John's island, stretching east and west along the coast for some 56 leagues [about 200 mi. = 320 km.]. It is 20 leagues in width at the widest part.... There is nothing to report about this island save that the said pilot Stephen Gomez states that when passing it, he saw many fires and signs of habitation. There is a passage between it and the mainland called St. Julian's channel, from five to six leagues in width.... In the neighbourhood are many small islands, all uninhabited. It stretches from 46° to 47°30'.[35]

Common opinion has it that Gomez, in voyaging north, stopped short of the Gulf of St. Lawrence. Hoffman, for example, has concluded from a study of maps published between 1525 and 1541, that Gomez

seems to have explored along the Maine and New Brunswick coasts as far as the St. John River, and to have stayed some time

96

in the Penobscot River. Turning eastward, he encountered the western coast of Nova Scotia, which he mistook for an island and named Isla de S. Iuan [St. John's Island]. He then returned to the mainland and to his landfall, and proceeded down the coast.[36]

Thus, according to Hoffman, "St. John's Island" is merely the bulk of Nova Scotia.

Prince Edward Island lies between latitudes 46 and 47°N and its land-side coastline is about 190 miles (300 km.) long. These data fit well with Santa Cruz's description of the St. John's Island that Gomez passed on his voyage. It is reasonable to conclude, therefore, that Gomez entered the Gulf of St. Lawrence and discovered Prince Edward Island on this voyage.

Giovanni da Verrazano
First official French expedition to the New World

Although French fishing fleets had been active off Newfoundland and in the Gulf of St. Lawrence since about 1504, French officialdom had ignored the Americas. France's foreign policy had been centered in the Mediterranean Sea from the time that Charles VIII led an expedition to Naples in 1494, to assert his claim to that kingdom. The return to Spain of Magellan's ship, laden with spices from the Molucca Islands, could not be ignored. France's reaction was immediate; the following year Francis I authorized Giovanni da Verrazano, a Florentine, to search for a way to the Orient in the region north of the Spanish-American possessions.

The voyage may have been initiated and it was probably financed, in part at least, by French and Italian bankers resident in Lyons[37] who had made the city a center for financial interests trading in France with Germany, Italy and Spain. They were familiar with international undertakings and prepared to back a venture that might result in a French discovery of a short, commercially-feasible route to the source of spices.

Verrazano left Dieppe with four ships in 1523 but a storm forced part of the fleet to put into a port in Brittany. Repairs took some time—too long to leave adequate time to cross the Atlantic and make the search in 1523. Verrazano had the ships refitted for fighting and spent the rest of the year privateering off the coast of Spain. Finally in January, 1524, he started across the Atlantic but not from France. It seems he had decided not to take the established route used by French fishermen and he probably did not dare to use the southern Spanish route from the Canary Islands. He chose a midway course—from a deserted island in the Madeira group (latitude

32.5°N), well to the south of France, off the coast of northern Africa.

Apparently Verrazano had made little effort to inform himself about what had already been discovered on the opposite side of the Atlantic by contemporary seamen, including French fishermen. He turned instead to the writings of the ancients whose speculations about the configuration of land and sea had been found to be wrong by Columbus, Cortereal, Magellan and others. The news that a large land mass lay between Europe and the Orient had escaped Verrazano; in a report to Francis following his return, he wrote:

> My intention was in this navigation to reach Cathay and the extreme east of Asia, not expecting to find such an obstacle of new land, as I found; and if for some reason I expected to find it, I thought it to be not without a strait to penetrate to the Eastern Ocean. And this has been the opinion of all the ancients, believing certainly our Western Ocean to be one with the Eastern Ocean of India without interposition of land.[38]

Verrazano encountered North America in latitude 34°N (near Wilmington, North Carolina). He turned south and cruised for about 150 miles (240 km.). Fearing he would meet the Spaniards, he came about near the present Georgia/Florida boundary, regained his original landfall and continued up the coast. Sailing alongside the Outer Banks—the 175-mile-chain of narrow sandy islands off the coast of North Carolina—he concluded they were an isthmus, and that the waters of the several sounds he could see on their western side were part of the "oriental sea." He sailed along the supposed isthmus hoping to find a strait or a way around it, so that he could "penetrate to those blessed shores of Cathay."[39] There was no opening.

Verrazano worked his way north; eventually he crossed the mouth of Bay of Fundy and moved up the coast of Nova Scotia. At Cape Breton Island he left the mainland and crossed Cabot Strait to Newfoundland, not realizing he had passed the entrance to the Gulf of St. Lawrence and an entrance to the interior of the continent. He continued north on the east coast of Newfoundland to latitude 50°N. Then, his supplies used up, he set a bearing for France.

In the course of the voyage, Verrazano went through the usual arrogant, meaningless ritual practiced by explorers of the day, claiming all the land he had passed for his king, Francis I. He is believed to have been the first to call the vast region from Florida to Labrador "New France." France used Verrazano's voyage as a basis for claiming much of the eastern seaboard of North America and the term "New France" appeared on some maps of the time. All of the coastline claimed by Verrazano, between the Spanish ventures in the south and the English enterprises in the north, had been previously traversed by navigators representing other nations including Spain's Estevan Gomez, probably in the same year.

Earlier explorers like Cortereal had inferred that the "New Founde Land," as America was called for want of a better name, was a vast continent that included Greenland as well as Florida. Verranzano's voyage confirmed the continental nature of the land discoveries beyond the Atlantic. Although he added little of a fundamental character to the world's knowledge of the geography of the east coast, he brought back the first detailed descriptions of the shoreline, the natives and how they lived, and the nature of their country. Also, his voyage marked the beginning of French participation in the exploration of Canada.

Verrazano reached France in the summer of 1524 to find that Francis I was again occupied with war in the Mediterranean. Francis was defeated and captured, and carried to Spain as the prisoner of the Spanish king. Although Verrazano was anxious to command another expedition across the Atlantic, under the circumstances official interest in "Terre Neuve" (as the French called the New World) flagged and the proposed voyage was postponed indefinitely.

Part Three

The Discovery of Canada

John Cabot had been followed soon to the northern part of North America—into the coastal waters of what is now Canada—by the Portuguese and Spanish mariners: Fernandes, Cortereal, Fagundes and Gomez. By the year 1524, only a quarter of a century after Cabot's voyage, they had rediscovered Greenland and Labrador, established that the new lands were part of a great continent extending from the frozen north to the Portuguese discoveries in South America, and had attempted to found a colony in the Gulf of St. Lawrence.

Undoubtedly history has failed to record some of the voyages to the northeast coast of North America made in the years between 1497, when Cabot first touched its shores, and 1534, the year that Jacques Cartier began the proper documentation of the geography of the St. Lawrence River system. The chronicles of such voyages—undertaken purposefully or by accident when they drifted off course—are lost, mislaid or destroyed, or perhaps news of the event was kept from the public record because the voyage was privately financed. Valuable and revealing historical documents continue to be found—in libraries, archives, museums and among the genealogical documents preserved by families. The last word about the precursors of Jacques Cartier, the man who is credited with the discovery of the St. Lawrence River for Europeans, has not been written.

Recently (1944), the historian Lanctot has presented evidence that shows Cartier took part in one of these obscure voyages ten years before his well-documented voyage into the Gulf of St. Lawrence. He traveled either as a member of Verrazano's 1524 expedition to "Terra Neuve" or as part of a privately funded venture to the Newfoundland area.

Lanctot found the principal evidence for a 1524 Cartier voyage in two sources. The first is a treatise written by a Father Pierre Biard in 1614, recounting his experiences in the New World. It includes a reference to Cartier that Biard may have found in Canada, or perhaps in the port of Dieppe where we can surmise he researched the local archives and shipping files to pass the days while waiting for passage to Terra Neuve. The reference states:

Canada...which extends along the banks of the great River of Canada, and the Gulf of St. Lawrence; this being only the most Northern part of New France...was discovered principally by Jacques Cartier in 1524 and then in a second voyage ten years afterward in 1534.[1]

The second source is the genealogical history of the House of Le Veneur preserved in the family archives in France—specifically, an extract prepared from these documents by Judge Henault, a relative of the family by marriage and a member of the French Academy. The extract supports the claim that Cartier voyaged to "Terre-Neuve" prior to 1532:

> ...in 1532, King Francis I had made a pilgrimage to Mont St. Michel.... [He was] received by Jean Le Veneur in the double capacity of Grand Almoner of France and Abbot of Mont St. Michel.
>
> It was during this pilgrimage that Jean Le Veneur presented to the king sieur Jacques Cartier, Pilot Mariner of St. Malo, a relative of the Bursur of Mont St. Michel Abbey, as being capable, in consideration of his voyages to Brazil and Terre-Neuve, of conducting ships in the discovery of new lands in the New World for the king.[2]

8

The Voyages of Jacques Cartier
1534–42

Cartier's introduction to Francis I in 1532 led to his appointment as "Captain and Pilot for the King" and a call from the king to continue the explorations of Verrazano and thereby to strengthen the claim to Terra Neuve that his 1524 voyage had given France. (In truth, compared to England, Portugal or even Spain, the French had done little to establish a claim in the part of America north of Florida; the claim was based entirely on the voyage of Verrazano.) In 1534, two years after meeting the king, Cartier undertook the first of three voyages under royal commission, to the New World. It began a new phase in the history of Canada.

Little is known about the early life of Jacques Cartier. He was born in 1491 and became a pilot domiciled in St. Malo, Brittany. In 1520, he married Catherine Des Granches, a woman whose family was more prominent than his own.[3] The records in St. Malo's Court of Justice and in its Registry of Vital Statistics include more than a hundred references to Cartier over a period of forty-seven years, testifying that he was active in the life of the town.[4] Curiously, despite these activities which reveal that he involved himself in such mundane activities as baptisms and acting as godfather to numerous children, his life in the town left only a shallow imprint on history.

1534—first voyage: Cartier explores the Gulf of St. Lawrence

Forty-one year old Jacques Cartier left St. Malo (latitude 48.5°N) on April 20, 1534 with two ships, each of about sixty tons burden, manned by sixty-one men in all. A royal order for the payment of equipment tells that he had instructions "to voyage to that realm of the Terres Neufves to discover certain isles and countries where it is said there must be great quantities of gold and other riches."[5] This meant, in plainer words, that he had orders to continue the search, begun by Verrazano, for a route to the riches of the Orient.

The Frenchmen enjoyed good sailing weather and intercepted the coast

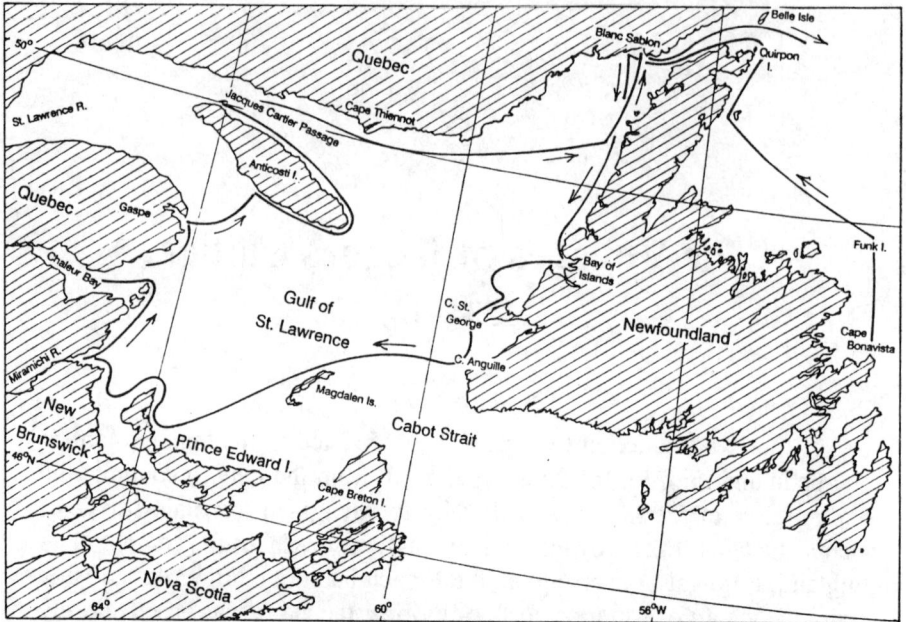

Figure 21. Jacques Cartier's exploration of the Gulf of St. Lawrence in 1534.

of North America on May 10, after twenty days at sea. Cartier had maintained a steady westerly bearing from St. Malo and it carried him to a landfall near Cape Bonavista, well down the eastern side of Newfoundland. The coastal waters were so adrift with blocks of ice that he put into Catalina harbor, about ten miles (16 km.) south of Bonavista, and stayed there for ten days waiting for the waters to clear. He used the time for rigging and fitting up his longboats with sails. The boats were small enough to be rowed if that became necessary, and they would be used for exploring openings that the ocean-going ships might be unable to enter for one reason or another.

They left Catalina harbor on May 21 and sailed northward with the purpose of passing around the north end of Newfoundland. As they approached Funk Island, they observed it was crowded with sea fowl including auks as large as geese. The island was surrounded by loose ice but the men got ashore with the longboats and easily filled the boats with the fat, tasteful birds whose wings were so small they could not fly.

The Gulf of St. Lawrence

They reached the Strait of Belle Isle on May 27 but the entrance to the Gulf of St. Lawrence was adrift with icebergs and Cartier decided it was not safe to attempt the passage. They anchored at Quirpon Island, off the northeastern tip of Newfoundland, in a convenient sheltered bay to wait for a more favorable time. On June 9, finally, they entered the strait and sailed through it into the gulf. Next day they anchored near Blanc Sablon on Quebec's south shore, twenty-five miles (40 km.) inside the gulf, to take on wood and water. We can assume from Cartier's decisive movements after he reached Newfoundland that he was familiar with the geography of the region either from a previous voyage or from talking with Brittany fishermen back in France.

Cartier used the next three days to explore the north side of the gulf with the longboats, searching for good harbors among the numerous off-shore islands. He met and went aboard a large ship from La Rochelle, France. Her captain intended to fish out of Blanc Sablon but had run past the bay in the night. Cartier guided him into one of the harbors he had discovered. Judging from the matter-of-fact manner in which Cartier reported the incident in his journal, he found nothing surprising about encountering an European ship in the gulf.

They made contact with natives along the coast and observed that they used furs to clothe themselves, and they decorated their hair with feathers and their faces with paint. They learned that the natives had come from "warmer countries" in birchbark canoes to hunt seals.

Cartier took the ships southward from Blanc Sablon on June 15, hugging the west coast of Newfoundland, past the entrance to the Bay of Islands. On June 18, when they were off Cape St. George, the wind blew strongly and as they could not find a harbor in which to anchor, they moved out into the gulf for the night. In the ensuing days, the stormy weather, head winds and overcast sky conspired to keep them out of sight of land until the 24th when they saw Cape Anguille, near the southwest tip of Newfoundland. The winds and fog prevented them from drawing near and on the following day Cartier chose to run westward before the wind, across Cabot Strait, leaving Newfoundland in his wake.

They passed by numerous islands in the gulf including the Bird Rocks and the Madeleines, and they were much astonished at the sight of walruses asleep in the sun. They came to the western corner of Prince Edward Island on June 29 and thought it was part of the mainland. They landed a number of times and saw Indians but did not make contact with them.

Chaleur Bay

They crossed from Prince Edward Island to the mainland on July 2 and went ashore briefly near the mouth of the Miramachi River, in New Brunswick. They continued north up the coast and next day (July 3) they

105

came to Chaleur Bay, twenty-five miles (40 km.) wide at its mouth and in places more than 300 feet (90 m.) deep. Cartier thought it might be the entrance to a strait leading into the "other" ocean and he anchored the ships in a small cove on the north side of the bay with the intent of testing this possibility.

Two days later, Cartier took one of the longboats into the bay to reconnoiter its trend beyond a prominent point which blocked the view inland from the ships. The Frenchmen had no sooner rounded the point and lost sight of their ships when they encountered forty to fifty canoe loads of natives crossing the bay before them. Some of the natives landed and set up a great clamor, motioning the white men to come ashore, holding up furs on sticks. Evidently white visitors were a familiar sight and known to have desirable goods to exchange for furs.

Cartier, with only one longboat, was badly outnumbered; he was reluctant to trust the natives and gave orders to row back to the ships. Seeing this, the natives closed in on the Frenchmen until seven canoes surrounded the longboat. Although they gave signs of joy and expressions of friendship, Cartier became uneasy and he waved them off. The natives persisted and Cartier felt compelled to fire his two small cannon over their heads to discourage them. The natives retired to the shore but then they came on again and this time Cartier dispersed them by setting off two fire bombs in their midst.

Next day (July 6), nine canoe loads of Indians entered the cove where the ships were anchored. Cartier sent out his two longboats to meet them and as they approached, the Indians made signs that they wanted to trade and held up furs. Cartier put two men ashore with gifts of knives and other iron goods, and a red cap for the chief. This seemed to establish good relations and soon all the natives had come ashore. They bartered all their furs, including those they wore, so that they were left quite naked. And they made signs that they would return with more furs.

On July 8, Cartier went up Chaleur Bay with both longboats. He was disappointed on the following day, to find the way barred by low mountains. He had reached the head of a bay—this was not a passage to that "other" sea. As the Frenchmen were returning to their ships at the mouth of the bay, they met natives again. They went ashore and presently more than 300 men, women and children joined them, singing and dancing and showing every evidence of joy at the presence of the white men. Trading was resumed and again the natives bartered everything they owned

> so that nothing was left to them but their naked bodies; for they offered us everything they owned, which was, all told, of little value.[6]

Cartier noted in his journal that these natives would be easy to convert to "our holy faith."

The Gaspé

Two days later, on July 12, Cartier continued his journey northward along the coast of the Gaspé Peninsula. Strong winds, fog and drizzle slowed their progress and caused them to anchor in Gaspé Bay. The weather deteriorated and Cartier was forced to move twenty or thirty miles (30–50 km.) into the bay to obtain adequate shelter. They remained there until July 25. During this time they met several hundred natives—men, women and children—who had come in canoes from several places in the interior to fish for mackerel with nets made from the thread of hemp. They appeared exceedingly poor but they were friendly and accepted small gifts—combs, tin bells and rings—with signs of great joy. They had brought with them Indian corn, beans, nuts and fruit of various kind. The Frenchmen observed that they ate their meat and fish almost raw, only warming it slightly in their campfires.

Cartier had a thirty-foot (9 m.) cross bearing the inscription—"VIVE LE ROY DE FRANCE"[7]—erected at the entrance to the bay and he marked the occasion with a ceremony. Later, the chief of the natives, with three sons and a brother, approached the ships in a canoe and in a long harangue, indicated that all the land in the region belonged to him and Cartier should have consulted him before erecting the cross. Cartier lured him close with the offer to barter an ax for the bearskin he was wearing—close enough to enable his men to seize the canoe and force the astonished Indians to come on board. Then Cartier told the chief that the cross was simply a landmark to guide Frenchmen back into the river. He said he intended to return to the bay and bring valuable goods with him. He said he wanted two of the chief's sons—Taignoagny and Dom Agaya—to come away with him and promised to bring them back. He greatly pleased the two young men by dressing each in a shirt, ribbons, a red cap and a chain to wear around the neck. He gave the chief and the others each a hatchet and two knives. The chief seemed satisfied with the arrangements and the next day brought thirty or forty natives to the ship to take their farewell of the sons and to give Cartier assurances that the cross would not be removed.

Cartier felt he had good reasons for inducing the brothers to leave the tribe and accompany him to France. He probably wanted to show the French king what kind of people lived in the New World and that they needed to be taught "the holy faith." Equally important, he wanted the two Indians to learn the French language so that when he returned, they could act as interpreters to help him learn what was known about the interior of this continent.

Anticosti Island and the Jacques Cartier Passage

Cartier left Gaspé Bay on July 25, sailing east-northeastward toward Anticosti Island. He thought the island was part of the mainland and that he was crossing the mouth of a bay. After intercepting the island, he followed its coastline eastward and passed around its eastern extremity. Then moving westward, he began tracing its north shore.

At sunrise on August 1, they saw to the north a thickly wooded shoreline and beyond that, inland, "a marvellously high coast cut into peaks."[8] (They were looking across Jacques Cartier Passage, which is the north entrance to the St. Lawrence River, alongside the south shore of Quebec.) Cartier crossed to the far shore, a distance of twenty-five miles (40 km.), and pressed on westward hoping this was a strait leading to another sea. The passage narrowed but when he reached the far end of the island, he saw that the expanse of water before him began to broaden to the west. This looked promising but now the ships encountered strong headwinds and they could make no progress. Cartier anchored and attempted to continue with the longboats but the tide had turned against him and the men could make no headway with the oars. Eventually they gave up and returned to the ships.

Back on board, Cartier assembled the captains, pilots, masters and sailors to receive their advice on how the expedition should proceed. The unsuccessful attempt to move ships and longboats through the passage suggested he would have to study the tides to find a more propitious time to make another attempt to pass through and explore the country to the west. It was August 1 and the sailing season was well advanced. They were in a strange land and they must think about the coming winter. The period of strong east winds, characteristic of the autumn, was approaching and soon they might have difficulty getting back to France. Either they should sail for France immediately or begin preparations to spend the winter in the New World. The assembled men decided, by a large majority, to sail for France.

Return to France

Cartier, taking advantage of a strong favorable wind, began the return voyage immediately, sailing eastward alongside the north shore of the Gulf of St. Lawrence. They sighted smoke rising from campfires as they passed Cape Thiennot but because the wind blew toward the shore, they did not attempt to land. Seeing the fleet passing by, some dozen Indians in two canoes came after them and readily boarded the ships. They intimated that they lived near the entrance to the Strait of Belle Isle. They said that all the ships that had come from across the Atlantic to fish in the gulf had already left the region with their season's catch.

Cartier took the ships across the gulf to the west coast of Newfoundland on August 8 in heavy weather and now the winds blew with "fury and violence."[9] He managed to work the ships back to the north (Quebec) shore, to a protected anchorage at Blanc Sablon. They remained there, waiting out the weather, preparing for the voyage across the Atlantic. On August 15, after hearing mass, they passed through the Strait of Belle Isle in fine weather and moved into the Atlantic. They reached St. Malo on September 5, 1534; the voyage had taken four and one half months.

1535–6, second voyage: Cartier enters the St. Lawrence River

Soon after he returned to France, Cartier began preparations for a second voyage to the New World. He had probably learned from his Indian captives that the expanse of water beyond the point of his most westerly progress was a great river. The second voyage would be a more ambitious project for he planned to spend the winter on that river. Early in May, 1535 all was ready and on the 16th, he and his crews

> each confessed himself and we all received our Creator together in the Cathedral of St. Malo. After communion we went and kneeled in the choir of the church before the Reverend Father in God Monseigneur St. Malo who, in his episcopal state, gave us his benediction."[10]

On Wednesday, May 19, "the wind came fair and in our favour and we set sail from St. Malo with three vessels"[11]—the *Grand Hermyne* (100–200 tons), the *Petite Hermyne* (60 tons) and the *Hemerillon* (40 tons) "for the completion of the discovery of the western lands."[12] They enjoyed good weather until May 26 when it turned stormy and they were plagued by headwinds and an overcast sky. On June 25 the ships became separated in foggy weather and could not find each other. Cartier, in the *Grand Hermyne*, reached Funk Island on July 7 and paused for a day to kill and load his two longboats with the birds in which the island abounded. He continued to the north, entered the Strait of Belle Isle and on July 15, dropped anchor at Blanc Sablon where he had arranged a rendezvous in the event the fleet became separated. The other two ships arrived, together, on July 26, sixty-eight days after leaving St. Malo. It had been a long voyage.

They sailed westward on July 29 after making minor repairs and taking on wood, water and other necessities. They moved along the north shore of the bay, examining the islands and looking for good harbors but primarily searching the shoreline for an opening into that "other sea" that would let them reach the Orient. They entered Jacques Cartier Passage and on August 9 they came to a "a very fine large bay, full of islands and with good entrances and anchorage for any weather that might prevail."[13] It was about as far west as Cartier had reached on the first voyage. He named it St. Lawrence's Bay; in time the name "St. Lawrence" was used for the gulf and eventually, also, for the great river that flows into it. Today Cartier's St. Lawrence's Bay is called Pillage Bay.

First Europeans of record on the St. Lawrence River

They left Pillage Bay on August 13, continuing westward, and this time easily cleared the Jacques Cartier Passage. Technically, they were now in the St. Lawrence River. They rounded the western tip of Anticosti Island and coasted along its southern shore, completing the circuit they had begun in the first voyage, establishing that it was an island and not part of the mainland as Cartier had concluded in the previous year.

Cartier crossed the river to its south shore on August 17. His captive Indians, Taignoagny and Dom Agaya, told him this was the start of the canoe route

> to Canada; and that two days' journey from this cape [the Gaspé]
> and island [Anticosti] began the kingdom of the Saguenay, on
> the north shore as one made one's way towards this Canada.[14]

Cartier thought the natives were talking about a territory or kingdom called Canada. The word canada, or kanata[15] was an Indian word for town[16] and the brothers were trying to make Cartier understand that the canoe route from the Gaspé ran alongside the south shore of the St. Lawrence River, past the mouth of the Saguenay River which comes in from the north, to the kanata (that is, the town) of Stadacona where they lived. The kingdom of the Saguenay was thought to lie somewhere northwest of the junction of the St. Lawrence and Saguenay Rivers.

Later, Cartier began using the word "Canada" to designate a region centered on the town of Stadacona (the site of modern-day Quebec) and including about a hundred miles of the St. Lawrence River. Cartographers picked up the name Canada from Cartier and used it on early maps of North America for the most northerly part of New France—the part bordering on

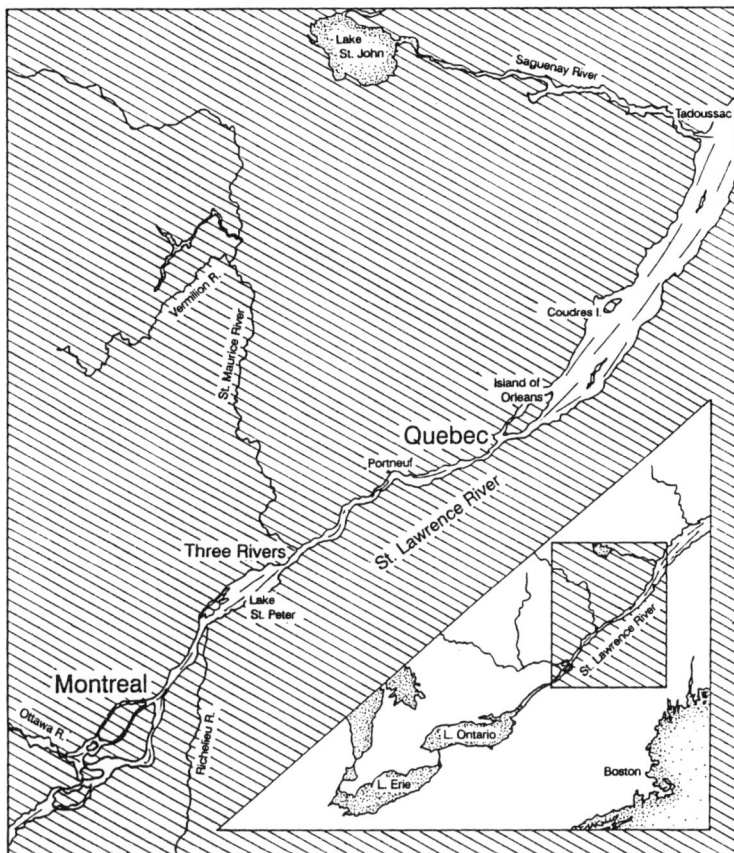

Figure 22. The St. Lawrence River between the Ottawa and Saguenay Rivers. Quebec and Montreal occupy the sites, respectively, of the Indian villages of Stadacona and Hochelaga.

the Gulf of St. Lawrence and the St. Lawrence River.

Taignoagny and Dom Agaya told Cartier the river became fresh as one approached Stadacona and it narrowed so that eventually it was possible to proceed only with small boats. They had never heard of anyone reaching its headwaters. Cartier concluded from these remarks that the river would take him into the deep interior of the Terra Neuve but it was unlikely to be a passage to the "other sea."[17] Therefore, he decided to make one more search for a strait before starting up the canoe route to Canada.

He crossed the river, and reached and anchored the ships at Sept-Iles on August 19. Then he used the longboats to examine the part of the north coast he had not traversed previously. By August 21 he had satisfied himself that no strait existed; he found only walruses. He returned to the ships intending to start up the river immediately but fog and headwinds kept them at Sept-Iles until August 24.

On September 1 they came to the Saguenay, "a very deep and rapid river, which is the river and route to the kingdom and country of the

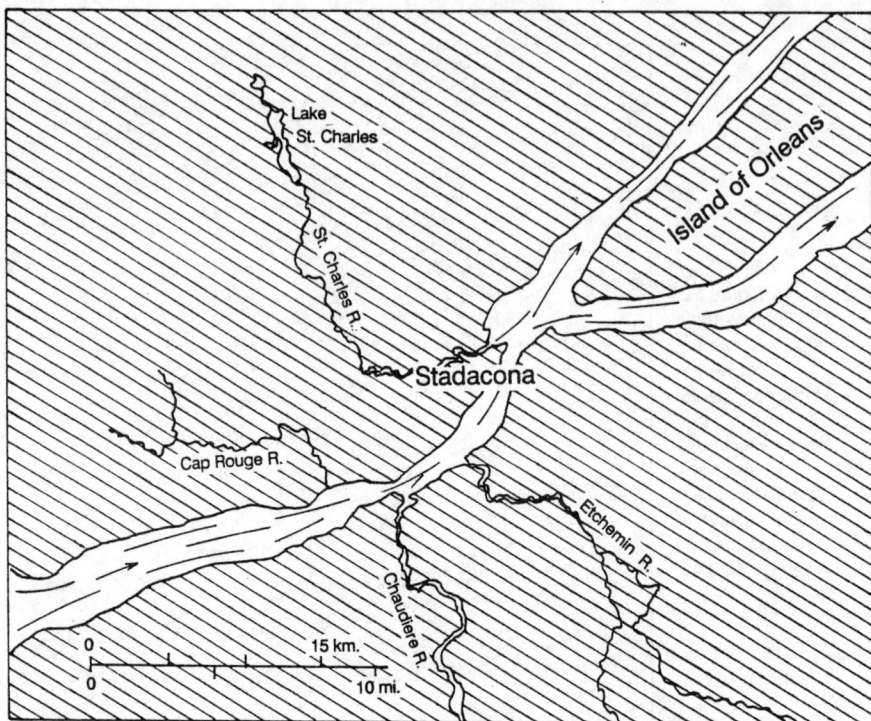

Figure 23. The St. Lawrence River in the vicinity of the Indian village of Stadacona (the site, later, of Quebec City). Cartier called this region of the St. Lawrence valley "Canada."

Saguenay."[18] The area was bare and rocky, and the Frenchmen were astonished to see various kinds of trees, some quite tall, growing on "this naked rock." They found four canoes near the mouth of the Saguenay, their native owners having come down the St. Lawrence from Stadacona to fish and catch seals. The natives seemed terrified of the ships and would not approach until Cartier's Indians called to them and identified themselves. Word of the French expedition had been carried up the St. Lawrence River and had preceded their arrival at the mouth of the Saguenay. The ships with their dark hulls and spread sails, and the sight and sound of their cannon being fired, had been likened by the messengers to great white-winged animals that spat fire and thunder.

Canada

As they continued up the river, reefs and extremely swift and transverse tidal streams made their progress difficult and at times, hazardous. Near Coudres Island (between the present-day cities of Rivière-du-Loup and Quebec), they came onto a school of beluga whales; natives told them, later, this was the only part of the river in which they were found. According to their captives, the island marked the beginning of the country controlled by the chief who lived in Stadacona; Cartier interpreted this as the beginning of the country of Canada.

On September 7, they reached the large island of Orleans. Cartier went ashore taking Taignoagny and Dom Agaya with him. He found the island inhabited by Indians whose main occupation seemed to be fishing. They would not come near the white strangers until the captives called to them, explaining they were Taignoagny and Dom Agaya from the town of Stadacona, who had crossed the sea with the white men and had returned unharmed.[19] Then the natives welcomed the Frenchmen and brought them gifts of food—eels and other fish, Indian corn and melons. After the white men had gone back on board, many canoe loads of Indian men and women came out to the ships to see and speak with the two captives, assuring themselves that they had suffered no ill treatment. Cartier distributed small gifts and although they were of little value, the Indians were much pleased with them.

Next day (September 8) Donnacona, the Lord of Canada as Cartier described him, came to the ships accompanied by twelve canoe loads of Indians. When he was opposite the smallest of the three ships, he "began to make a speech and to harangue us, moving his body and his limbs in a marvellous manner, as is their custom when showing joy and contentment."[20] It was obvious he was delighted to see his sons again.

After the visit from the Indians, Cartier went upriver with the longboats to find a suitable place to lay up the ships. He had learned of the existence of a large village called Hochelaga (on the site of present-day Montreal) well up the river and he planned to visit it. It was clear from what he had been told about the river above him, that he would have to leave the large ships and journey to Hochelaga with his longboats. He chose the mouth of the St. Charles River, which flows into the St. Lawrence from the north at the western tip of the Island of Orleans, (near present-day Quebec City) as the site for his base. Nearby lived the tribe of which Donnacona was chief, in the village of Stadacona.

Cartier moved the ships to their new anchorage on September 14 and there he was met by Donnacona supported by twenty-five canoe loads of his people and his two sons, Taignoagny and Dom Agaya, who had rejoined the tribe. The French were well received by all the natives except the latter two. They had suddenly changed their attitude to Cartier; they were unfriendly and refused to come back on board.

Next day when Cartier went ashore, he was greeted by a large number of natives from the village but now Donnacona and a number of his people joined the two previous captives in distancing themselves from the French.

Cartier sought out the group and spoke with them. Taignoagny told him that Donnacona was displeased because Cartier and his men carried so many weapons. Cartier replied it was the French custom as Taignoagny well knew. It came to Cartier that Taignoagny spoke for himself, that he was bent on making trouble for him with Donnacona. Taignoagny was determined to prevent Cartier from going upriver to the village of Hochelaga; he wanted the people of Stadacona to be the principal contact with the French and thereby control the distribution of metal goods—knives, hatchets, needles, kettles and other cooking utensils—that the French could bring to the New World. He had observed the practice of commerce in France and had learned, quickly, that control meant power and profit. The language barrier made it difficult for Cartier to discuss matters of mutual interest with Donnacona; he depended on Taignoagny and Dom Agaya to act as interpreters and he was sure the brothers had begun distorting each conversation to suit their own ends.

On the following day (September 16), the Frenchmen were greeted by more than 500 men, women and children, and Donnacona came on board with a dozen of the headmen of the village. Taignoagny said the purpose of the visit was to inform Cartier that the chief was annoyed about the proposed journey to Hochelaga. Cartier replied that his mind was made up; he had orders from his king and he was going to visit the village.

Next day, at a ceremony, Donnacona presented Cartier with a ten or twelve year old girl and two small boys. Taignoagny explained that the purpose of the gift was to induce Cartier to forego the journey to Hochelaga. Cartier replied that if that was the price of the gift he would have to return the children. He said he intended to make the journey but he did not return the children to the chief.

Hochelaga

Two days later (September 19), Cartier left Stadacona and started the 40-ton *Hemerillon* and two longboats up the river, leaving the two larger ships at anchor. Neither of the brothers accompanied him. Cartier was impressed with the country alongside the St. Lawrence River:

> Along both shores we had sight of the finest and most beautiful
> land it is possible to see, being as level as a pond and covered
> with the most magnificent trees in the world.[21]

The forest had been cleared in places to provide space for villages and fields for growing crops. Cartier noted that fishing seemed to be one of the main occupations of the natives. The people were friendly and unafraid; it was evident that the visit of the Frenchmen afforded them a pleasurable diversion and they were eager to exchange food and whatever else they had for French wares.

At the village of Achelacy (near the present town of Portneuf) situated just below the Richelieu Rapid, the local chief presented Cartier with two of his children—a boy of two or three, and a girl of eight or nine. Cartier refused to take the boy; he was too young.

The expedition came to a halt on Lake St. Peter. The river immediately above them was composed of four or five branches and none at this time of the year was more than six feet (2 m.) deep where it entered the lake. They would have to leave the *Hemerillon* on the lake and go on with the longboats. They met five Indians here, hunting for game. They showed no alarm at sight of the white men and greeted them in an open and friendly manner. When one of the longboats grounded, a particularly big Indian picked up Cartier as if he were a child and carried him to shore. They indicated by sign language that it would take another three days to reach Hochelaga.

Cartier had the longboats provisioned, and accompanied by his captains, four "gentlemen" and twenty-six sailors, he pushed on in fine weather. The party arrived before the palisaded Indian village of Hochelaga on October 2 to a greeting by more than a thousand people. It seemed to the white men that they were received like gods, particularly when the women brought their babies to be touched by Cartier and his companions. Cartier distributed knives, beads and other trinkets and the Indians showered their visitors with fish and bread made from Indian corn. There was much dancing and even after the whites returned to the longboats to sleep, the Indians continued to dance all through the night by the light of their fires.

Next day (October 3) Cartier, elaborately clothed and accompanied by his "gentlemen" and twenty sailors, visited the Indian establishment. They were welcomed into the village by girls and women who crowded around the Frenchmen, rubbing the faces and the upper parts of the visitors' bodies (it seemed to be their way of signifying welcome), weeping with joy and holding up their babies to be touched. Their chief, suffering from total paralysis, was carried into the crowd and Cartier was invited to touch his limbs. Then the sick, blind, lame and old people were brought before Cartier so that he might lay his hands on them. Clearly, the white strangers were considered to be more than mere mortals. Cartier made the sign of the cross over them and read passages from the Bible and a prayer book. He gave gifts to everyone and then, to the delight and astonishment of all, he had the trumpets and other musical instruments sounded.

The Frenchmen estimated the village consisted of about fifty wooden houses, each measuring about 150 by 40 to 50 feet (45 x 12–15 m.) in size. It was circular in shape, built against the foot of a mountain and completely enclosed by a three-tiered wooden palisade thirty feet (9 m.) high. Several hundred cultivated acres of corn lay within easy reach of the village.

They climbed to the top of the mountain, which Cartier named Mont Royal[22], and obtained a view of the surrounding country for a distance of almost a hundred miles (160 km.). They saw the Lachine Rapids on the St. Lawrence River above the position of their longboats, and the broad river itself, flowing in from the southwest as far as the eye could see. They saw to the north, the Ottawa River and were informed that the Indians living along it were an aggressive people, constantly at war with other tribes; they dressed themselves in "armor" made of wood slats bound together with cords for protection in fighting.

Cartier was concerned about the safety of the *Hemerillon* and the seamen he had left to guard her. As soon as his party had descended the mountain and reached the longboats, he had the sails raised and they started down the river, much to the regret of the people of Hochelaga who followed them a considerable distance. They reached the *Hemerillon* next day (on October 4) and found nothing amiss. It took a week to reach the mouth of the St. Charles River where the other two ships lay at anchor.

Cartier spends the 1535–6 winter in Canada

Cartier found relations with the Indians at Stadacona tense. The men who had stayed behind, fearing they might be attacked, had built a fort before the ships and surrounded it with a palisade made of logs planted upright in the ground. They had mounted artillery to guard the approach to the fort from the land. At Donnacona's invitation, Cartier visited the village accompanied by his gentlemen and a force of fifty seamen. It was an impressive display of power and it earned him respect and a welcome from the villagers.

Cartier learned about Indian warfare and the treatment of enemies when Donnacona showed him five scalps "stretched on hoops like parchment."[23] The chief said they had been taken from Indians who lived south of the St. Lawrence River and waged continuous war against his people. Two years previously, they had massacred almost two hundred of his men, women and children one night when they were camped on an island in the St. Lawrence, opposite the Saguenay. They had set the camp afire and killed his people as they rushed from the shelters to escape the flames. Only five had survived.

The Indians resumed coming to the ships after this meeting, bringing food to barter for knives, awls, beads and other items. Cartier had been cautioned by the chief of Achelacy to trust neither the two brothers nor Donnacona and his headmen. And Taignoagny and Dom Agaya did continue to undermine attempts to maintain good relations, telling the natives that the food they gave the white men was worth much more than the wares they got in exchange.

Donnacona tried to recover the children he had presented to Cartier, saying he had given them on condition that Cartier would not journey to Hochelaga. When Cartier refused to part with them, the girl escaped. Cartier assumed she had been induced to leave his ship. To show his displeasure and lack of trust in the people of Stadacona, he strengthened his defenses by digging a deep ditch around the palisade, and adding a gate and drawbridge. And he maintained a strong watch throughout the nights.

These actions upset the Canadians and they attempted to get back into Cartier's good graces. At first Cartier dealt harshly with them. He called them traitors and rogues, and he upbraided Taignoagny for going back on his promise to accompany him to Hochelaga and for stealing the girl. Within days the girl was returned to Cartier and the natives were at pains to persuade him that they had not counseled her to run away, that she had done so on her own volition because the cabin boys beat her. Cartier reciprocated by entertaining the natives with bread and wine, and friendly relations were resumed.

Cartier heard many fanciful stories that winter. He was told that the people of the kingdom of the Saguenay were as white as the French, that they dressed in woolen clothes and owned great stores of gold, copper and rubies. It was said that men in another region had no anus because they never ate and had no need to evacuate; their bodily functions consisted simply of making water through the penis. In another country, the people had only one leg.

In December Cartier "received warning that the pestilence had broken out among the people of Stadacona to such an extent, that already, by their own confession, more than fifty persons were dead."[24] He feared a plague but there was no escape for the white men; their ships were caught in the frozen river. He immediately broke off all contact with the Indians but despite this, the Frenchmen were soon affected. The disease sapped the strength of the men. Their legs and then their upper extremities became swollen and blotched in appearance, and their gums rotted exposing the roots of the teeth which became loose and fell out. By the middle of February, 1536, not ten men could be considered healthy. They suffered terribly through that winter. Men died and the dead had to be buried temporarily in the snow for the living did not have the strength to dig graves in the frozen earth. Curiously, Cartier was not affected.

In the belief that "he who is on guard against everything, escapes something,"[25] Cartier took elaborate pains to hide their plight from the natives, fearing they would be attacked if the true extent of their weakness became known. To account for the absence of his men outdoors, he pretended they were busy at various tasks below deck in the ships. To support this fabrication, he had the sick men make noises with sticks and stones inside the ships, giving the impression they were hard at work.

> During this period there died to the number of twenty-five of the best and most able seamen we had, who all succumbed to the aforesaid malady. And at that time there was little hope of saving more than forty others, while the whole of the rest were ill, except three or four. But God in His divine grace had pity upon us, and sent us knowledge of a remedy which cured and healed all.[26]

Cartier learned of the remedy one day in April when he was outdoors and saw Dom Agaya, who recently had been very sick, walking about apparently in good health. He inquired about his rapid recovery and the Indian told him he had cured himself by drinking a juice obtained by boiling the leaves and bark of the hemlock tree. He instructed two squaws to show Cartier the tree and explain how to prepare the drink. The juice worked a miracle in the ships; within a week, the men, although still weak from their ordeal, were free of scurvy, for that was the disease that had afflicted them. Some of the seamen declared it had also completely cured the French pox from which they had suffered for five or six years. Twenty-five seamen died before the remedy was discovered; they were given a decent burial in the spring.

Donnacona and Taignoagny began brewing more trouble in the spring. The two men went off in February, ostensibly on a deer hunt, but they were away for two months and Cartier feared they were seeking assistance to do him mischief. They returned in April and now the village seemed to harbor an inordinate number of strange Indians. Moreover, Cartier's seamen were no longer welcomed into the houses of the village and this confirmed Cartier's suspicions that Donnacona was keeping something from him.

Cartier prepares to return to France

Meanwhile, Taignoagny was plotting treachery of his own design. He sent word that if Cartier would capture Agona, a local chief who had slighted him, and carry him off to France, Taignoagny would agree to do whatever Cartier asked of him. Cartier had already decided he could best protect himself and further his ends, by seizing Donnacona, Taignoagny, Dom

Agaya and the headmen of the village. He was particularly bent on carrying Donnacona to France because he wanted the king to hear, first hand, the chief's tales of white men on the Saguenay and their wealth. It would be a strong inducement for financing another voyage to the New World.

Donnacona, perhaps sensing something was afoot, became wary and would not come near the ships. To allay his fears, Cartier told Taignoagny the king had forbidden him to carry adults to France but he offered to convey Agona as far as Newfoundland and put him off there. This satisfied Taignoagny and in turn, it seemed to assure Donnacona that he was in no danger of being forced to accompany Cartier to France. Still, the Indians did not totally trust Cartier's intentions.

On May 3 in the early afternoon, Cartier observed a large party of natives approaching the ships. He thought his opportunity had come and he ordered his men to prepare to seize the chief, Taignoagny, Dom Agaya and two headmen when he gave the word. He greeted Donnacona and invited him and Taignoagny to come on board to eat and drink as usual. The chief was uneasy but presently, although Taignoagny had counseled against it, he entered the fort with Cartier. Seeing this, Taignoagny warned the Indian women to flee before fighting began and forgetting caution, rushed into the fort to rescue the chief. There was now a considerable number of Indian men gathered in front of the palisade and they were extremely agitated. Cartier decided to make the first move. He signaled his men to take hold of the Indians whose capture he had planned and then he commanded that the others be driven away. They were already fleeing; Cartier's determined actions had decided the issue.

At nightfall a large number of natives appeared on the opposite bank of the river and began clamoring to speak with the chief. Cartier would not allow it and they kept at it all night. About noon the next day they accused Cartier of killing the chief. To prevent them from doing something desperate, he had the chief brought on deck. Cartier told the chief he would be returned to his people after he had spoken with the king, and that the king would give him a fine present. This seemed to satisfy the chief and his people, and Cartier permitted them to come alongside the ship in their canoes so that they could converse more comfortably.

The next day (May 5) the natives gathered on the river and sent four women to the ships in a canoe with a large quantity of food—Indian corn, fresh meat and fish—for the chief. Cartier allowed them on board and at Donnacona's request, he told them that their chief would return to them "within ten or twelve moons."[27] The tribe had to be satisfied with this.

The loss of twenty-five men to scurvy had left Cartier shorthanded and he was obliged to abandon the *Petite Hermyne* for want of men to work her.

He gave the hull to a group of visiting Indians that they might extract the nails; iron was a much prized item, used for many purposes. On May 6, he took the other two ships out of the St. Charles River and started down the St. Lawrence. He kept to the south shore, skirted the Gaspé Peninsula, passed by the northern tip of Cape Breton Island, crossed Cabot Strait and arrived at Cape Ray on the southwestern corner of Newfoundland on June 4. He remained there for two days and then sailed on to the St. Pierre and Miquelon Islands where they tarried to take on wood and fresh water; and they stored one of the longboats at Cape Race on the southeastern tip of Newfoundland. They encountered several ships from France and Brittany while they were at anchor.

Having completed all preparations for the Atlantic crossing, Cartier embarked on June 16 and set a course for France. They were favored by good weather and arrived at St. Malo on July 16, 1536.

Cartier's third voyage: 1541–2

Francis I and his court were fascinated by Cartier's description of his discoveries, and the prospect of finding a wealthy white kingdom along the Saguenay River was intriguing. The king was anxious to share these riches but France was at war with Spain again and the war absorbed time and money. Serious preparations for a third voyage did not begin until the Treaty of Nice was signed by the two nations in 1538, two years after Cartier's return. The next voyage would be a more elaborate undertaking for the plan that took form called for creating a settlement in Canada—a base for establishing and expanding the influence of France in America.

Word that Francis proposed to dispatch another expedition to "a river in the land of the Cod [commanded by]...a Breton pilot named Jacques Cartier"[28] began to circulate in 1539. Charles I of Spain was apprised of the French preparations by his ambassador to France in 1540. The scope of the expedition—not only to explore the region but to found a colony—had a sound of permanence that disturbed Charles. He immediately instructed the Cardinal of Toledo to call in the French ambassador and protest these actions. He claimed they were a violation of the Treaty of Tordesillas—that the territory visited by Cartier was in the Spanish sphere of influence. He charged that the real purpose of establishing a French settlement on the great river was to stage an attack on Spain's Indies from the rear.

Not content with this approach, Charles ordered the governing authority for the Indies to consider the matter. It deliberated for a month and then recommended that spies be sent to discover the nature of the proposed expedition; that the defenses of the Indies be strengthened and its Spanish population armed; that a fleet be prepared for the defense of the Indies; that officials of Seville begin storing, secretly, a quantity of food supplies; that Indies-bound ships from Seville travel in convoys and be armed; and that Spain negotiate a mutual defense-alliance with Portugal. It did not recommend any aggressive action against France.

Charles also appealed to the pope for support (the Treaty of Tordesillas had papal sanction). The French king countered by declaring that one important aim of the settlement was to begin the work, long delayed, of converting the "heathens" in the northern reaches of the American continent to the Roman Catholic faith.[29]

Francis awarded Cartier a commission in October, 1540 and authorized him to choose fifty prisoners to be the first settlers in Canada. When this news reached Charles, he instructed the Cardinal of Toledo to order his fleet to sea and in company with the Portuguese fleet, to destroy any of Cartier's ships they might encounter and kill all his seamen.

The Cardinal was reluctant to commit Spain to such a provocative act and risk open hostilities with France. After meeting with the various pertinent councils, he recommended to Charles that a spy be sent to the port of St. Malo where Cartier was preparing his fleet; that a commander be designated for the Spanish fleet and 1000 men readied for action; that a survey of Andalusian ports in Spain be made to find ships that could be usefully requisitioned; and that Portugal be asked to close its ports to French ships.

Charles approved the Cardinal's recommendations and related that he had complained to the pope about the French king's actions. The Cardinal answered that little help could be expected from the pope or, for that matter, from the Indies. Treasuries had been exhausted by recent wars; neither Spain nor France had the finances to mount a decisive action.

Cartier sails for Canada

French preparations for the expedition continued unchecked. Francis appointed Jean-François de la Rocque, Lord of Roberval, to act as "his Lieutenent and Governour in the Countreys of Canada and Hochelaga and [he named] the sayd Cartier Captaine generall and leader of the shippes."[30] Roberval, a Protestant, was an odd choice for governor since Francis had declared that one of the principal reasons for founding the colony was the conversion of the Indians to the Catholic faith. Few Frenchmen were volunteering to live in Canada, and Francis ordered that any prisoners thought to make good settlers should be turned over to Roberval.

In April, 1541 the Spanish ambassador in France obtained a secret report which claimed that

> Canada, where they [the French] intend to take the said army...faces the Indies of the [Holy Roman] Emperor [Charles V = Charles I of Spain] and is certainly a cape of these. And [at that place] where they wish to harbor the ships of the Very Christian [French] King there flows a great river with gentle waters towards the said Indies.[31]

The report seemed to imply that the French were readying an army to attack the Spanish Indies from Canada using the St. Lawrence River for access. Obviously, the writer of the report had not the vaguest knowledge of the geography of North America. But the report confirmed Charles' suspicions that the French objective in the New World was not Canada but the Indies.

Rumor had it that Francis had provided funds for ten ships, 400 seamen, 300 soldiers, some skilled tradesmen, a few women, and quantities of livestock and supplies.[32] It was reported that Cartier would sail from St. Malo with six ships; Roberval would leave France from further up the coast with four ships.

The Spanish immediately prepared and sent out two light fast ships to search for the expedition. One was dispatched to Newfoundland and the other to the Cape Verde Islands in the event that the French were planning a frontal attack on the West Indies. It was learned at the islands, that four French ships had passed that way, steering west-southwest. The Spanish ship gave chase but a storm forced it to abandon the hunt.

Cartier was on his way well before the Spanish began searching for him, having sailed from St. Malo with five ships on May 23, 1541. Bad weather scattered his fleet and severely lengthened the passage across the Atlantic. He was carrying cattle, goats, hogs and other animals intended for the settlement. The fresh water supply was exhausted before he reached Newfoundland and the animals had to be given cider to slake their thirst. He was still at sea when the Newfoundland-bound Spanish ship reached America. Her captain was informed that Cartier had already passed into the Gulf of St. Lawrence and he abandoned the chase.

Cartier reached Newfoundland in August and rendezvoused at Quirpon Island, off the northeastern tip of Newfoundland, with his five ships and waited for Roberval. But Roberval was still at anchor in France, waiting for the delivery of his guns and ammunition; he would not leave until the armaments were in place. Finally, the season now well advanced, Cartier passed through the Strait of Belle Isle into the Gulf of St. Lawrence and entered the St. Lawrence River. He arrived at his previous anchorage in the mouth of the St. Charles River on August 23.

Cartier was greeted by Agona at the head of six or seven canoe loads of Indians from Stadacona. Agona, who ruled Canada in Donnacona's absence, asked after the Indians Cartier had taken to France in 1536. They had not fared well in the intervening five years; all except the little girl had died. Cartier admitted that Donnacona was dead but he told Agona the others had become "great Lords" and were married, and had decided to remain in France. The natives' earlier treatment at Cartier's hands had given them little reason to trust him and they may have surmised that his report on the fate of their countrymen was mainly lies. Still, the natives showed no antagonism toward the white men and Agona, for one, was not unhappy at the news about Donnacona; it meant he would continue as the chief of Canada.

The Cap-Rouge settlement

Thinking, perhaps, that it would be wise to select another location for his base, Cartier took his ships up the St. Lawrence River another twelve miles (20 km.) to a more commodious anchorage where the Cap-Rouge River flows in from the north. It was a small river "not past 50. pases broad"[33] at its mouth, twisting through wooded country and open meadows thick with grass. A high rocky promontory at its mouth could be fortified to command passage along the St. Lawrence River and defend against entry to the Cap-Rouge River. This is where Cartier chose to establish the first settlement in Canada. The move to Cap-Rouge and the plans to build and fortify a settlement did nothing to improve relations with the people of Stadacona.

Cartier had decided to send two of his five ships back to France. He removed their cannon and positioned them on shore at river level to protect the proposed settlement and the three vessels he intended to keep with him. That done, he began building a fort on the promontory. He had brought provisions enough for two years but to add fresh vegetables to the crews' diet, he set twenty men to prepare and till about an acre of land and sow it with turnips, cabbages, lettuce and other vegetables. It was the fall of the year but the seeds sprouted within eight days in the rich soil.

The bedrock rising out of the river valley was visibly mineralized. The rock was

> a kind of slate stone blacke and thicke, wherein are veines of mynerall matter, which shewe like gold and silver: and through-out all that stone there are great graines of the sayd Myne. And

in some places we have found stones like Diamants, the most faire, pollished and excellently cut that it is possible for a man to see. When the Sunne shineth upon them, they glister as it were sparkles of fire.[34]

By September 2 the food and goods intended for the settlement had been taken ashore and stored, and the two ships were on their way back to St. Malo with letters for the king describing Cartier's preparations for wintering in Canada.

There was still time for exploration before the winter set in. Cartier wanted to visit the kingdom of the Saguenay in the spring to investigate the stories of white people, woolen clothing and precious metals and stones. He had been told the best way to reach the kingdom was not by way of the Saguenay River, but up the Ottawa River which entered the St. Lawrence a few miles above Hochelaga. He knew he would have to ascend several rapids above the village to reach the Ottawa. The rapids were said to be a serious obstacle and he wanted to see them so that he could use the winter to plan the logistics for taking a force of men and all their supplies to the Saguenay kingdom.

He started up the St. Lawrence on September 7 with two longboats. He stopped at Achelacy with gifts for the chief who had given him a little girl in 1535, and left two French boys to learn the language. On September 11 he arrived at the foot of the rapid of St. Mary. It looked to be a difficult ascent and Cartier decided to leave one of the boats and double-man the other. In vain—the bed of the river was so rock-strewn and the strength of the current so great, they could not gain the top. They landed and found a well beaten trail beside the river; clearly the local people carried their canoes and goods along this part of the route.

They walked up the portage and above the rapids they came onto a village where the people were exceedingly friendly. After Cartier had got the natives to understand that he wanted to visit the kingdom of the Saguenay, four young men offered to show him the way. They accompanied him to a village at the foot of a second rapid (the Lachine) where Cartier learned he would have to ascend a third rapid (the Long Sault) to reach the Ottawa River. He was informed, too, that the Ottawa was not navigable over its full length.

It was now obvious to Cartier that he would have to depend on Indian canoes and paddlers if he intended to travel in the interior of this continent with its many portages between the navigable stretches of river. The French longboats were heavily-built craft, designed for use in coastal waters and never intended to be moved any distance on land, and certainly not over

Indian portages. Champlain reached the same conclusion in 1603 when he came onto the Lachine Rapids:

> I never saw any torrent of water pour over with such force as this does...and whenever it falls from some small height, it boils up extraordinarily, owing to the force and speed of the water as it passes through the said rapid...he who would pass them must provide himself with the canoes of the savages, which a man can easily carry...besides this first rapid, there are ten more, for the most part difficult to pass; so that it would be a matter of great toil and labour to be able to see and do by boat what a man might propose, except at great cost and expense, besides the risk of labouring in vain. But with the canoes of the savages one may travel freely and quickly throughout the country, as well up the little rivers as up the large ones.[35]

Cartier learned also, at the village, that the Ottawa River would not take him all the way to the kingdom of the Saguenay. He would have to leave the river at some point and strike northeast across country along the height of land that is the source of the rivers that flow into the St. Lawrence from the north. He had seen and heard enough to know a journey to the Saguenay would be no small undertaking. He turned back, picking up the two French boys he had left at Achelacy; the chief was not at the village.

Cartier reached Cap-Rouge to find that relations with the Stadacona Indians had chilled. The supposedly friendly chief of Achelacy had taken it upon himself to turn Agona, the new lord of Canada, against Cartier in his absence. The Indians' lack of trust in the words and deeds of the French had turned to hostility. The natives no longer brought the much-needed gifts of fish to the white men. It appeared they were gathering in large numbers in the village and conspiring to rid themselves of the Frenchmen and the settlement.

There is no official French account of Cartier's winter (1541–2) at Cap-Rouge; historians have had to rely on the stories brought home by French, Spanish and Portuguese seamen who fished the waters around Newfoundland. Apparently Cartier lost about thirty-five men during the time they were constructing the buildings—killed by Indians armed with bow-and-arrow and carrying wooden shields. Early in June, 1542, he abandoned the Cap-Rouge settlement and sailed for France with the remainder of his company.

Roberval's attempt to re-establish the Cap-Rouge colony

Roberval had been delayed almost a year in France by difficulties in obtaining guns and ammunition. He finally sailed from La Rochelle on April 16, 1542 with three ships carrying two hundred prospective settlers, both men and women, some taken from the jails of Paris. The start of the voyage was not auspicious. The Atlantic was stormy and the fleet was immediately driven to seek a sheltered anchorage for the night. They ventured out again the next day and had favorable winds for a few days but then they faced headwinds and they returned to Brittany where they remained for a number of days.

The fleet reached St. John's harbor in Newfoundland on June 7. Roberval found seventeen fishing boats in the harbor; St. John's was already an important center for the cod-fishing trade. While he was at anchor there, Cartier arrived from Canada. He told Roberval that his force was too small to combat the Indians who had begun assailing him on a continuous basis; he said he was returning to France. He showed Roberval specimens of the "diamonds" and a quantity of "gold ore" he had collected near the Cap-Rouge settlement. Roberval commanded him to come about and accompany him to Canada but Cartier had had enough; he slipped out of the harbor in the night and sailed for France.

Roberval spent the greater part of June in St. John's, settling quarrels between French and Portuguese fishermen and taking on fresh water and wood. He got away toward the end of the month and reached Cartier's settlement in July. He occupied it and during August and early September, he kept everyone busy strengthening the fort and preparing the settlement for the 1542–3 winter. A survey of supplies revealed that they did not have sufficient food to see them through the winter and Roberval immediately began rationing meat, bread, beans and butter. Their lot improved somewhat when a number of natives arrived at the fort with a large quantity of fish which they bartered for knives and other trifles.

On September 14, Roberval sent two of his three ships back to France with instructions to return in the spring, should it please the king, with food and other necessities. He also wished to be informed how Cartier's "diamonds" had been received by his majesty.

The settlement suffered terribly from scurvy that winter (1542–3); about fifty of its company died from the disease. It seems that Roberval was totally unprepared for its appearance. Apparently, Cartier never understood the cause of the mysterious illness that killed twenty-five of his men in the winter of 1535–6, or that it would recur if men were forced to live on a restricted diet over a period of months. We can assume that in their preparations for the voyage, the two men never discussed the killer disease or the miraculous recovery that could be effected by drinking a juice prepared from hemlock bark.

The kingdom of the Saguenay continued to intrigue the French. On June 6, 1543 Roberval started up the St. Lawrence River with a flotilla of eight boats carrying seventy men, intending to ascend the Ottawa River to the kingdom. He left instructions with the remainder of his people to sail for France if he was not back by a certain date. One of the eight boats returned on June 14 with the news that a boat had been lost and eight men drowned. On June 19, another boat came down the river with a quantity of corn and orders for the settlers to remain at Cap-Rouge.

Roberval was unable to ascend the St. Lawrence River past the Lachine Rapids. Neither he nor his men had the proper experience for the venture and, like Cartier before him, he learned that his French-built boats and equipment were not suited to the task. Little else is known about his attempt to find the kingdom of the Saguenay. He returned to Cap-Rouge and, abruptly, he began preparations to return to France with all his people. The continuous aggressive hostility of the native Canadians, the hard struggle to provide adequate food for the settlers, and the long, cruel, cold, disease-ridden winter had sapped his energy and resolve. We can surmise the discovery of the difficulty he faced to pass the rapids to the Ottawa River was the last straw. He felt overwhelmed by this beautiful, bountiful but savage land and he decided to abandon the settlement.

Roberval arrived in France in September, 1543, to find that Spain and France were at war again. The failure of Cartier and Roberval to establish a colony in New France and penetrate the interior to the kingdom of Saguenay was disheartening for Francis. Discouraging, too, had been the analysis of Cartier's "diamond" and "gold ore" samples; they consisted of common quartz and iron pyrites. The king, occupied with funding the war, disappointed that the three expeditions, seemingly, had gained nothing for France, allowed his interest in the northern lands to languish. The search for the Saguenay and the colonization of the New World had lost its allure and it would not be rekindled until new incentives presented themselves. It was sixty years later—in the next century—before the French again took an active official role in the New World.

9

The English Renew the Search for a Northwest Passage
1576–87

The discovery of mainland North America by Cabot in 1497 had inextricably linked England to the new continent and it offered the challenge of a new world to explore. But, after an initial flurry of activity, no official English voyages were sent across the Atlantic to build on Cabot's discovery. It was left to cod fishermen, soon followed by fur traders, to bind the region of the discovery—around Newfoundland—to England with economic ties. This was in marked contrast to the behavior of the Spanish and Portuguese governments who moved quickly to explore, occupy and develop their discoveries far to the south.

The new continent continued to be ignored by the English government during the first three quarters of the sixteenth century. The reason for this neglect was due in part, to the War of the Roses (1455–87) which had exhausted England economically and emotionally. Henry VII (1485–1509), who had sponsored Cabot, was fully occupied with restoring England and consolidating his position as king.

His son, Henry VIII (1509–47), involved with personal matters and the politics of religion, was left with little inclination to exploit Cabot's discoveries. But he was persuaded to send two ships, in 1527, "to explore a certain region in the north between the Labrador's land [Greenland] and the Cod-fish land [Newfoundland]."[1] The expedition's orders were to search in this region for a "strait towards the northern parts"[2]—a strait that would lead to the other sea and "the land of the Great Khan."[3] The ships had the misfortune of being separated in a storm and one was lost. The surviving ship held the course to the north even though some of the seamen died of the cold. Eventually they encountered floating icebergs and then a frozen sea and they were forced to alter their course. Their adventures were not yet at an end. An account of the voyage has it that they "ran into a sea as hot as water in a boiler."[4] They feared it would melt the pitch of their ship and, therefore, they left the area and sailed southward to Newfoundland where their pilot was killed by Indians. This rather fanciful tale brought to an end for a time, the official English attempts to find a northwest passage.

At Henry's death his son, Edward VI, gained the throne. He was a minor and control of the government passed to the king's council. Edward's short reign (1547–53) was marred by strife over the country's economy, with Scotland which resulted in the abandonment of that country to the French, over taxes to finance the fighting, but particularly over religion.

Nevertheless there were signs of an awakening of the English temper for maritime adventure. The king's council, urged by its most powerful member, the Earl of Warwick (afterward Duke of Northumberland), encouraged English merchants to find new overseas markets with the object of lessening England's dependence on trade with the nearby and competitive European countries. The merchants responded by disputing the Portuguese claim of a monopoly of the trade with Africa, sending ships into African ports in the Mediterranean and along the west coast, loading merchandise for shipment to England and elsewhere. And in 1553, Sebastian Cabot, then governor of the Merchant Adventurers, sent three ships to Vardo (on the northeastern tip of Norway) and beyond, to search for a Northeast Passage to the Orient. The voyage ended tragically for the commander, Sir Hugh Willoughby, and his ship but his second-in-command, Richard Chancellor, reached the White Sea. He and his company spent the winter in Moscow and established trade relations with Ivan the Terrible. Northumberland initiated other plans to increase maritime trade and improve England's economy but the fruit of many of his projects was delayed until the time of Elizabeth I.

The reign of Mary I (1553–8), daughter of Henry VIII and Catherine of Aragon, was undistinguished except for her religious zeal. It is best remembered for her efforts to restore the country to Roman Catholicism; they absorbed the nation and hindered the expansion begun under Edward VI. Isolated from English politics before her accession, Mary turned to her cousin, the Roman emperor Charles V, for counsel and was persuaded to marry his son (later Philip II of Spain), eleven years her junior.

One of Mary's first acts was to legitimize her birth by having Parliament annul Henry's divorce of Catherine; it cast a slur on the birth of Elizabeth, her younger sister and daughter of Anne Boleyn. Then she forced repeal of the antipapal laws put in place by Henry VIII and Edward VI, and England was accepted back into the Roman fold and a measure of papal authority was restored. Old statutes that empowered the clergy to take action against heretics were revived. It resulted in the persecution of Protestants with such energy that in the space of three years, almost 300 men and women were burned at the stake on the charge of heresy. These events brought a hatred of Rome to England and cast the shadow of infamy on Mary's reign.

When Mary's resolve to go ahead with the marriage to Philip became known, it provoked a dangerous rebellion and only Mary's determined stand saved the throne for her. The marriage, in 1554, allied England with Spain but it did not prevent Philip from closing the ports of Spanish and Portuguese colonies to English traders. It brought England into war against France alongside Spain, and it threatened to place England's resources into the hands of the Roman emperor. The marriage was perhaps the most unpopular of all Mary's acts and she was unable to get Parliament to agree to Philip's coronation.

The succession of Elizabeth I (1558–1603) gave England a government headed by a strong monarch, something the country had lacked since the time of Henry VIII. She had "the body of a weak and feeble woman, but...the heart and stomach of a king." Elizabeth appointed the country's most competent men to the Privy Council (her private counselors); its secretary and leading member, William Cecil, became one of the ablest ministers of the realm. She set about achieving peace in the land and restoring the strength and prestige that had been dissipated in the reign of Mary. Toward these ends, she replaced the bishops appointed by Mary but she cautioned that the conversion to a predominantly Protestant clergy must not stir up controversy in the kingdom—she was more concerned with the unity of England than the predominance of Protestantism. She made peace with Scotland and France. Protestants gained control of the Scottish government and the French were expelled from "the back door into England"[5] thereby rooting out one source of trouble.

Elizabeth's foreign policy was marked by moderation. She tried to maintain friendly relations with Philip II of Spain while warding off his attempts to marry her, gathering her strength at home and building English maritime power. She played France against Spain, neutralizing the Spanish military might occupying the Netherlands and keeping alive Dutch resistance with intermittent aid to the rebels.

Still, there was continuing trouble with Spain. In 1563–4 for example, the Spanish attempted to curtail English trading rights in the Netherlands. The disagreement was enhanced in 1567 when the main Spanish army arrived in the Netherlands after the Dutch rebelled against Philip's religious persecution. Having the Spanish army so dangerously close to England did nothing to improve the quarrel over trade. In 1568, English attempts to trade with Spanish America ended with the destruction of English ships. Elizabeth countered by capturing a treasury ship bound for the Netherlands with pay for the Spanish troops. Philip responded by seizing all English ships in Spanish ports and stopping all trade with England.

Elizabeth's problems with Spain coincided with plots at home to drive William Cecil from office and, with Spanish help, to assassinate her and secure the throne for Mary Stuart, a Catholic. The plotters were discovered and decisively beaten, and the 800 executions that followed effectively crushed the opposition; Mary just escaped being beheaded in 1572. The pope excommunicated Elizabeth but Spain was too occupied with the Dutch rebels and a French threat to aid the rebels to take advantage of the situation and intervene on Mary's behalf.

Elizabeth's success in avoiding a debilitating war during these troublesome times made possible a remarkable expansion of England's maritime commerce and adventure abroad. English merchants penetrated new markets in Germany, the Netherlands, the Baltic, Russia, Spain, the Mediterranean Sea and the west coast of Africa, supported by the queen's growing sea power. English privateers including Sir Francis Drake, ranged the Caribbean Sea and attacked the Spanish main. In 1577, Drake passed through Magellan's strait and raided ports and shipping along the Americas' west coast—a Spanish preserve. To avoid retracing his route past the furious Spanish, he crossed the Pacific Ocean and rounded Africa into the Atlantic, his ship laden with Spanish treasure. This bold adventure typified the growing confidence in the English strength to tweak the Spanish nose.

Up to Elizabeth's time, the world's knowledge of the North American coastline north of Newfoundland had advanced little beyond what the Vikings had discovered in traveling their route to America—from Greenland's west side across Davis Strait to Baffin Island and down the coast of Labrador. The very early English mariners who voyaged to America had argued that because there was a southwest passage into the Pacific Ocean (Magellan's Strait), there must be a northwest passage as well. Experience with the frigid and stormy waters of the far north (for example, the voyage in Henry VIII's time) had been discouraging but toward the end of the sixteenth century there was renewed interest by Englishmen, not only in America's far north but also in the eastern seaboard between Florida and Newfoundland.

Martin Frobisher

Martin Frobisher (c.1539–94), was the first of a number of Elizabeth's adventuresome mariners to enter the Arctic Ocean to search for the elusive passage to China. He was born in Yorkshire, of Welsh ancestry.[6] He went to sea at the age of fourteen when he shipped on a voyage to Guinea, in West Africa, and was imprisoned by the Portuguese who regarded this part of the world as their private trading preserve. He was given the command of a ship when he was still in his early twenties. In 1563, as captain of the *Anne Appleyard*, he was awarded letters-of-marque against French Catholics and captured five vessels in the English Channel. He also privateered off the west coast of Africa and was charged with piracy in 1566. Early in the 1570's, Frobisher was in Elizabeth's navy, serving off the Irish coast.

Frobisher's first voyage to Davis Strait: 1576

Frobisher is said to have harbored an interest in searching for a northwest passage from an early age. He was persuaded there was a short and easy northern route to China and he determined to find it "knowing this to be the only thing of the world that was left yet undone."[7] He spent much time with the maps of the day, devising a plan and discussing it with his friends, approaching English merchants as early as 1560 to finance a voyage. Eventually he turned to the Queen's court, laying his plan before wealthy and learned men and there he succeeded in gaining the interest of the Earl of Warwick (son of the earl in Edward VI's time), a powerful figure at court. There was an obstacle. The Muscovy (or Russian) Company had the sole English right to search for the passage and the company would neither undertake an exploratory voyage nor permit anyone else to make the venture. At last in 1575, Michael Lok, treasurer of the company, a well-to-do merchant from London and an enthusiastic supporter of Frobisher's proposal, persuaded the Queen to lend her support and the monopoly was broken.[8] Thereafter, Lok and Frobisher were able to arrange financing by eighteen sponsors—the charter "venturers"—of whom ten were shareholders of the Muscovy Company. Lok was a member of this group and its most active participant. Now, finally, Frobisher had the opportunity to indulge his wish. It was fifty years after the failure of Henry VIII's expedition.

The money enabled Frobisher to ready two barques—the *Michael* (25 tons) and the *Gabriel* (20 tons)—and a 7-ton pinnace, and to provision them for a voyage of twelve months. It was a tiny force to invade the North Polar Sea. The little fleet left its anchorage in the Thames on June 7, 1576 and turned into the North Sea, Frobisher commanding the *Gabriel*. After passing the Shetland Islands, they sailed a northwesterly course and encountered a great storm in which the barques were separated for a time and the pinnace with its crew of four was sunk. On July 11, in latitude 61°N, the two barques sighted the southeast coast of Greenland, ringed by an icefield. A dense fog descended on the scene and the captain of the *Michael*, "mistrusting the matter,"[9] slipped away and returned to England, reporting that Frobisher had gone to the bottom with the *Gabriel*.

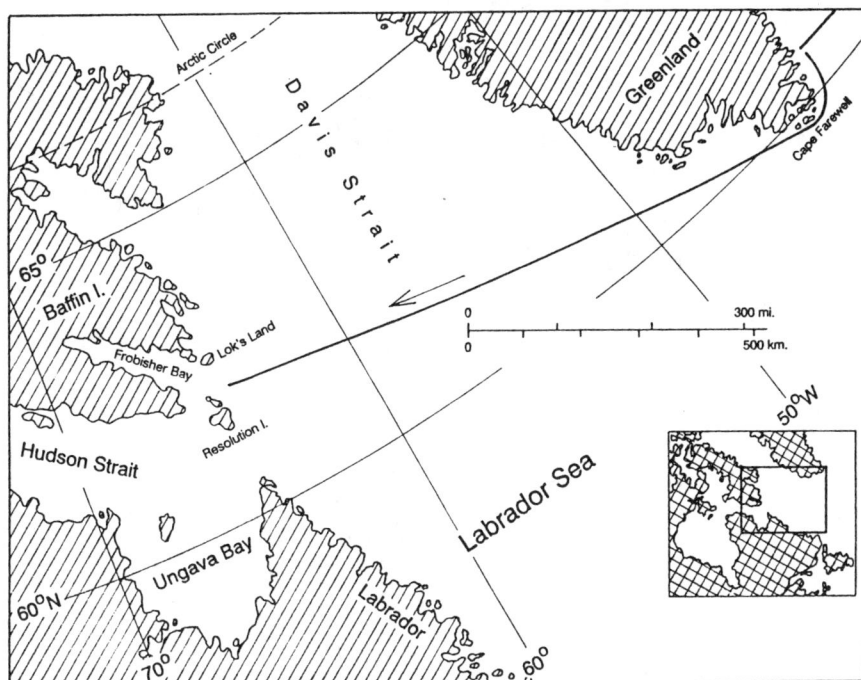

Figure 24. Martin Frobisher's route to Baffin Island in 1576.

The *Gabriel* had suffered considerable damage; nevertheless and despite the loss of the *Michael* and the pinnace, Frobisher continued the
voyage. He rounded Greenland and set a northwest bearing across Davis
Strait. On July 26, Christopher Hall, master of the *Gabriel*, noted that

> we had sight of a land of yce: the latitude was 62 degrees, and
> two minutes.
>   The 28. day in the morning was very foggie; but at the clearing
> up of the fogge, wee had sight of lande, which I supposed to be
> Labrador.[10]

It was not Labrador; in latitude 62°N they were a degree-and-a-half of
latitude (about a hundred miles) north of mainland North America. The
landfall, if it occurred in 62°N, was the southeastern tip of Baffin Island, on
the south side of the entrance to Frobisher Bay.

They cruised the entrance to the bay, searching in the fog for a protected
place to anchor. Ice rimmed the shore and stretched into the bay, preventing
them from getting in close and that night they stood well clear of the land
to avoid collision with shifting masses of ice. Early in the morning of July

133

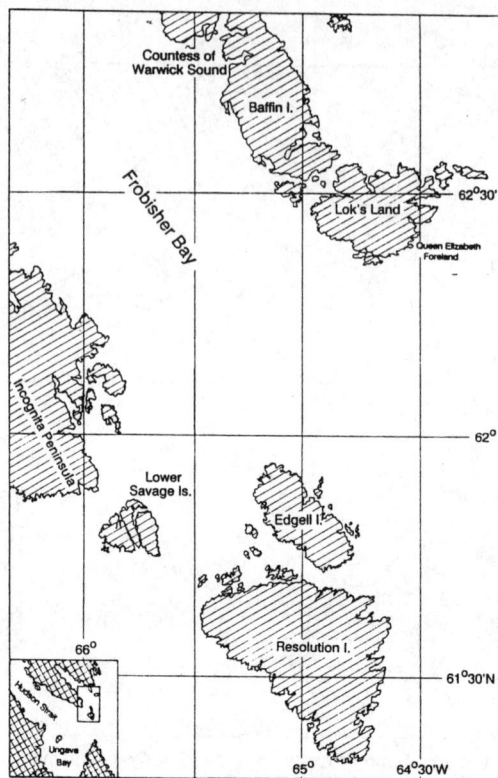

Figure 25. The entrance to Frobisher Bay.

30 there was no fog to obscure their vision and they saw a headland to the northeast[11]; it was probably Lok's Land—an island and the northern portal of the bay.

On August 10 they finally got ashore on an island "one league from the maine" and detected a tide setting to the west alongside its shoreline. The direction of the tide led Frobisher to conclude he had made landfall at the entrance of a channel (Hall called it a "streight")[12], which he could hope, would lead westward into another sea. Next morning (August 11), he took the *Gabriel* into the channel. It trended northwestward and after penetrating it for some days, he was convinced it was a strait between two continents (with Asia to the north and mainland America to the south), leading to the South Sea and Cathay. Recalling that Magellan had named the Southwest Passage after himself, he called it Frobisher's Strait. It was merely the bay which is presently known as Frobisher Bay.

They moved gradually deeper into the bay, anchoring at night, taking the opportunity of a sandy beach to caulk the ship. The morning of August 19 being clear with no wind, Frobisher went ashore with a small party to a high point inland to look for inhabitants. Presently they became aware that they were being observed from a distance; natives were peering at them from behind rocks and paddling through the waters of the bay in their leather kayaks. They were Eskimos. Frobisher thought they were trying to encircle him and he hurried back to his boat.

It took patience to persuade the native Americans to come to the ship but eventually curiosity overcame suspicion and fear. They began visiting the ship, bringing gifts of salmon and the meat of animals, and bartering the skins of seals and bears for trinkets such as glass beads and bells; bells seemed to fascinate them. Frobisher thought the people looked like

> Tartars, with long blacke haire, broad faces, and flatte noses, and tawnie in colour, wearing Seale skinnes, and so doe the women, not differing in the fashion, but the women are marked in the face with blewe streekes downe the cheekes, and round about the eyes.[13]

Frobisher did not altogether trust the Eskimos and he warned his men to be wary. The men were less fearful and contrary to his wishes, they dealt quite casually with the native Americans. The day after the initial contact it had a tragic result. Frobisher had sent five of the seamen to set a native ashore, telling them to keep well out of reach of his companions. The men ignored the instructions, choosing instead to row among the natives "and so were taken themselves, and our boate lost."

On the morning of August 21 the snow lay a foot deep on deck. It was time to think about the return voyage but Frobisher was reluctant to abandon the men the Eskimos had captured. He kept the ship in the vicinity, firing his cannon and sounding a trumpet but there was no sign of the men. The Eskimos, knowing they were in bad repute with the white men, were wary about approaching the ship. Frobisher was convinced his men were being held against their will and he determined to capture a native and hold him as a hostage against their return. Using the offer of a bell as a lure, he was able to entice one to come close enough to take the bell from his hand and in the process he seized the Eskimo by his wrist and yanked him and his craft aboard. In the struggle to free himself, the native bit a piece off his tongue.

There was no reaction from the Eskimos to the seizure of one of their number; they made no attempt to barter for his return. The seamen they had captured, and their boat, were not seen again. On August 26, Frobisher reluctantly weighed anchor and began the homeward voyage. He carried the captive Eskimo back to England as proof of having visited a strange new land. The native died of a cold in England.

Among the various items brought back to England as curiosities by Frobisher, was a heavy black rock, apparently collected by one of the seamen with the thought that it might be coal. The specimen was to have an enormous impact on future voyages to the northwest. The events that brought the black rock to prominence are not exactly known. One story has it that Frobisher gave portions of it to friends as souvenirs of the voyage and by accident or design, one piece was thrown into a fireplace by the wife of a recipient. It lodged there for some time and when it was removed and cleaned, it was seen to glisten not unlike gold.[14]

The rock was assayed by the goldsmith Giovanni Agnello, who reported its gold content as twenty-five ounces per ton of rock—a phenomenally high value. A number of other assayers tested the rock but only Jonas Shutz, a German assayer resident in London, confirmed the presence of gold in the "ore." Despite the contrary results, several prominent men of the Queen's court were convinced of the correctness of Agnello's results. Frobisher's name was on everyone's lips and London was in the grip of a gold fever.

Michael Lok organized the Company of Cathay to sponsor another voyage to Baffin Island. The main purpose of the expedition was to exploit the gold discovery but time permitting, Frobisher was to continue the search for a northwest passage. Lok had no difficulty selling shares in the company. Investors were attracted to the prospect of taking part in a gold mining operation and Frobisher was enjoined to expend most of his effort on that part of the venture.

Frobisher's second voyage: 1577

Frobisher left Blackwall, England May 26, 1577 with three ships: the 280-ton *Ayde* and the two barques, *Gabriel* and *Michael,* of the first voyage. He carried almost 150 persons—"gentlemen," seamen, soldiers, miners, metallurgists and a London goldsmith. He had provisions enough for half a year.

The fleet passed up the east coast of England and reached the Orkneys on June 7, where they took on fresh provisions, and then set a westerly course. On July 4 they came onto Greenland ringed by solid packice extending for as much as thirty-five miles (55 km.) out to sea; beyond the ice, icebergs floated on the open water. They spent four days trying unsuccessfully to land.

The expedition reached Lok's Land on July 16 and found the opening into Frobisher Bay so clogged with ice they dared not risk entrance with the ships. Frobisher had two pinnaces prepared and having ordered the ships to stand well offshore out of reach of the shifting, grinding ice, he entered the bay and began searching for the "black gold-bearing ore" on a small island off Lok's Land, where the original find was thought to have been made. They could not locate a piece even as small "as a walnut." They had more success the following day on a larger island and Frobisher returned to the ships on July 19 with the news that he had found gold-bearing rock "which shewed it selfe in the bowels of those barren mountaines."[15]

Overnight the wind had driven the ice out to sea and Frobisher now felt easy about taking the ships into the bay to a "fair" harbor he found on its southern shore. Then, after giving thanks to God for their safe arrival and promising to use every endeavor to bring the "barbarous people" of this land to the "true religion", he "tooke possession of the Countrey" for Queen Elizabeth.[16]

Frobisher used ten days to prospect the south shore of Frobisher Bay. He satisfied himself that it contained no great riches and moved the ship and barques to the northern shore, into the Countess of Warwick Sound. He anchored off Kodlunarn (White Man's) Island where the miners began extracting a "black ore" and loading it on the ships. The Eskimos soon found the Englishmen and readily approached them, but the initially friendly contact between Europeans and Americans quickly turned into an ugly arrow-shooting altercation in which several people were hurt.

Leaving the miners to their task, Frobisher moved deeper into the bay intending to continue his explorations of the bay and search for the five men he had lost on the previous voyage. toward that end, his men pursued the Eskimos whenever they sighted them and on one occasion, managed to corner three wounded men, two women and a child. Rather than submit to capture, the native men leaped off a cliff into the sea and were drowned. The Englishmen found the older of the women so ugly, some of them suspected she was a witch and they tore off her footwear to see if she was cloven-footed. Finding she had normal feet, they let her go but they kept the younger woman who was quite comely, and her child.

The possibility of friendly relations with the Eskimos was lost by this time and Frobisher's men showed little concern for the natives. When they came upon their tents, they took what they fancied. On one of their forays they found articles of clothing that had belonged to the white men but it was no proof they were still alive. The chance encounters between Europeans and Americans continued; sometimes the natives seemed to want to be friendly, leaving gifts of food along the shore. Frobisher and his men were always wary of them, suspecting they were engineering a trap to capture a few whites and exchange them for Frobisher's prisoners.

By the last week in August, 158 tons[17] of the "black ore" had been loaded into the three ships. Frobisher expected that after smelting, it would defray in large part, the cost of the two voyages. They left Frobisher Bay on August 24, steering to pass near the southern tip of Greenland. The ships became separated during a three-day storm in the Atlantic but happily, the *Ayde* sighted Land's End on September 17 and soon after, one of the barques landed at Bristol and the other at Yarmouth. Only two men had been lost on this voyage; one had died of natural causes on Baffin Island and the other had been swept overboard in the storm.

Frobisher's third voyage: 1578

One of Frobisher's first acts after reaching England, was to assure the Queen that the expedition had returned safely with a large quantity of the gold ore. He had not found the passage to Cathay, but he held hopes that it would yet be discovered. He must have impressed Her Majesty for she immediately appointed a commission to look into organizing a third voyage. And she proclaimed that the peninsula on the southwest side of Frobisher Bay, would be known as Meta Incognita (Latin for unknown limits).

Apparently few assays had been made on Baffin Island while the miners were at work; the main thrust of the operation had been to extract a quantity of the ore and load it on the ships. Back in England, a sample was quickly submitted to Jonas Shutz, the assayer who had confirmed the presence of gold on the original sample. He reported favorably on the value of the Kodlunarn rock. The Queen's commissioners, having received the results and considered the commercial advantages of a northwest passage to Cathay, recommended that a third voyage be undertaken without delay. They were of the opinion that a colony should be established on the peninsula and the already-discovered ore bodies mined during the winter. To facilitate this, they advised that a building to house the miners be constructed in England, taken apart for shipping and reconstructed near the mining site. They concluded that the proceeds from the mining operation would pay for the voyage and provide funds for future voyages. To support the operation, five small assay furnaces were set up in London and the construction of a metallurgical works was begun near Dartford in Kent.[18]

There was no shortage of volunteers to spend the winter in the north-west. The organizers settled on a complement of about 400 consisting of 150 miners and 6 assayers, and the men (cooks, bakers, carpenters and soldiers) to service the miners and sail the ships. Fifteen ships were employed to carry the company, the provisions needed to feed it and the equipment required for mining. The discovery of a northwest passage had become incidental to the establishment of a gold mine. The fleet left England on May 31, 1578 and moved westward through the English Channel and around the south end of Ireland, and set a northwest course for Meta Incognita.

They reached Greenland on June 20 and although there was considerable drift ice near the shore, Frobisher managed to reach land in the ship's boat. He came onto several shelters made of the skins of animals but was not able to converse with the people who fled at sight of the Englishmen. They searched the tents and found nails and wooden boards, products almost certainly manufactured in Europe, but took nothing except two large dogs for which they left a few trifles. Quite ignoring the rights of these people, Frobisher claimed the land for Elizabeth and renamed it West England.

Soon after leaving Greenland, Frobisher had to take a more southerly route to avoid masses of drift ice that far exceeded what he had encountered on the two previous voyages. They were also troubled by thick fogs which made sailing in the ice-infested waters doubly dangerous. On June 30 they found themselves amongst a pod of great whales and struck one with such force that the ship was stopped in its tracks.

They came to Resolution Island, at the south entrance to Frobisher Bay, on July 2 through seas that were thick with ice. They entered the bay and despite the difficulties, managed to sail a considerable distance before they were confronted by ice piled into mountainous heaps. Still, the icepack moved, opening and closing, and they worked the ships ahead, one by one, from one opening to the next. Inevitably, the ships became separated and isolated from each other. A storm rose and increased as the night wore on, and it drove the ice before it, pressing in on them—so close they could not avoid contact with it. To their horror, the *Dennis* was rammed, her timbers splintered and she began to sink. Fortunately all of the ship's crew was rescued. They passed a terrifying night (July 2–3), the ships imprisoned by the ice that threatened to overwhelm and crush them. The men worked with timbers, pikes and oars to fend it off—sometimes going over the side onto the ice and putting their shoulders to the ship's side, straining to lessen the pressure on her timbers. The storm eased in the morning and the fog lifted so that they could see their way. Aided by a northwest wind that drove the ice out to sea, they got clear of the bay and moved seaward to lie well offshore, waiting for the sun and wind to disperse the ice. The next day (July 5) the fleet was enveloped in fog so thick it hid the ships one from the other.

On July 7, having been carried well out to sea, they worked the ships shoreward, still in a heavy fog, until they could discern land on the starboard side. Frobisher thought they were in Frobisher's strait (Frobisher Bay), alongside its north coast but when he consulted with his people, there was no general agreement about their location. Christopher Hall, the chief pilot who had been on the first voyage, said he had never seen this coast.

Even as they lay there in the fog, several ships lost contact with the fleet. Fortunately the water was relatively clear of ice and on July 10, still in a dense fog, Frobisher directed the fleet to take a westerly course expecting that this bearing would take them deeper into the "strait." After sailing for "sixty leagues,"[19] with the land always on the starboard side and the open sea before them, he conceded that this was not the "true strait" (Frobisher Bay) but another strait. He ordered the ships to turn back and on July 21, in clear weather, they passed and recognized Resolution Island[20] and came to the entrance of Frobisher Bay where they found two of their ships waiting for them.

An examination of a modern map of the North Polar Sea region suggests that they had been in Hudson Strait, sailing northwestward alongside the south shore of Baffin Island. Frobisher confessed later that had it not been for his obligation to set up a gold mining operation in Frobisher Bay, he would have continued sailing westward in this other (Hudson) strait. He expected it would have taken him to the South Sea, thereby erasing all doubts about the existence of a northwest passage to Cathay.

Spells of fog and floating ice continued to delay their entry into Frobisher Bay. Little more than a month remained before the winter packice would close in and hold the ships in the grip of winter. They needed to get on with the business that had brought them to the bay, yet some of the ships were still missing. There was much grumbling among the men and talk about immediately returning to England, and this was amplified near the end of July when a six-inch fall of snow accompanied by a bitter wind, added to their misery. Frobisher was firm; he persisted in his efforts to get the fleet into the bay and on July 30, he succeeded in reaching the Countess of Warwick Sound with nine ships. He found two of the missing ships waiting for him and this cheered the company. And late in August, two of the three other missing ships found and joined the fleet; the captain of the third ship, certain that the fleet had gone down, had sailed away one night and headed back to England.

The idea of erecting a building had to be abandoned; some of its components had gone down with the *Dennis* and others had never been put on board the ships in England. There would be no over-winter operation. Frobisher wanted to push further up the bay, hoping to prove that it led into the South Sea and bring the welcome news back to England. His captains demurred; they mentioned the shortage of food and fresh water, the continuing fog, the daily fall of snow, and the cold which each night built up frost on the ships. They felt it was essential to get the ships loaded with ore and leave the north country with all possible speed. Frobisher had to give in. He left Baffin Island having extracted and loaded about 1250 tons of "black ore" from shallow pits at seven localities.

The fleet was scattered on the homeward voyage but early in November all of the ships had reached ports in the British Isles. About forty men had been lost in the venture.

The bulk of the ore was unloaded at Dartford, England. It had been proven by mid-1578—in Frobisher's absence—that the early (Jonas Shutz) assays of the black rock from the second voyage were wrong; the rock did not contain a commercial quantity of gold. Nevertheless, six tons from the new shipment were processed at the recently-constructed Dartford metallurgical works. It confirmed the new findings; the gold content was negligible. However, 354 ounces of silver were extracted in the process, giving reason to be optimistic. But even this was a false result. The silver was probably accidentally introduced by the inadvertent use of a silver-bearing lead in the extractive process. The works closed in February, 1579, after less than four months of operation and much of the untreated ore was used around 1580 to repair the west wall of the Manor House built by Henry VIII for Anne of Cleves.[21]

It seems incredible that the Queen's commissioners, with the investigative resources of the kingdom at their disposal, failed to determine that the rock was worthless until the third voyage was organized and underway. The art of recovering gold from ore was well known several thousand years before Frobisher's time and it was practiced by the Spanish and Portuguese in America in his time. It raises the question: was this a fraud and if so, who perpetrated it? Michael Lok risked and lost a fortune on the enterprise but he bore the brunt of the shareholders anger. They made him the culprit when the Company of Cathay failed and he was sent to a debtor's prison.[22] Elizabeth invested money in the ventures but in spite of the dubious end of the affair, Frobisher remained in her good graces.

What was Frobisher's contribution to man's knowledge of the far north? He did his limited traveling in a region that had probably become well known to the Norsemen. The Eskimo reaction to the Frobisher visits suggests that their folklore included references to overseas visits from people of a different culture—likely the Vikings. Frobisher did not discover any new lands or bodies of water but he did establish an English claim to land in the New World's far north. Furthermore, he was instrumental in reviving interest in voyaging into these waters and he was followed by others. His voyages led, within a quarter century, to the discovery of Hudson Bay which, like the St. Lawrence River system, was a way of reaching into the deep interior of present day Canada.

Frobisher continued to serve the queen after the voyages. In 1585 he was vice-admiral of Sir Francis Drake's expedition to the West Indies. In 1588 he commanded a squadron of English ships in the battle with the

Spanish Armada and was knighted during the operations. He was still in the queen's service in 1594 and was wounded leading an assault against the Spanish at Brest. He was carried to Plymouth where he died, at the age of fifty-five. His entrails were interred in St. Andrew's parish church in that city; his body was buried in London.

The voyages of John Davis: 1585–7

The promise of gold on Baffin Island had been allowed to divert Martin Frobisher's backers from their original design of finding a northwest passage. The discovery that there was no gold—that the last two voyages had been based on erroneous, if not deceitful assay results—may have tarnished Frobisher's image. A proposal in 1581, three years after his third voyage, to send him back to the arctic to continue the search for the passage, came to nothing.

Despite the failure of the Frobisher voyages to find the Northwest Passage, various merchants and gentlemen of Elizabeth's court remained interested in the idea and willing to risk money in another venture. In 1585 Adrian Gilbert, brother of Sir Humphrey Gilbert, obtained a patent to renew the search. He and his associates—among them Sir Walter Raleigh, William Sanderson and Sir Francis Walsingham—chose John Davis, an experienced and practical sailor, and versed in scientific navigational methods, to be their captain and chief pilot.

John Davis was born near Dartmouth, on the shores of the English Channel, about the year 1550; he was ten years younger than Frobisher. Like Frobisher, he lived his life at sea and served Elizabeth against the Spanish Armada. He became one of the most skilled and literate navigators of his day; in 1594 he published an 80-page booklet entitled *The Seamen's Secrets* which went through eight editions, the final in 1657.[23] It seems he became interested in searching for a northwest passage about the time that Frobisher was making his voyages, and already in 1583 he began trying to interest various people in England in a plan he had formulated.

Davis' first voyage to North America: 1585

Davis left Dartmouth on June 7, 1585. He commanded the 60-ton *Sunshine* with twenty-three persons aboard; Captain William Bruton had charge of the 35-ton *Moonshine* carrying nineteen people.[24] Davis' crew was unusual in that four of his seamen had been chosen because they were also musicians.

The expedition was repeatedly delayed at sea by bad weather but finally,

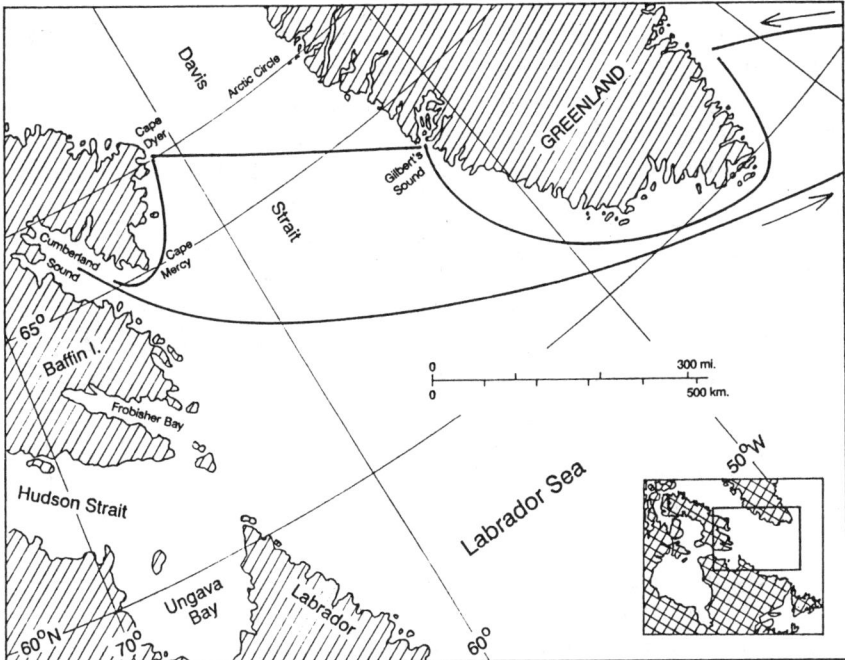

Figure 26. John Davis' first voyage, in 1585, to Baffin Island.

on July 19, while passing through a fog so dense the ships could not keep eye contact, they heard the grinding, crunching sound of drift ice. Next day the fog lifted and they saw to the west, the bleak rock-bound eastern shore of Greenland, its mountains covered with snow, with "no view of wood, grass or earth to be seen."[25] Davis called it the Land of Desolation.

There was no chance of getting ashore through the shifting masses of ice that would surely have reduced the ships' timbers to splinters. The next day, before they could begin the search for another landing site, their course of action was decided when a strong wind took hold and blew them southward along the south-southwest trending coast. On July 24 they reached its southern tip (Cape Farewell), and next day Davis set a course to the northwest and they soon lost sight of the land.

They held their bearing for four days and on July 29 they sighted land to the northeast. They bore toward it and came to a group of islands lying off the west coast of Greenland in latitude 64°N. They anchored in an inlet which Davis named Gilbert's Sound (the location of Godthab, or Nuuk on modern maps), and went ashore for wood and fresh water. The region was devoid of large trees but driftwood for firewood was plentiful.

Almost immediately they found evidence of humans—discarded footwear and sewn leather goods—and then they heard the cry of voices, and when one of Davis' men gave a shout it was returned. Presently they saw a number of people in the distance. Davis, hoping to titillate the curiosity of the natives and lure them close, had his musicians play their instruments and he and his men leaped and gyrated to the beat of the music. The natives approached in their kayaks (they were Eskimos) but they were wary. Finally one stepped ashore and when Davis tossed gifts to him, it seemed to reassure them.

The next day (July 30) the native Greenlanders came in thirty-seven one-man kayaks. They rowed past the ships and went ashore, signaling to the Europeans to join them and waving furs. Soon the two groups were actively trading and the white men acquired kayaks, mukluks, and fur garments off the backs of the natives. Relations became friendly and relaxed; Davis' men were even allowed to handle the Eskimo weapons and oars, and they learned from them by signs, that "towards the north and west there was a great sea."[26]

Early on August 1, a favorable wind rose and although they had arranged to meet the natives for more trading, Davis made sail and took the ships out at 4 a.m. He set a northwest course "thinking thereby to pass for China."[27] But five days later (on August 6) they intercepted land in latitude 66°40'N. They had reached Baffin Island immediately south of Cape Dyer, which was marked by a mountain Davis named Mount Raleigh. They spent about a week at the anchorage collecting firewood, exploring the region, and hunting polar bears for their meat. The bears were plentiful and large—the forepaws of one they killed measured fourteen inches from side to side.[28]

On August 8 they began following the coast southward; three days later they reached Cape Mercy in a heavy fog. They rounded the cape, keeping to the shoreline, and when the fog lifted, they saw they had moved some distance into an opening (Cumberland Sound), sixty or more miles (100 km.) in width, trending northwestward. Davis thought he had reason to hope that this was the passage he sought for it was free of ice (suggesting it had a current) and the water was the same color as the Atlantic. They sailed northwestward for days, finally halting at a cluster of islands in the passage. Davis decided the ships should separate, one going around to the north of the islands and the other to the south but before he could execute the plan, the weather turned foul and they had to take shelter. It was the beginning of a spell of bad weather. Davis used the time to investigate the islands, rowing amongst them with the ships' boats.

They came onto a pod of whales on the far side of the islands. They had not seen any east of the islands and Davis felt this was evidence they were in a strait—that the animals had come up the strait from a western sea. There were other hopeful signs that this was a strait. For one, the water looked to be ocean water, not much adulterated by run-off from the land.[29] For another, the men rowing the boats thought they sometimes felt the meeting of two strong tides, presumably one from Davis Strait to the east and the other from the western sea they sought.

On August 20 the ships were still confined to the vicinity of the islands, facing an adverse wind with the sailing season fast coming to an end. Davis consulted with Captain Bruton and next morning, the wind still barring their progress to the northwest, they left the shelter of the islands and turned back, moving along the south shore of the sound. It was August 26 before they regained the headland at its entrance and laid a course for England.

They reached Greenland on September 10, intending to go ashore, but they could not find a safe anchorage and they lay well off shore, planning to renew the search in the morning. A great storm rose in the night; it separated the ships and three days passed before they regained contact. With no sign of improvement in the weather, they left Greenland and resumed the voyage back to England. toward the end of the month they had to endure another storm. Again the ships were lost to each other but both put into Dartmouth on September 30, within the space of two hours.

Davis' second voyage to the North Polar Sea: 1586

John Davis was commissioned by his backers to return to the North Polar Sea to resume his exploration of Cumberland Sound—"to search the bottom of this strait because by all likelihood it was the place and passage by us laboured for."[30] He left Dartmouth for Ireland on May 7, 1586 with a fleet of four ships—the *Sunshine* and the *Moonshine* of the previous voyage, the 120-ton *Mermaid* and a 10-ton pinnace, the *North Star*.

They reached 60°N (the latitude of Cape Farewell, Greenland) on June 7, and here Davis divided the fleet. He sent the *Sunshine* and the *North Star* northward to search for a passage between Greenland and Iceland, and around the north end of Greenland and down its western side. He gave orders that they should search as high as 80°N, land and ice permitting, and to rendezvous with him at Gilbert's Sound on Greenland's west coast. Having seen the two ships off to the north, he sailed westward with the *Mermaid* and the *Moonshine* and on June 15 he came to Cape Farewell. The shore was so clogged with ice there was no thought of landing. He rounded the cape and following the coast, reached the previous year's anchorage at Gilbert's Sound on June 29.

The voyage of the previous year had shown that a small pinnace would

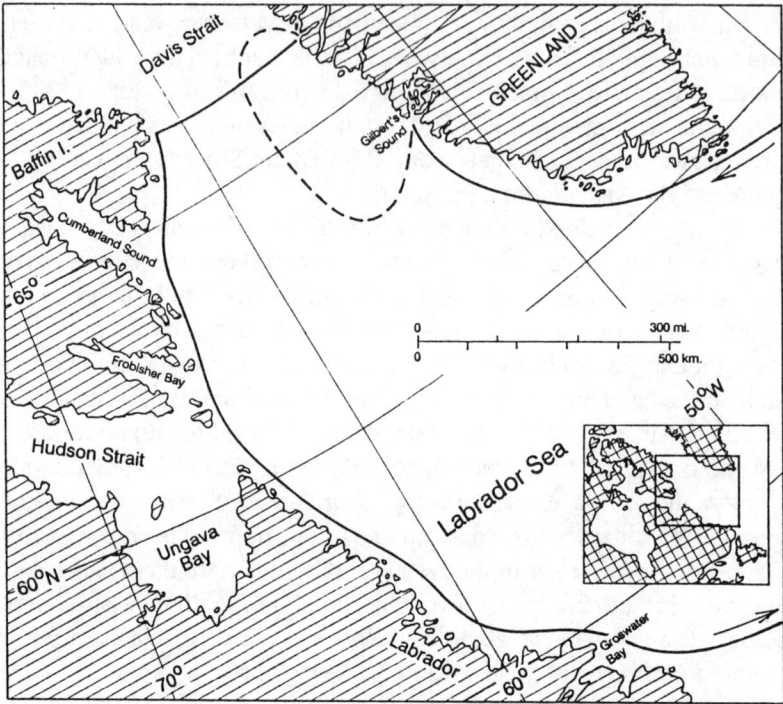

Figure 27. The probable course of Davis' second voyage, in 1586, to Baffin Island.

be useful for exploring shoreline that was inaccessible to the *Mermaid* and the *Moonshine*. To this end, the *Mermaid* carried the parts of a pinnace in her hold and now Davis had the pieces removed to the shore and the carpenters set about fitting them together. The Eskimos were happy to see the Europeans again and within a day of their arrival, as many as a hundred one-man kayaks surrounded the ships at a time, offering gifts of fur, meat and fish. The pinnace was completed on July 4; she was heavy but they easily launched her with the aid of about forty natives.

On one of their forays into the interior, the Englishmen had an opportunity to observe an Eskimo make fire:

> He took a piece of board which had a small hole bored part-way through it. Into that hole he thrust the end of a round and pointed stick, the tip of which he first dipped in seal oil. Last, he wrapped a thong of leather about the stick and then, in the fashion of a turner, he employed the thong to rapidly twirl the stick. Very speedily, he produced fire. That done, he added bits of moss and turf.[31]

The friendly relations the Europeans enjoyed with the Greenlanders began to deteriorate after only a week. The natives were strongly attracted to anything made of iron and they began taking items made of the metal whether they were nails or an anchor. The thefts increased to include clothing, arms and oars. The Greenlanders' behavior became mischievous: they cut the *Moonshine's* boat adrift and severed the ship cables. It became dangerous when they began lobbing stones, a half-pound in weight, onto the decks of the ships with their slings; one struck a boatswain with such force that he fell to the deck.

Nothing Davis did caused the Eskimos to curb these actions for more than a short time. Finally, on July 9, he seized the principal mischief-maker saying to the others he would give him up only after the ship's anchor was returned. There was no response and Davis, despairing of a return to the easy-going ways, made sail and left the inlet, setting a course to the west across Davis Strait.

On July 17, when they were in latitude 63°N, the little fleet encountered a great mass of ice in the strait, in waters that had been relatively clear on the first voyage. Visibility was severely limited by fog and it forced them to move cautiously alongside the mass—first to the south and then to the north—looking for an opening to the west. It was very cold; they suffered in hand and body, and the ships were difficult to work because the ropes and sails were stiff with frost. Reluctantly, on July 30, Davis ordered the ships to come about and they steered east-southeast—back to Greenland. Two days later, on August 1, they were back on Greenland's west coast, in latitude 66°33'N, some 175 miles (280 km.) north of Gilbert's Sound. To their astonishment, the weather was very warm, the shore was free of snow and mosquitoes were out in full force.

There had been much grumbling and talk about going home among the men during the unsuccessful attempt to find a way through the ice in Davis Strait. Davis decided to send the discontented to England in the *Mermaid*; she was not particularly useful because of the difficulty of maneuvering her amidst islands and ice floes. He kept the smaller *Moonshine* and the most physically-able-and-willing men to man her. On August 12, at six o'clock in the morning, he left the *Mermaid* riding at anchor and sailed the *Moonshine* back into the strait. The seas had cleared of ice during the twelve-day interval and they passed unimpeded across the strait and within two days, on August 14, they sighted Baffin Island.

Meanwhile, early in July, the *Sunshine* and the *North Star* had encountered solid ice between Greenland and Iceland and although the day for the rendezvous with Davis was almost a month away, they left the region, not waiting to see if the seas would become passable. They reached Gilbert's

Sound and anchored on August 3, two days after Davis regained the Greenland coast some 175 miles (280 km.) to the north. The ships were still there, expecting to rendezvous with Davis, when the *Mermaid* came down the coast after parting with the *Moonshine* on August 12. She passed Gilbert's Sound, not stopping to see if the *Sunshine* and the *North Star* were waiting there, and entered the Atlantic.

The Eskimos found the *Sunshine* and the *North Star* anchored in Gilbert's Sound and soon they were quarreling with the seamen. The trouble quickly erupted into outright fighting and several seamen were wounded and four Greenlanders were killed in the altercation. Despite the danger, the Englishmen remained at the anchorage until August 31, waiting for Davis to join them.

Davis intercepted Baffin Island in latitude 66°19'N (near Cape Dyer) and he lay anchored there through the night of August 14–15. In the morning he ordered a southward bearing and they crossed the wide mouth of Cumberland Sound, not recognizing it as the body of water he had spent so much time exploring the previous year and the principal objective of the present voyage. The south shore of the sound seemed to be all islands and this fact plus the presence of a strong current flowing westward into the opening, again roused Davis' hopes that this might be the entrance to a through passage.

It began to snow in the evening of August 19 and the weather turned foul with much wind. It may have decided Davis to leave the vicinity because the next afternoon, with a fair wind from the north-northeast, he ran southward "for the express purpose of searching the coast in the hope that God would, in His mercy, direct us to the passage."[32] They sailed down the coast of Baffin Island, passed Frobisher Bay and crossed the open water of Hudson Strait. On August 28, in latitude 57°N, they saw land to the west; they were well down the coast of Labrador.

In the afternoon of September 4 they passed Groswater Bay, the prominent entrance to Hamilton Inlet—"a mightie great sea passing bet-weene two lands West."[33] Was this an entry to the northwest passage? Davis wanted to explore westward into the opening but the wind was against him and he had to give up the idea.

Two days later, as they were preparing to leave North America, tragedy struck. Davis had sent five men ashore to retrieve fish they had laid out to dry on the beach. The men were ambushed by "the brutish people of this country" who killed two and severely wounded two others. One escaped by swimming toward the ship with an arrow through his arm.

They left on September 11 and reached England early in October.

Davis' third voyage to America: 1587

Davis reported to William Sanderson, his principal backer, that on the basis of the knowledge he had gained from the two voyages, he felt certain if there was a northwest passage, it had to be in one of four places.[34] The accounts of the two voyages suggest that the four possibilities were Hamilton Inlet, Hudson Strait, Cumberland Sound and perhaps Baffin Bay. He added that he had acquired 500 seal skins and 140 half-skins and pieces-of-skins on the second voyage. If the company of associates would back him for a third voyage, he was sure he could obtain enough furs from the natives to pay for the entire cost of the voyage—perhaps he could even return a profit. Sanderson was willing and the following year, in 1587, Davis made his final and most productive voyage to Canada's North Polar Sea region.

Davis left Dartmouth on May 19 with two barques—the *Elizabeth* and the *Sunshine*—and a pinnace, the *Helene*. The *Elizabeth* carried the parts of a pinnace. The plan called for the barques to accompany the *Helene* to Gilbert's Sound where the carpenters would assemble the pinnace. Thereafter, the barques were free to go commercial fishing off Newfoundland.

The *Helene* was in trouble before they came abreast of Plymouth when the tiller broke. Repairs were made and she continued on her way but a week later, in fair weather, her foremast split and then went overboard. She demonstrated before long, that she was an exceedingly slow sailer and could not stay with the barques in calm weather. Fearing to lose her, Davis took her in tow whenever the wind was less than brisk. Still, she rode well in rough seas and this seemed to indicate she was staunchly built.

They anchored in Gilbert's Sound on June 16 and next morning the carpenters transferred the parts of the pinnace from the *Elizabeth's* hold to an island and began fitting them together. During the next two days the site was visited by numerous natives, professing by gestures that they came in friendship. But very early in the morning of the third day, the Europeans saw from aboard their ships, that the Eskimos were literally tearing apart the nearly-completed pinnace for the nails in her. Davis drove them off with gunfire but he was not able to prevent them from carrying away some of the planks. They were found later, with the nails removed, but so badly damaged the plan for completing the pinnace had to be abandoned. The pieces were taken aboard the *Elizabeth* with the thought that they might be used to build a small fishing boat.

The *Helene* had begun to leak badly while standing at anchor in the harbor and she had to be pumped to keep her afloat. Some of the seamen iterated their fears that she was badly built and unsafe and declared they would not board her much less sail into the arctic on her. They were angling

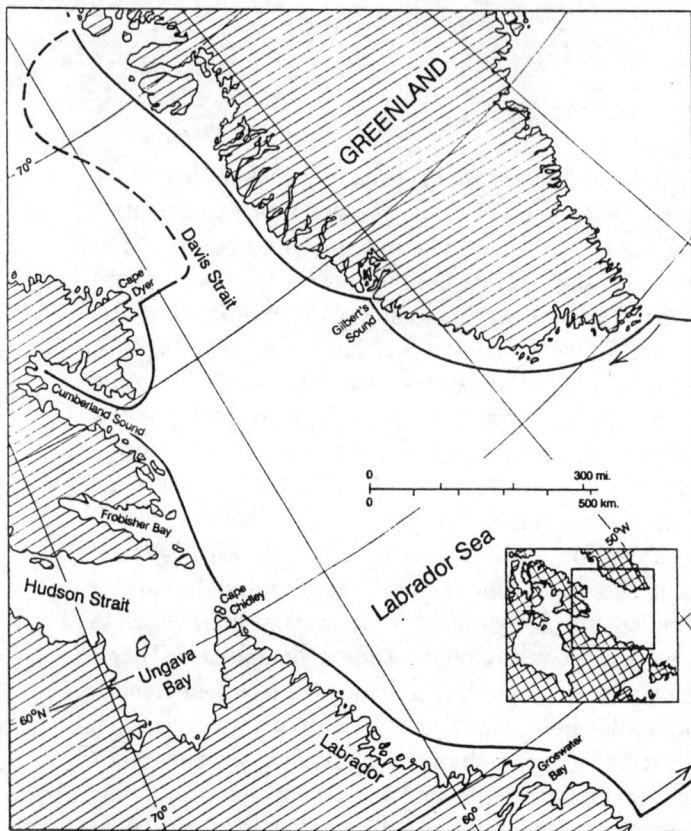

Figure 28.
The probable course
of Davis' third voyage,
in 1587, to America.

for Davis to return to England but he was adamant—there would be no thought of turning back.

Late in the morning of June 21, the fleet left Gilbert's Sound, the barques sailing southward for Newfoundland's fishing grounds, the *Helene* with Davis aboard, steering northward alongside Greenland's west coast. The *Helene* ran to the north for nine days—into Baffin Bay, searching for the passage to the Orient. On June 30 they were in latitude 72°12'N—the most northerly penetration of Davis Strait of record. The sea before them was open but that night the wind shifted and blew in from the north. They could not move up the coast against it and Davis set a course to the west, into Davis Strait. Greenland fell away behind and presently all sight of land was lost. They sailed in open water until July 2 when they intercepted an ice field that stretched endlessly north and south. The wind still blew strongly from the north and it forced them to search southward for a way around or through the field.

They moved cautiously alongside the ice field, at times lying idle when the wind failed, until July 12 before they succeeded in reaching Baffin Island; it was ringed with ice. They searched for an anchorage that would allow them to shelter for a few days—to give sun and wind the opportunity to rid the strait of ice—but they could not find an inlet with water shallow enough to hold the anchor. Fearing the ice might shift and trap them in the night, they put out into the strait again.

On July 19 they were near shore again. They had endured days of wet and foggy weather with visibility too limited to fix their position. Suddenly, early in the afternoon, they saw looming above them, a mountain many of them recognized from the first voyage. It was Davis' Mount Raleigh, in latitude 66°37'N, immediately north of Cumberland Sound. By midnight they were opposite the sound and they entered it. Davis used the next four days to penetrate the sound to its western extremity, discovering it was not a strait into the western sea as he had thought on the first voyage.

They regained Davis Strait on July 27 and continued southward and three days later they were opposite "a wide gulf, or inlet" between latitude 62° and 63°, its entrance totally blocked by ice. It was Frobisher Bay but Davis named it Lumley's Inlet, not recognizing it as the bay which Frobisher had extensively explored and from which he had extracted the supposed gold ore. On July 31 they passed a prominent headland which Davis named Warwick's Foreland; it was Resolution Island.

They crossed "the mouth of a great gulf" through a turbulent sea that "behaved as though a great tide from the east was being met by one equally great from the west."[35] Davis thought the "great gulf" might be a connection between two oceans and, therefore, worth investigating. It was the entrance to Hudson Strait.

They continued southward and on August 1 they reached the North American mainland at Labrador's most northerly point. Davis named it Cape Chidley.

Davis followed Labrador's coastline south and now he began looking for the *Elizabeth* and the *Moonshine*. He had arranged to meet them somewhere between latitude 55° and 54°N and to return to England in their company for he was uneasy about sailing the *Helene* across the Atlantic without an escort. By August 15 he was gravely concerned; he was already well south of the rendezvous and had seen no sign of the barques or the markers they were to set out on islands and headlands. His men felt there was nothing to be gained from remaining in the vicinity. Davis agreed and on August 16 they began the month-long but fortunately uneventful journey back to Dartmouth.

The accounts of Davis' second and third voyages point up the difficulties under which pilots labored in his time. Davis had explored Cumberland Sound in considerable detail in 1585. Yet, when he passed its entrance in 1586 he did not recognize it. And when he came onto Frobisher Bay and

Resolution Island during his third voyage, he did not identify them with features that Frobisher had discovered and named ten years earlier. It was not that he was unacquainted with Frobisher's voyages; the rocks of Greenland's west coast reminded him of the ore that "M. Frobisher brought from Meta incognita."[36]

The reality of earth's features is that a cape or an inlet looks different from one season or even one day to the next—its appearance is affected by a variety of factors including the weather, the direction from which it is approached, even the time of day. Its physical appearance may not be particularly distinctive on a coastline hundreds of miles long and monotonous with not very different capes and inlets.

The problem for mapmakers and pilots in Davis' day lay in their inability to describe the position of a cape or island or strait with coordinates that would enable another navigator to take his ship directly to the feature. Modern mapmakers locate physical features quite unambiguously by their geographic coordinates—that is, their latitude and longitude. The sixteenth-century navigator could determine latitude by measuring the height of the sun at noon or of the North Star at night, provided these celestial bodies were not obscured by clouds or fog. There was no way of accurately determining longitude. Davis' values for longitude were in error by as much as 5° (equivalent to about 350 miles (560 km.) at the equator)—good enough for warning a pilot that he should be on the look-out for a large island but totally inadequate for guiding him to Cape Dyer on Baffin Island's east coast.

Both Frobisher and Davis experienced trouble in dealing with the natives; they found their behavior unpredictable and they learned not to trust them with life or property. It is not known to what extent the white men provoked this behavior.

There were other difficulties for explorers in the Arctic Ocean. Davis had disagreements with his own men when they became mentally exhausted by the daily struggle with the forbidding environment. The seaworthiness of the *Helene* was a constant worry, especially in Davis Strait which was blocked by ice when he first tried to cross it with the pinnace. And time was always at a premium because the sailing season was lamentably short. For these reasons and others, Davis was able to examine only one of the four waterways he thought might lead into the "other sea"—Cumberland Sound and it proved to be merely an inlet of the sea.

10

The Discovery of Hudson Bay
a Second Entrance to the Canadian Interior
1610

The Muscovy (or Russian) Company, an offspring of the Merchant Adventurers which had operated out of England under a charter dating back to 1407, was founded by a group of English merchants about 1552, with Sebastian Cabot, then in his seventies, as governor. The original intention of the founders was to sponsor voyages to search for a route around the top of Europe and Asia to the markets of China and the Indies. Cabot had gained a wide range of maritime experience beginning with the preparation for his father's 1497 voyage to North America and he may have accompanied his father on the voyage. Thereafter he was employed in a variety of positions: commander of an English expedition to America about 1508, cartographer for Henry VIII in 1512, pilot major and official examiner of pilots for the Spanish navy in 1518, commander of a Spanish expedition that explored the south coast of South America between 1525 and 1528, and an appointment to the British navy in 1548.

The first expedition organized by Cabot for the Muscovy Company left England in 1553. It consisted of three ships of which only one, under Richard Chancellor, survived the voyage. Chancellor reached the White Sea where he and his men were taken ashore by Russian fishermen and conducted to the court of Ivan the Terrible in Moscow. As a result of this visit, the company developed a profitable trade overseas with Russia, principally through the port of Archangel in the White Sea.

The flourishing trade between Russia and England excited the envy of the Dutch who, like the English, depended upon maritime trade for their economic well being. In the time that John Davis was exploring the North Polar Sea, Amsterdam was a thriving port for the distribution, in Europe, of merchandise from the Middle and Far East. The movement of Dutch shipping from the Indian and Pacific Oceans, through the Southeast and Southwest Passages, was hampered by restrictions and Dutch merchants chafed at the restraints. They determined that if there was a passage around the north side of Europe and Asia, its discovery would be made by someone in their employ and not by a competing power; they wanted a Dutch Northeast Passage. In 1594, they sponsored the first of three voyages, under the direction of Willem Barents, to search for the passage.

Conditions in the arctic seas north of Europe were unbelievably harsh. In 1596, on the third voyage, Barents' ship was engulfed by ice after rounding the north end of Novaya Zemlya and he was forced to winter on the east coast of the island. The ship did not come free in the spring and Barents and his men abandoned her and set out for the Netherlands in two open boats. He died on the voyage but most of his men survived.

Henry Hudson

Dutch competition in the arctic had materially reduced the Muscovy Company's advantage in trade with Russia and now the Dutch exploratory voyages were threatening to make the waters above Europe and Asia a Dutch sea. In the drive to cross the Arctic Ocean, Barents had reached the Kara Sea, well past the most easterly advance of the English. In 1607, ten years after the return of Barents' men from Novaya Zemlya, the Muscovy Company responded to the challenge. It called on Henry Hudson, an English navigator, to renew the English thrust into the arctic above Europe and Asia, and find a way to reach the Orient.

Hudson's voyages in 1607 and 1608

The voyages of Frobisher, Davis and Barents had confirmed earlier observations that the far north seas were frozen. Still there were influential voices that claimed it was possible to sail across the North Pole to the other side of the earth. The Church of England's Reverend Samuel Purchas, for one, postulated that because latitudinal circles decreased in circumference from the equator, to a point (or nothing) at the North Pole, a voyage across the pole should amount to a mere nothing. It is said that Hudson was a religious man but he was probably too much of a practical seaman to be swayed by the Purchas doctrine; nevertheless, he decided to attempt to voyage across the North Pole.

Hudson left England in May 1607, in the 40-ton *Hopewell* with a crew of eleven, including his son John, and started up the east coast of Greenland. Eventually, in latitude 73°N, he was stopped by ice but he had reached farther north on this coast than anyone before him. He turned east and traced the boundary of the ice to Spitsbergen, attaining a latitude of almost 80°N.

On the voyage back to England, between Spitsbergen and Iceland, he discovered the island of Jan Mayen in latitude 71°N.

Hudson had found the way across the North Pole blocked by ice but his voyage had some positive results for his backers. He brought back the news that whales were plentiful in the waters around Spitsbergen. It led to the establishment of an English whale fishery in the arctic and the Muscovy Company was pleased to employ him in 1608 for another attempt to cross the Arctic Ocean.

It was Hudson's intention, on the next voyage, to attempt a crossing of the Pole further to the east—in the waters between Spitsbergen and Novaya Zemlya. If he found the arctic region bound by ice, he planned to turn eastward and probe for a way past Novaya Zemlya into the Kara Sea. There was not much hope of a passage around the north end of that island where Barents' ship was frozen fast in 1596. Since Barents' time, English and Dutch explorers had passed around its south end into the Kara Sea but they had found the sea here clogged with ice. Hudson planned to search for a passage or strait through the center of Noyaya Zemlya in the hope of finding the Kara Sea open in this region. A chart prepared by Barents suggested that such a strait did exist. Hudson sailed from England late in April 1608. Early in June he sighted North Cape on the northern tip of Norway and set a course for the North Pole. He encountered an ice field within a few days and, as planned, he followed its edge eastward. It brought him to the western side of Noyaya Zemlya on June 26. As expected, the northern tip of the island was enclosed in ice, forcing him southward and he moved down the coast, searching for Barents' strait. Early in July he found a promising opening and sent the ship's boat to investigate it. The channel grew steadily shallower as they advanced inland until there was only four feet (little more than a metre) of water under the keel; obviously this was not a passage into the Kara Sea.

The voyage had yielded nothing but there was still time to round the southern tip of the island and see if the Kara Sea was blocked. But Hudson abruptly gave up the search for a way east and turned back, and on July 17 he was opposite Vardo, Norway. It has been speculated that he had decided to make only a token effort to cross the seas above Europe and Asia—that he was convinced that the waters above the Americas offered the only possibility of finding a northern sea passage. He may have ended the search in the east early to give himself time to take the ship into Davis Strait and probe its waters before the sailing season ended. If so, the crew forced him to give up the idea and that ambition had to be put aside for a later year. He reached England before the end of August.

The Muscovy Company was disenchanted with the prospect of continuing a costly search that had given no promise of finding a northern passage to China and did not offer to finance another voyage. The Dutch, however, were not discouraged by Hudson's failures. Officials of the Dutch East India Company had followed news of his voyaging and they were impressed with him. The Dutch company was anxious to press the search east across the Kara Sea and late in 1608, Hudson visited Amsterdam to discuss the matter. The Dutch offered to sponsor another voyage into the northeast and an arrangement was quickly and easily concluded.

Voyage up the Hudson River: 1609

Hudson left the Netherlands in April 1609 in the 60-ton *Half Moon* and entered the Barents Sea early in May. His crew was a motley collection of sixteen Dutch and English seamen who soon showed they had no stomach for the task. By the time the ship reached the vicinity of Noyaya Zemlya they had had enough of the ice-infested waters and the search for the Northeast Passage, and some of them threatened to mutiny if he did not turn back. They were a rough lot, drawn from the docks of two countries and Hudson could not hope to stand against them. He agreed to come about but he refused to return to the Netherlands. To abandon the voyage before it had fully begun would have ruined his reputation. He insisted that the crew agree to a search for a Northwest Passage—either from Davis Strait in the north or along the east coast of America between Virginia and Nova Scotia. They could make the choice. The men accepted the proposition and chose the second alternative.

It was about the middle of May when Hudson set a course for Virginia, planning to strike the coast of America some 300 miles (500 km.) north of the Jamestown colony founded two years earlier (in 1607). He had been informed by John Smith, the governor of Jamestown, that a channel almost a mile wide at the coast, led into the interior at this point. Smith had heard reports from Indians, of the existence of large bodies of water to the west. The governor probably associated these waters with the Pacific Ocean and thought the channel might lead to it. Few if any Europeans suspected at this time, that 3000 miles (5000 km.) of continent lay between Virginia and the Pacific Ocean.

Hudson and his crew sighted the coast of Maine on July 12. They cruised leisurely southward for a month, taking time to replace a mast when they found a suitable stand of timber, fishing, trading with Indians, and searching for the opening into the interior. They came about just above Cape Hatteras and began searching to the north for John Smith's opening. Their conduct left a poor impression on the native Americans. In the course of their contacts with them, they stole a boat, drove off the inhabitants of one village and ransacked the houses of whatever they fancied, and they got a native drunk for the fun of watching as he "leapt and danced" after they put him ashore. Hudson took part in some of these activities and he must have sanctioned others.

Early in September Hudson anchored in the mouth of an outflow of water sheltered by a large Island (Long Island) and set about examining the region with the ship's boat manned by five sailors. The local Indians visited the ship and seemed happy to have the white men among them. But only a few days after the *Half Moon's* arrival, the men in the boat were attacked by two canoe loads of natives and one of Hudson's men took an arrow in the throat and was killed. Hudson retaliated by seizing two hostages when a number of natives came aboard to barter corn and tobacco for knives and beads. The crew mocked the captives, forcing them to wear red coats, needlessly antagonizing them.

Hudson started the *Half Moon* into the interior on September 11. His hostages escaped within a few days and when they reached the safety of the shore, they expressed by gestures their scorn of the white men and vowed revenge. The ship reached the vicinity of modern-day Albany within a week (on September 19). The flow of water was decreasing and Hudson must have suspicioned that this was not a channel to another sea. Nevertheless, next day he sent the ship's boat upstream to see what lay ahead. The men reported that the channel continued to narrow and it grew shallower—it was a river. In spite of this evidence, Hudson sent a party upriver for another look a few days later. They rowed a distance of twelve miles (20 km.)—to near Waterford—before returning to the ship with the same conclusion. Hudson was convinced there was no point in continuing into the interior and he turned the ship for the journey back to the Atlantic. The Jamestown governor's channel had proved to be the Hudson River; the "large bodies of water in the west" were probably the Great Lakes.

In that same summer, Samuel de Champlain and about eighty Algonquin and Huron Indians met and defeated the Iroquois at Lake Champlain, only a few days' travel north of Hudson's highest point of ascent.

The crew (and perhaps Hudson too) marred the passage up and down the river with their treatment of the native Americans. Like many Europeans who had preceded them to the New World, they assumed the Indians were savages and could be used for pleasure and profit, as they chose. They were not above using liquor to gain an advantage when they wished to barter with them as well as for the sheer amusement of getting them drunk. They seized Indian property, apparently without a qualm, but they would not tolerate petty thieving on the part of the natives—maiming or killing them for the slightest offense.

Hudson brought the *Half Moon* into Dartmouth on November 7 and immediately sent notice of his arrival to his Dutch employers in the Netherlands and described his success in finding and exploring an important river that emptied into the Atlantic along the American coast. He requested them to support another voyage in the following year, this time to search for a passage to the Orient around the north end of America. He asked that certain of his men be replaced by more responsible sailors. The communication was delayed by bad weather and meanwhile, word that Hudson had discovered a navigable river into the interior of America got around the port and eventually it was heard by people in authority. They acted swiftly; the *Half Moon* was detained in the port and Hudson and the English members of his crew were ordered to reserve their services for their own country.

The discovery of the Hudson River was a significant event. The Dutch founded the town of New Amsterdam on Manhattan, the island between the Hudson and East Rivers; it eventually formed a part of the city of New York. The Hudson became a Dutch river for a time but Hudson was to have no part in the development of the region for the Dutch.

Voyage to Hudson Bay: 1610

The Muscovy Company had given up on Hudson after his failures, in 1607 and 1608, to cross the Arctic Ocean. Now he had discovered a river in America that could have important trade implications for the Dutch; it raised his stature in England. It had the effect of inducing influential Englishmen to take seriously his proposal for a new adventure: to renew the search for a Northwest Passage in the waters visited by Frobisher and Davis in the years between 1576 and 1587. Davis had come away from the voyages with the conviction that several openings in Davis Strait should be investigated as possible channels for reaching the western sea. For one, he had noted a "furious overfall"—a rush of tides and currents—when he crossed from Resolution Island to Cape Chidley in Labrador, and he had marked it as possibly a passage to the "Other Sea." (He was referring to Hudson Strait.) This was the body of water Hudson had proposed to investigate for his Dutch backers. Now that interest in a Northwest Passage had been revived in England, a syndicate headed by Sir Thomas Smith, Sir Dudley Digges and John Wolstenholme was formed to enable Hudson to undertake a probe of Davis' "furious overfall."

Hudson left London on April 17, 1610, dropping down the Thames in the 55-ton *Discovery*. His crew of twenty-two included:

Robert Juet: mate;

Edward Wilson: 22-year-old surgeon;

John King: quartermaster;
Francis Clemens: boatswain;
Silvanus Bond: cooper;
Robert Bylot: navigator;
Bennett Mathues: cook;
Philip Staffe: carpenter;
John Williams: gunner;
Thomas Woodhouse: mathematician;
Abacus Prickett: servant and representative of Sir Dudley Digges;
Michael Butt, Syracke Fanner, Arnold Lodlo, Adame Moore, Adrian Motter, Michael Perse, John Thomas and William Wilson: able-bodied seamen;
John Hudson and Nicholas Syms: cabin-boys.

Juet, Lodlo, Perse and Staffe had served previously with Hudson; Juet had been one of the principal trouble makers on the voyage up the Hudson River.

At Gravesend, Henry Greene—young, clever, a well-born scapegrace who enjoyed the company of prostitutes, pimps and panders—was taken on board. It was soon evident that Greene enjoyed a special relationship with Hudson and this stirred resentment among the crew.

Favorable winds carried them rapidly up the east coast of England; on May 5, they were off the Orkneys and three days later they passed by the Faeroe Islands. They sighted Iceland on May 11 and here their progress was interrupted by fog and contrary winds which held them on Iceland's west coast for a fortnight. The crew members happily amused themselves at fishing, shooting and bathing in the hot springs. Greene, however, caused trouble. He fought with Edward Wilson, the surgeon, and when Hudson took his side, Wilson had to be persuaded to continue the voyage and Juet muttered that Greene's role on board ship was that of informer to Hudson. The words reached Hudson only after the ship had left Iceland; they caused him to consider returning to Iceland and putting Juet ashore. Had he done so, the voyage might have had a different ending for him.

There was much ice surrounding Greenland when *Discovery* reached it, ruling out any chance to land. Hudson continued his westerly course and toward the end of June, they came to Resolution Island and entered Hudson Strait.

Hudson Strait is a part of the Hudson Bay water system which includes Hudson and James Bays, Foxe Basin and Foxe Channel, and Ungava Bay.[1] The system is considered to be an extension of the Atlantic Ocean. It is a huge area covering almost 500,000 square miles, half of it occupied by Hudson Bay which thrusts deep into the interior of Canada. The waters of

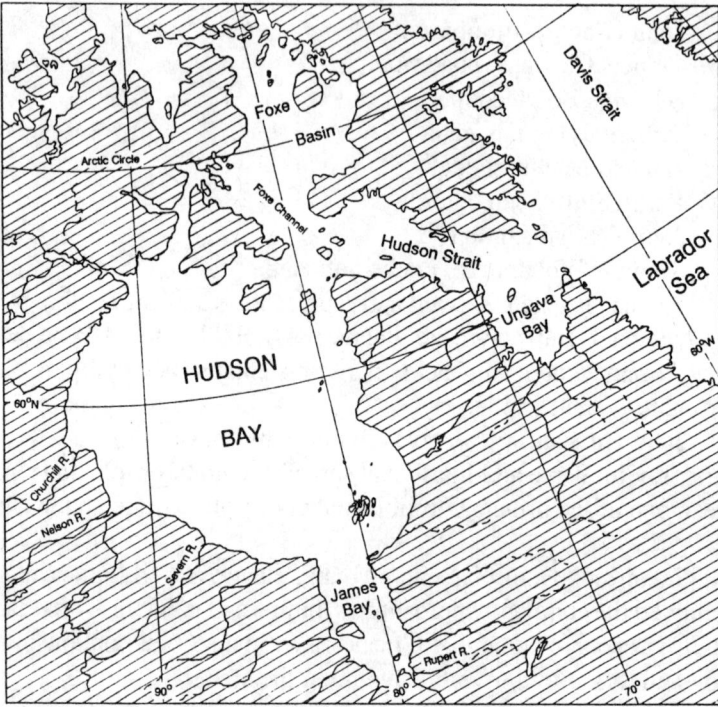

Figure 29. The Hudson Bay water system.

Hudson Bay, fed by numerous tributary rivers, flow northward through a narrow gap into Hudson Strait. In the north, arctic sea water funnels southeastward through Fury and Hecla Strait into Foxe Basin, and southward through Foxe Channel into Hudson Strait where it joins the Hudson Bay water. The joining of these waters creates a strong eastward discharge along the south shore of the strait into the Labrador Sea. The north side of the strait is dominated by an inflow of water from the Labrador Sea; it flows westward until it is overcome by the outflow from Foxe Channel and Hudson Bay, and is forced southward until it joins the main discharge to the east. The consequence of this mingling of conflicting currents, flows and tides is to make Hudson Strait a turbulent rush of boiling water. It made passage difficult for ships; John Janes, mate on the *Helene* when John Davis crossed the eastern entrance of the strait in 1587, noted in his journal:

> This day and night we passed by a very great gulfe, the water whirling and roaring as it were the meetings of tydes.[2]

160

The ice that rafts out of Hudson Bay and Foxe Basin, carried this way and that by the shifting waters, makes the strait all the more hazardous for shipping. It is usually free of ice only by late summer.[3] Hudson arrived at its entrance late in June, two to three weeks before the recommended beginning of the sailing season.

Both shores are visible to a ship moving through the strait in fair weather. Neither the weather nor the season favored Hudson. He could not see the shore for the fog and he could not steer the ship by compass for it was rendered useless in the strait "owing to the excessive dip of the needle"[4] which was due to the close proximity of the magnetic pole. The masses of ice drifting haphazardly in the unpredictable currents, visible only at close range in the fog, filled the men with terror. Hudson moved the ship to the Labrador coast, then crossed the strait to Baffin Island, then recrossed it to Ungava Bay, seeking a clear safe passage to the west.

The men came close to mutinying in Ungava Bay but Hudson talked them out of it. He showed and explained his chart to them, telling them what he hoped to accomplish and how much had already been done, suggesting

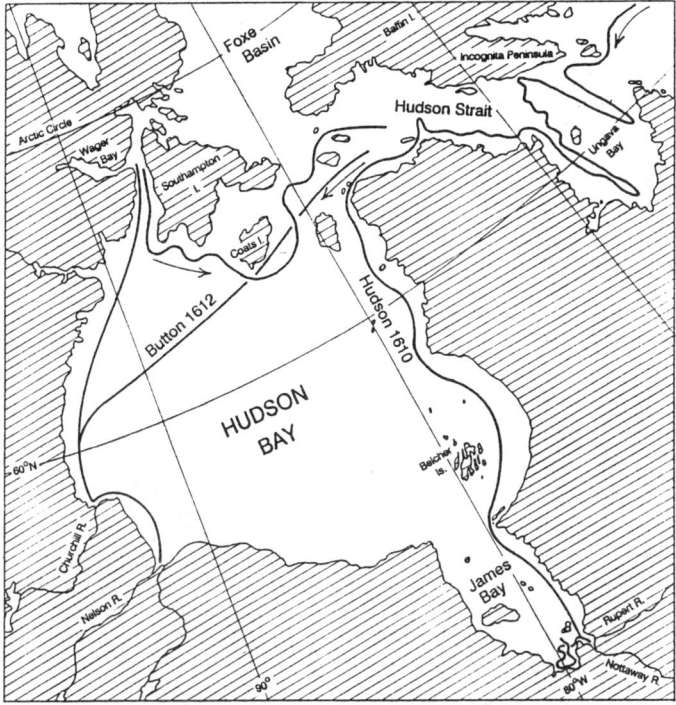

Figure 30. The voyages of Henry Hudson (1610) and Thomas Button (1612–3) into Hudson Bay.

that those who faltered had "wren's hearts," challenging them to go on. He was able to persuade them; it might have served him better had he made an example of the dissenters, especially old Robert Juet.

They left Ungava Bay in their wake on July 19, sailing along the south shore of the strait. On August 1 they passed between Charles Island and the mainland and next day they were through the strait; the most difficult part of the voyage was behind them.

Hudson now set a west-southwest course to pass through the gap between the towering Labrador headland of Cape Wolstenholme and the vertical cliffs of Digges Islands, two miles to the west. The air was filled with the scream of sea birds nesting on every square inch of rock. After a short stop to explore Digges Islands, Hudson took the ship south—into the open water of Hudson Bay. They were the first Europeans on that inland sea. They saw before them an apparently limitless expanse of water stretching to the south and the west. Hudson was certain he had "won the passage" to the Orient but instead of continuing to the west, he drove the ship south, keeping the eastern shore of the bay in view. And after a time they reached James Bay—the bottom of the bay.

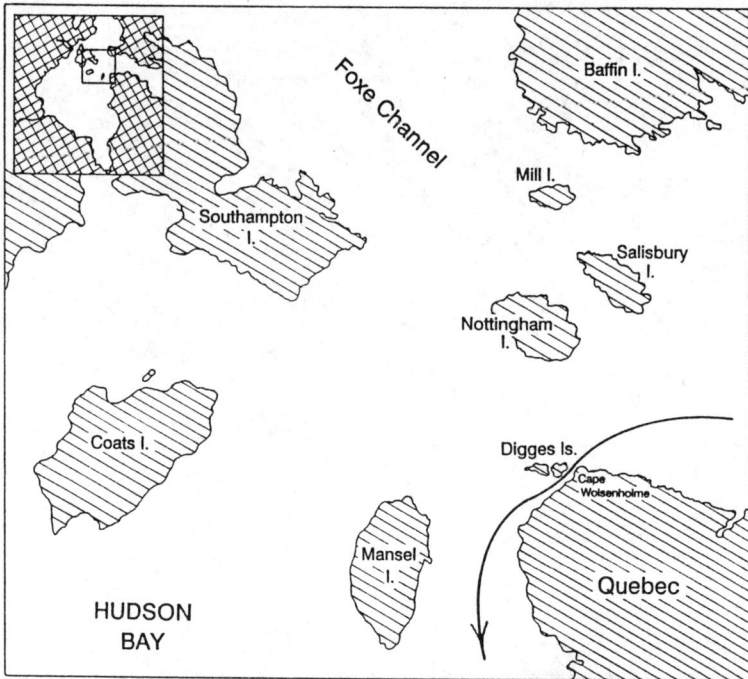

Figure 31. Henry Hudson's route between Digges Islands
and Cape Wolsenholme into Hudson Bay.

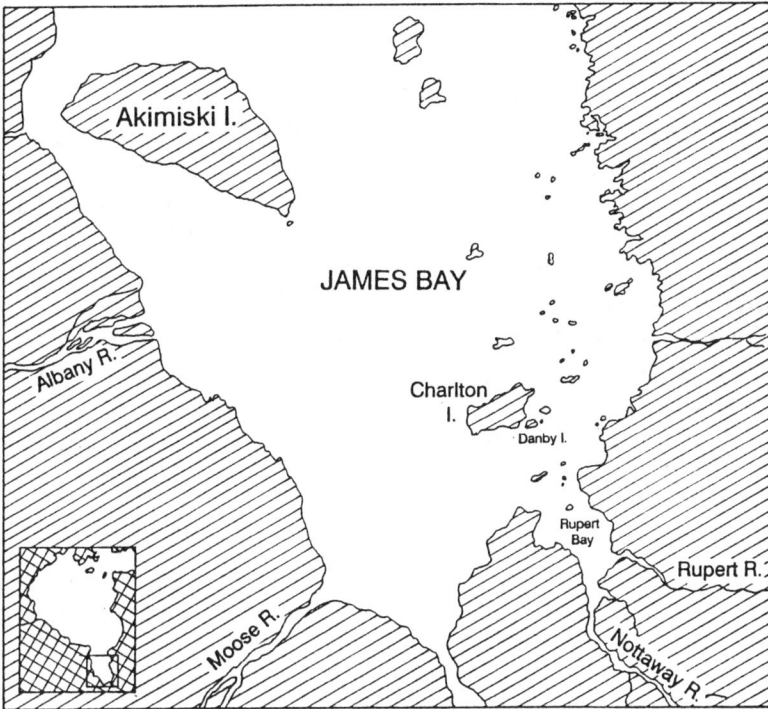

Figure 32. James Bay where Henry Hudson spent the winter of 1610-1.

Hudson spent several weeks in James Bay, searching for a hidden outlet to the south, sailing back and forth as if he could not believe he had come to a dead end. One wonders why he did not leave James Bay and direct the ship westward; west was the most obvious direction in which to continue the search for a Northwest Passage. Some of the crew, led by Juet, began to mutter again. It irritated Hudson and he charged the old mate with disloyalty. Juet asked to be accused and tried before the full crew, expecting them to be sympathetic and support him. The trial was held on September 10 but it did not have the result Juet expected. A number of crew members related damning incidents giving Hudson just cause for demoting Juet. He appointed Bylot in his place as mate and he replaced Clemens, the boat-swain, with William Wilson.

Winter in James Bay: 1610-1

Hudson continued his scrutiny of the shores of James Bay until near the end of October when he anchored the ship in the southeast corner of the bay in the mouth of the Rupert River, in latitude 51°10'N. The nights had grown long and cold and the ground was covered with snow. Soon there would be no open water in the bay and indeed, within ten days—by November 10—the ship was frozen into place.

Soon after they became immobilized in the bay, John Williams, the gunner, died. It was the custom at sea to auction a dead man's clothes but Hudson ignored the practice and arbitrarily decided to sell Williams' homespun cloak to Greene who had come on board without proper dress. This appeared to the crew to be another display of favoritism and it did not sit well with them.

Friction between Hudson and his crew increased as winter conditions forced them into close confinement. Hudson planned to spend the winter on board the *Discovery* and refused to listen when the carpenter, Staffe, suggested erecting a shelter on shore. Later he changed his mind but now the carpenter demurred, citing the difficulties of working outdoors in the cold of winter. Hudson lost his temper with the carpenter who was a loyal supporter, abusing him with foul names and threatening to hang him for insubordination. Greene openly sided with Staffe and to punish Greene, Hudson allowed Bylot to buy John Williams' cloak. Despite the altercation, Hudson and Staffe came to some kind of reconciliation and the shelter was soon built.

Hudson had not considered wintering in America and had not stocked the ship with enough food to last them through to spring and back to England. He began rationing the provisions and he offered rewards to the men for shooting bird and beast. Near Cape Wolstenholme they had fed well on birds nesting on the Digges Islands and now they eked out their provisions with ptarmigans. As winter wore on the birds became scarce. Hunger gnawed at the men's bellies and they suffered from scurvy, frost bite, stomach cramps and other diseases brought on by the cold and the scarcity of nourishing food. They ate what they could find, including moss. Edward Wilson, the surgeon, had the sense to brew buds "full of a turpentine substance" into "an oily substance." It proved an effective cure for scurvy and other ills related to their diet. With the approach of spring they were able to shoot geese and ducks flying north in incredible numbers. And they ate frogs. When the migratory birds had gone their way, the hunters found little game even though they ranged widely.

One day when the ice in the bay had begun to melt, a native appeared, evidently drawn by the sight of the ship. Hudson presented him with a few gifts—a mirror, some buttons and a knife—hoping he would return with companions or food. He did return with a few skins and some meat, and he offered them in payment for the items Hudson had given him. Hudson, anxious to have the native bring more food but thinking he must give the impression that he was not in need of it, began to haggle, trying for a better bargain with the native. The native agreed to Hudson's terms and left, but he did not return.

Finally there was open water in the bay and the men went fishing with a net and enjoyed a catch of 500 on the first day's try. They thought their food worries were at an end, but successive catches dwindled and soon they were again short of provisions. Hudson had seen smoke on the horizon to the southwest and he surmised it marked a native camp on a river near the coast. Taking a week's supply of food, he set off alone across the bay in the ship's boat to find the camp and bargain for food. The natives would have nothing to do with him; they even set fire to the brush when they saw him approach.

Hudson returned to the ship totally discouraged and in a fit of senseless anger, he dismissed his mate, Bylot, and replaced him with King, a man who did not enjoy the same respect of the crew. It was an unfortunate time to lose control of his emotions. The men—particularly Juet, Greene and William Wilson—had been brooding and talking of mutiny in Hudson's absence. Bylot, one of the most influential men in the crew, had stood in their way and now Hudson had traded his loyalty for the doubtful qualities of King.

Early in June Hudson began preparations to leave the anchorage. In an effort to augment the food supply, he sent men out in the ship's boat to have another try at fishing. They returned after two days with only a meager catch. He took what bread remained and with his own hands, he divided it among the men—"hee wept when he gave it to them" for it came to only a pound per man. They left the bay on June 12 and almost at once hunger became a pressing problem. To appease the men, Hudson divided among them the cheese remaining in the larder—a week's supply; it amounted to three and a half pounds per man. It made matters worse because most of the men were so hungry, they ate the week's ration in a day or two, and one devoured all of his portion immediately and "laid in bed two or three days for his labour."[5]

Despite the critical shortage of food and no prospect of improvement, Hudson was not ready to give up the venture. He planned to use the short summer sailing season to continue the search for the Northwest Passage and then return to England. When he thought he detected "mighty tides" from the northwest, he was inspired to hope they rose from another sea and the passage was there for the finding. Apparently he had the support of his officers but the rest of the crew were tired of the long adventure and anxious to quit America. And they held the suspicion that Hudson was keeping back food and sharing it with his favorites in the privacy of his cabin.

Hudson, too, had suspicions. He suspected that the men had food hidden in their cabins and he ordered one of the cabin boys to search their sea chests. The action angered the crew for they felt it was an invasion of their privacy—but it did turn up food. It solved nothing; the men's resentment and their distrust of Hudson and his plans festered and came to dominate the atmosphere aboard ship.

Mutiny in James Bay: 1611

Matters came to a head on the night of June 23 as the ship lay anchored to an ice floe near Charlton Island in James Bay. Greene, William Wilson, Juet, Thomas, Perse, Mathues and Motter chose this night to mutiny. They gathered in Prickett's cabin in the dead of night to plot their foul deed—an act as brutal as any recorded in seafaring history. Greene swore an oath that "hee would doe no man harme, and what he did was for the good of the voyage, and for nothing else."[6] The others did likewise. The oath was a sanctimonious lie for no man among them could believe other than what they intended meant a slow, dreadful death for at least some of their victims.

The familiar cheery sound of Mathues, the cook, going to the water butt at sunrise to fill his kettle, signaled the beginning of the insurrection. King, the new mate—enticed to enter the hold—had the door slammed and bolted behind him and as Hudson emerged from his cabin, Mathues, Thomas and Wilson fell on him and bound his hands. Hearing the noise, Edward Wilson, the surgeon, made to come out of his cabin. He was met by the mutineers who asked if he was well and when he said he was, they told him "he should keepe himself soe"[7] by not interfering.

The ship's boat was quickly hauled alongside and Hudson was hustled into it by Mathues and Thomas. Now a meaningless rage took hold of the chief perpetrators—Greene, Juet and Wilson. They cared not who else was put into the boat as long as the deed was quickly done for they were desperately anxious to finish their work and be rid of the sight of their treachery. But for the intervention of the other conspirators, Greene would have left Mathues and Thomas in the shallop to share the fate of Hudson. Lodlo and Butt, although no friends to Hudson, were forced to replace them. Woodhouse, pleading to be spared, was seized and thrust into the boat and he was quickly followed by Moore and Fanner, both too sick to resist, and Hudson's son, John.

Meanwhile Juet, the former mate, had gone to the hold to vent his fury on King, the present mate. But King had his sword with him and as soon as the bolt was withdrawn, he attacked Juet and would have killed him had the others not heard Juet's cries for help. They overpowered King and pushed him over the side of the ship into the boat. This seemed to satisfy the mutineers and they were about ready to cut loose when Staffe, the carpenter, came forward. A bit slow to comprehend what was happening, illiterate and unpolished, yet he knew right from wrong and he had not taken long to decide where his loyalty and duty lay. He told the mutineers in plain and certain terms what he thought of their actions and he said he preferred to "commit himself to God's mercy." He would not stay on the ship unless they forced him. They could not shake his resolve and they let him descend to the boat in dignity with his chest of tools, a musket, some meal, and an iron pot."[8]

The mutineers took the *Discovery*, now with thirteen men aboard, away from the ice into open water and cut the boat free. Then, with top-sails up, they steered to the north and the shallop fell off behind and was lost to view. What passed through the minds of the men in the shallop—actually eight men and a boy—as they saw the ship dwindle into the distance? They could not sail any distance in their small vessel. They would have to learn to exist in this country and hope that someone would come out from England to search for them. They had passed one dreadful winter here; could they go through another with even fewer resources?

As soon as the mutineers were out of sight of Hudson, they lowered the sails. They were intent on searching the ship and did not want the risk of ramming an ice floe while they bent to their work. They scoured the *Discovery* from bow to stern in a frenzied effort to find the food that would justify for them their act of mutiny, their belief that Hudson had starved them while he and his favorites fed well. And they found food—food that Hudson probably had held back to continue the search for the Northwest Passage and not for his own eating. They had forgotten the shallop in the excitement of the discovery until one of their number on deck cried out that it was coming up with them. Then, acting the part of guilt-ridden men, they let fall the sails and with all possible speed, fled northward from Hudson's view.

Return voyage of the *Discovery*: 1611

Bylot, as the most capable navigator on board, took charge of directing the ship but Greene soon came to dominate the company of mutineers. Prickett had demonstrated on the voyage, that he was literate and could speak persuasively. He was to claim, later, that he had been spared against Greene's wish because the others thought he would be useful in devising a plausible reason for taking over the ship and explaining it to the authorities in England. Indeed, Greene immediately set him to work to remove any incriminatory material from Hudson's journal. Apparently Hudson had complained at length about his crew, for only a small part of the journal ever reached England.

The ship passed the Belcher Islands and presently they came to another island where they anchored to fish; they were unable to catch anything. The food they had discovered in the ship was long gone and they were hungry again. They fed on two birds that Perse killed and "cockle-grass" which grew in the mud near shore. They stayed a day and a half at the island and when they resumed their flight, Bylot steered a northerly course against the objections of Juet who was certain they should be on a northwest bearing. Presently they came up with the ice, drifting northward into Foxe Channel; it held them up for ten days during which time there was much arguing about the direction they should be steering. Only Bylot and perhaps Prickett had any idea where they were or how to get out of Hudson Bay.

They lived on cockle-grass, gathered whenever they could get ashore, and on the expectation of finding Digges Islands. There they would have birds aplenty to eat but also, they would be able to orientate themselves and know the correct direction for reaching England. Bylot said he would get them to the islands but as the hungry days passed one by one, they lost faith in him. But then one day, incredibly, they saw through the morning haze in the distance, the islands and Cape Wolstenholme and as they drew nearer, the sight and sound of the birds that would provide the meat to get them home. They killed about thirty birds that morning.

They had a surprise encounter with a party of fifty or sixty Eskimos when they went ashore next day. The men were wary at first but presently the Europeans and Americans mingled in apparent friendship. The mutineers got as many birds as they could handle and laden with gifts from the Eskimos, they returned to the ship.

Next day, six of the Englishmen went ashore carrying trifles which they hoped to trade for meat and fur garments. Prickett, who was lame, was left in the ship's boat. No sooner had the others, all unarmed, begun to bargain than an Eskimo climbed into the boat and tried to knife Prickett. It was the signal for a general Eskimo attack on the white men. Prickett got his dirk free and drove it into the man's throat. Thomas and William Wilson, their bowels opened by spear thrusts, and Perse and Greene, both mortally wounded, managed to tumble into the boat. Motter had to swim for it while Perse held the Eskimos off with a hatchet. They got the boat turned, and Motter and Perse bent to the oars. At this, the natives sent a flight of arrows into their midst, killing Greene and wounding Perse and Prickett. The seamen were still some distance from the ship when Perse fainted from his wounds. Fortunately, the natives had chosen not to pursue them, probably fearing they would be raked by cannon fire from the ship, and the badly shaken Europeans reached their ship.

They threw Greene's lifeless body into the sea and got the wounded aboard. The Eskimo Prickett had stabbed and John Thomas died that day. William Wilson, "swearing and cursing in a most fearfull manner,"[9] and Perse followed two days later. And then they were nine.

Unless they made for Newfoundland, this was the one and only place on the homeward voyage where they could replenish their stock of food. The birds of Digges Islands represented their only chance of reaching England and they had not yet loaded enough birds to get them even as far as Newfoundland. Going ashore represented a fearful risk but they had to take the risk. They made two more trips to the island, although in another place, and managed to kill about 300 birds. They salted them against the long voyage across the Atlantic.

They entered Hudson Strait around the beginning of August, passed out of it about two weeks later, and set a course for the southern tip of Greenland and then Ireland. They rationed themselves to half a bird a day. Nothing was wasted; Juet concocted a soup from bird's skin after the feathers had been burned away[10] and they fried the bones in candle grease until they were crisp and then ate them seasoned with vinegar. And they ate seaweed. They grew steadily weaker until none among them could stand while steering the ship. They lay about the deck, too listless to mend sails even though they knew it would speed their return. In time Robert Juet died from "mere want."

They reached Ireland on September 6 to find that the people were too poor to feed them. They had to barter the ship's cable and anchor for food.[11] Finally, a Captain Taylor came to their aid and helped to get the ship and crew to Plymouth.

After the voyage

The actions of the mutineers were examined by authorities on October 24, a little more than a month after the ship docked in England. Prickett and Bylot cleverly manipulated the proceedings by playing to the avarice of their inquisitors. They said they had detected a heavy flow of tides and currents out of the west in the vicinity of Digges Islands. They produced Hudson's map of Hudson Bay; it left the west coast of the bay tantalizingly uncharted, implying that one need only search there to find the source of the tides and the Northwest Passage. Their presentation excited the greed of the merchants so effectively that instead of being indicted, Bylot, Prickett and Wilson were included as members of a new syndicate called "The Discoverers of the North-West Passage" with a royal charter to find the passage.

The company sent two ships—the *Resolution* and the smaller *Discovery*—to the bay in May 1612 under the command of Thomas Button. Francis Nelson served as master of the *Discovery*; Prickett and Bylot were members of his crew. Button probed about 600 miles (950 km.) of the west side of the bay, from the Nelson River which he named after his sailing master, north to the Churchill River and Wager Bay, in latitude 65°N, where he was stopped by ice. He wintered at the Nelson RIver. The sailing master and a number of his seamen, sick from scurvy, did not survive the winter. There were other misfortunes; five seamen were killed by Eskimos on Digges Islands and Button had to abandon the *Resolution* before sailing back to England. Despite these losses and failures, Button remained convinced there was a Northwest Passage out of Hudson Bay. Nor was the enthusiasm of English merchants much diminished; they sent out expedition after expedition in the succeeding years. The little *Discovery* made six voyages into the North Polar Seas.

The authorities looking into the mutiny summoned Bylot and Prickett in 1616 and again in 1617 to give evidence. In 1618, Prickett, Wilson, Mathues and Clemens were charged with "the ejection of Henry Hudson and John Hudson and others from the ship *Discovery*, in a boat called a shallop without food or drink and other necessities and the murder of the same."[12] They were tried before twelve "honest and selected men" from County Surrey who returned a verdict of not guilty.

Virtually nothing is known about the fate of Hudson and his men. The sole reference to the men is attributed to Captain Thomas James who spent the 1631–2 winter on Charlton Island in James Bay. He discovered on nearby Danby Island, a row of stakes that could only have been sharpened with a European ax. James was the first European after Hudson to enter James Bay and, therefore, it is safe to assume that the stakes were the work of Philip Staffe, Hudson's carpenter, and that Hudson visited this island or settled on it after the mutineers finished with him.

We can surmise that Hudson brought the shallop in to shore somewhere in James Bay soon after he lost sight of the *Discovery*. His immediate objective would have been to prepare a shelter and obtain food—any kind of food to sustain them while they worked out a plan to improve their lot. After their most pressing needs were satisfied, Hudson's thoughts would have turned to the longer term—preparations to get them through the winter while they waited for a rescue expedition to find and take them back to England. The Indians lived off the land; surely they could do likewise. It was not outside the realm of possibility for men determined to survive. Hudson had among his people two loyal, capable and reliable men in Philip

Staffe and John King. They had a box of carpenter's tools, an iron pot and at least one musket. With most of the summer before them, there was ample time to build an adequate if not comfortable camp, lay in firewood, forage for food and make another attempt to contact the local Indians.

Whatever preparations Hudson may have made to survive until he and his men were rescued, they failed to save him. The authorities looking into the mutiny, and the financial backers of the voyage, simply ignored him. The historical record includes no reason to believe that Button or Nelson, who explored Hudson Bay in the year after the incident, or any any of the voyagers that followed them into the bay in succeeding years, searched for Hudson. It was 1631, twenty years after the mutiny, before anyone next entered James Bay. Incredibly, Hudson was simply abandoned by his countrymen and left to his fate. In retrospect, it seems he would have given himself a better chance to survive after the mutiny, had he made for Digges Islands—to position himself where he was most likely to be seen by a ship entering Hudson Bay, and to live off the birds and their eggs while he waited.

As a result of the voyages of Frobisher, Davis, Hudson and Button, the principal physical features of the northeast coast of Canada had been identified and were included on maps published about this time (for exam-

Figure 33. Part of Samuel de Champlain's 1612 map of New France.

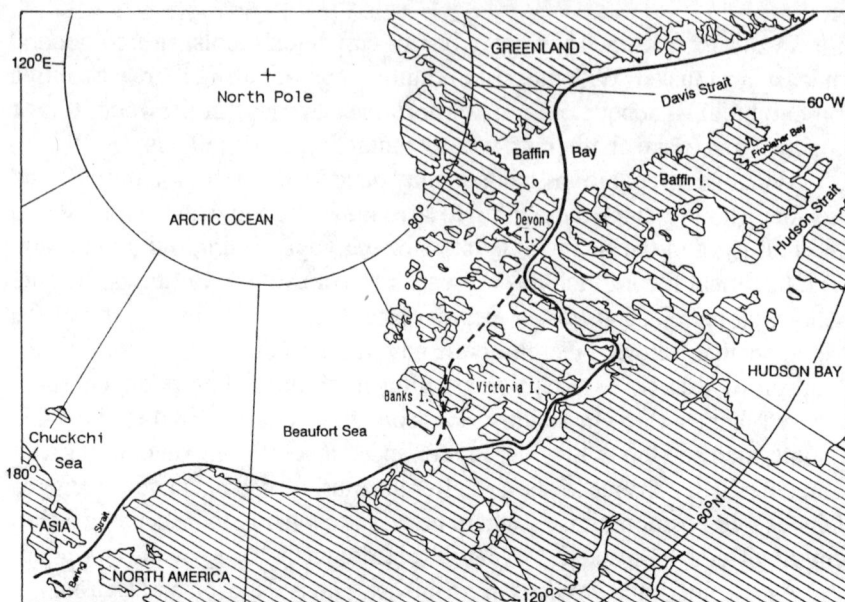

Figure 34. The Northwest Passage; an alternate route passes between Banks and Victoria Islands (after Lopez: *Arctic Dreams*, 1986, pp. 340–1).

ple, Samuel de Champlain's 1612 map of New France). The voyages had led to finding another way into the North American continent. Now there were two routes into the center of present-day Canada from the east: the St. Lawrence River/Great Lakes system discovered by the French, and Hudson Bay by the English. One phase of the discovery of Canada had been concluded.

The English were relatively slow to exploit their discovery of Hudson Bay. The representations of two disaffected French fur traders, Groseilliers and Radisson, finally roused the interest of Charles II of England in 1666. The two men advocated the establishment of trading posts where major rivers (the traffic arteries of the interior) emptied into Hudson Bay, to barter English merchandise for the natives' furs. At this time furs taken in the south and east part of the Hudson Bay drainage basin were carried to Quebec—up river, across a height of land, and down to the St. Lawrence River. The journey from the west side of the bay was long and intricate. Charles quickly grasped the English advantage. The natives would be able to reach the posts on the bay by traveling a relatively short distance downriver. Moreover, because the posts could be serviced by ocean-going ships, his traders would be able to offer the natives superior merchandise at a competitive price.

Hudson Bay held another attraction for Charles. English mariners were

172

certain that a Northwest Passage would yet be discovered and that the bay would be the key to that discovery. Voyages around Africa and South America to Asia and its offshore islands were long, difficult and costly. A Northwest Passage offered the prospect of a much shorter route and therefore, better profits for the trade with the Far East.

Charles began planning an expedition to Hudson Bay and in the course of the preparations, Prince Rupert, his cousin, became interested. It led to the formation, in 1670, of the Hudson's Bay Company. The company was to have a profound effect on the exploration of the interior of what is now Canada. Charles granted its associates a monopoly, in perpetuity, over any trade originating in Hudson Bay and the lands that drain into it.

Adjunct:

The First Colonies North of Florida

John Cabot's discovery of mainland North America in 1497, presented the English with an opportunity to exploit a new world, a mere three weeks' sailing time from an old country that held few prospects for the disadvantaged. But except for Sebastian Cabot's ill conceived and abortive attempt to found a settlement about 1507, almost a hundred years passed before the government—in Elizabeth I's time—sanctioned the first serious attempts to colonize North America.

The Spanish and Portuguese had acted quickly, after the voyage of Columbus, to consolidate their new empires far to the south. And in the years between 1520 and 1525, the Portuguese explorer, John Fagundes, had ventured into the northern part of the continent and organized a settlement in what is now eastern maritime Canada.

The French, preoccupied with political ambitions in the Mediterranean, had come later to North America. Jacques Cartier found the St. Lawrence River for them in 1536, and to consolidate their hold on that discovery, the French tried in successive winters (1541–3) to establish a colony at the mouth of the Cap-Rouge River. The Indians already had reason to distrust Cartier, and his relations with them deteriorated steadily. His colonists were not welcomed and the natives harassed them on a more or less continuous basis, killing them when they could. Moreover, the climate was not kind to them; they suffered from hunger and disease through the long cold winter. In the spring, after less than a year in the Cap-Rouge settlement, Cartier left Canada, beaten by the Indians and the savage country. For the next sixty years—until the next century—the French presence in the St. Lawrence valley was represented by fishermen and fur traders.

11

Early English and French Settlements in America
1583–1621

The first Anglo-American colonies

Cabot's 1497 landfall, in the vicinity of the Strait of Belle Isle and his subsequent "coasting voyage" along the north shore of the Gulf of St. Lawrence and down the west coast of Newfoundland, gave England a claim to the Gulf of St. Lawrence, the principal entrance to Canada by sea from the east.

One of Elizabeth's advisors was Sir Humphrey Gilbert, soldier and navigator, who from very early in her reign became an ardent and persistent advocate of English colonization. His first attempts to form a colony—in Ireland in the 1560s—failed. Thereafter, he began planning the founding of English communities in America in the area of Cabot's discovery[1] and in the more favorable regions (from the standpoint of climate) to the south along the Atlantic seaboard of what is now the United States. In 1577 he put forward a plan to seize foreign fishing fleets in Newfoundland and make the island an English outpost. Within a few years he had the support of Sir Walter Raleigh, his half-brother, who had begun urging the establishment of land bases in America, the better to carry out privateering missions against the Spanish in the New World. In 1578 Elizabeth granted Sir Humphrey a patent to go in search of and occupy "heathen lands not actually possessed of any Christian prince or people," a vague enough designation to give him leave to choose a location anywhere on the Atlantic coast, between Labrador and Florida, not inhabited by Europeans. The patent was probably the first English colonial charter[2]—the first of many granted to different individuals in the next seventy-five years.

After a series of misfortunes, Sir Humphrey sailed in 1583 with five ships varying in displacement from 200 to 10 tons. The largest turned back after two days and the others became separated at sea. Still, the four ships remaining with him safely crossed the Atlantic and rendezvoused in St. John's harbor, Newfoundland, on August 3.

Gilbert found the harbor occupied by fishing ships—thirty-six in all—from England, France, Spain and Portugal. He immediately ordered all the ships' personnel to assemble before him on shore where he announced that he was taking possession of the island in the name of the Queen. He proclaimed three laws: the Church of England would be the official religion; any prejudicial act would be considered treason; and a dishonorable remark about Queen Elizabeth would result in the loss of the offender's ears and worldly goods.

Gilbert decided to make his "western planting," not on Newfoundland, but on the mainland south of the island. He dawdled, enjoying himself immensely, using up supplies. Finally, late in August he was ready to leave, but now two of his captains and a number of seamen announced they would not accompany him. He sent the recalcitrants back to England aboard one of the ships and sailed with three ships on August 20, bound for Sable Island. He had been told the island was stocked with cattle left there years ago by a European ship and Gilbert intended to use the stock to replenish his provisions. One of his ships was wrecked on the dangerous approaches to the island with the loss of eighty-five men and he was left with two ships: the *Golden Hind*, displacing forty tons, and the ten-ton *Squirrel*. There were no cattle on the island.

His resources were so depleted, Gilbert decided to give up the venture and return to England. On the voyage home a great storm rose. The tiny *Squirrel*, with Gilbert aboard, could not withstand the weather and sank off the Azores. It put an inglorious end to the first English effort at colonization in America.

Two years later (in 1585) the British Admiralty sent Sir Bernard Drake to establish a military presence in Newfoundland. He entered St. John's harbor and found fishing ships of a half dozen nations at anchor. He immediately took a number of Spanish and Portuguese ships into custody and sent their crews to England as prisoners. It was part of the campaign to weaken Spain's naval strength and threaten her links with her American colonies. The basic object was to disrupt Spanish preparations for assembling the Armada, the great fleet that was sent to invade England three years later.

Roanoake Island: 1584–90

Sir Walter Raleigh—soldier and seaman, explorer, author and favorite of Elizabeth I—took over the patent for finding and occupying "heathen"

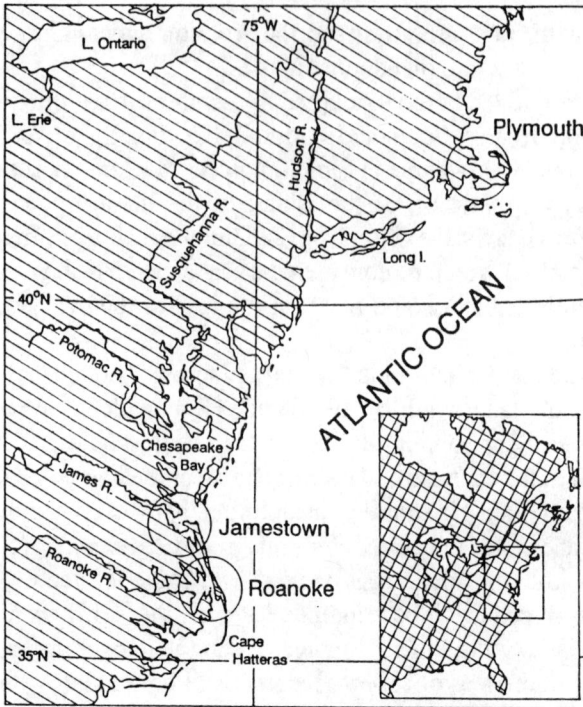

Figure 35. Roanoake, Jamestown and Plymouth—early
Anglo-American settlements in the United States.

lands after Gilbert's death. In 1584, he sent Philip Amadas and Arthur
Barlowe to America to choose a site for a colony somewhere near but north
of Florida. The two men landed on the North Carolina Outer Banks, near
latitude 36°N. Assuming the country was there for the taking, they immediately claimed possession of it for Elizabeth "as rightfull Queene, and
Princesse of the same."[3]

The two captains found the region bountiful—the land was well forested and full of game, and the seas held an abundance of fish. The Indians
soon located them and approached the ships without fear. The Englishmen
learned later that except for some shipwrecked sailors, they were the only
white people the natives had ever seen. The Indians impressed them as
having a pronounced sense for law and order. They were friendly, clean and
unwarlike except, the English were given to understand, when threatened.
They were industrious and grew various kinds of vegetables and fruits to
augment their diet. The Europeans were taken to a village of nine houses
on an island (Roanoake Island) in the sound between the Outer Banks and
the mainland, where they were welcomed into the ruler's five-room house

and royally entertained. Amadas and Barlowe returned to England with two Indians, specimens of tobacco and potatoes, and high praise for the coast of North Carolina.

The following year (1585) at Raleigh's bidding, Sir Richard Grenville left England with seven small ships carrying 108 men. They landed in America in August and established themselves on the north shore of Roanoake Island, near the village Amadas and Barlowe had visited. Raleigh named the new land Virginia in honor of the virgin Queen Elizabeth. The name Virginia soon became the designation for all the land England could occupy and hold against other claimants and in this respect it was similar to the French use of the name New France.

Sir Francis Drake stopped at the island in June 1586 on his way to England after carrying out a number of raids upon Spanish possessions in America—San Domingo, Cartagena and St. Augustine. He found the colonists generally in good health; their crops were growing and the corn was within a fortnight of being ripe enough to harvest. They complained about some shortages and they were concerned that promised supplies had not arrived from England. They asked Drake to leave two or three ships with them, saying they felt a need to have a way of returning to England if their supplies failed to appear. The true reason for their uneasiness lay, perhaps, in their relations with the natives who had grown hostile. The settlers feared death in payment "for the cruelty and outrages committed by some of them against the native inhabitants of that countrey."[4]

Drake agreed to leave three ships. As he was preparing to sail, a great storm swept the island and drove most of his fleet out to sea. The colonists, afraid they would be left without transportation, rushed aboard the ships remaining at anchor, abandoning belongings in their haste. Drake took them all back to England. A few days after their departure, Grenville arrived with supplies and new settlers; all but fifteen of the new settlers decided to return to England with him.

The following year (1587) Raleigh dispatched a second group consisting of 150 men, women and children[5] under the governorship of John White. They sailed in three ships with Simon Ferdinando as master of the fleet. White had instructions to pick up the fifteen men left on Roanoake Island by Grenville and transport all the settlers to what was deemed to be a better location on the shores of Chesapeake Bay, further up the coast. The expedition arrived at Roanoake Island late in July, to find the settlement deserted. The fort had been leveled to the ground but the houses were unharmed except that they were overgrown with vegetation and deer were feeding in them.

White learned from visiting several villages, that at least one of the fifteen men had been killed when a number of them were lured into an ambush by overtures of friendship. The others took refuge in the fort but the Indians set fire to it, forcing them into the open where they fought with the natives for about an hour. One Indian was killed and an Englishman died after he received an arrow in the mouth. His companions broke free and escaped from Roanoake Island by boat, landing on a small island near the entrance to the sound. It was said that the men remained for a time but eventually they quit the island. No one knew their whereabouts[6] and nothing more was heard about them.

On August 18, Eleanor, the daughter of John White and wife of Ananias Dare, gave birth to a daughter, the first child born of English parents in the New World. She was christened Virginia Dare.

Ferdinando now refused to go on to Chesapeake Bay, claiming that the sailing season was too far advanced. He forced the would-be settlers off the ships and on to the island, and insisted on sailing back to England. John White was persuaded by the settlers to accompany Ferdinando; of all the company, he was thought best able to obtain the supplies and equipment they needed and return quickly with them.

Help for the colony was delayed for three years by the campaign against the Spanish Armada and when John White did reach the island in August 1590, there was no trace of the settlers. The fate of the colony remains a mystery to this day.

Jamestown, the first permanent English colony: 1607

Discouraged by the disasters of Roanoake Island Raleigh, in 1606, transferred his equity in Sir Humphrey's charter to a group, mainly merchants, who styled themselves the Virginia Company of London. The company had a number of objectives—to found a Protestant English colony; to preach the Christian faith to the "heathen" people; to establish trade with the New World; and as an aid to accomplishing this last aim, to build a strong merchant navy staffed by well trained seamen. The company's first recruits, 144 in total, left England late in 1606 and reached the Chesapeake Bay area in May 1607. They chose to settle on the James River in the present-day state of Virginia where they established Jamestown, named for James I (1603–25) who had succeeded to the English throne. Jamestown became the first permanent English settlement in America.

The people suffered severe privations and within six months fifty of them died of disease and hunger. Matters would have been much worse except for the efforts of John Smith who pacified the Indians and somehow obtained food for the Englishmen. The odds against their survival in the face of hunger, disease (the land was marshy and they were plagued by mosquitoes that carried malaria), inadequate housing, polluted water and hostile Indians were considerable and worsened after Smith sailed back to England in 1609. The first governor, Lord de la Warr (after whom Delaware is named), reached Jamestown in June 1610 with more people and ample supplies—just as the survivors were preparing to weigh anchor and abandon the site. His arrival saved the settlement.

Jamestown was not a true colony in the beginning—the people did not own land but worked for absentee stockholders. They were encouraged to search for gold (of which there was none), rather than to farm and grow their food, and de la Warr ran the place like a military establishment, punishing laggards.

As a consequence of their role as employees rather than owners in the community, the people had little incentive to improve the site. A system of landownership and freedom to make personal decisions was needed but almost a decade passed before these reforms were instituted. The good life immigrants sought in America was slow in becoming a reality. In time, industries such as tobacco growing were begun and the settlement spread to adjacent areas and in 1619, the company sent over about a hundred young women to become the wives of the men. By the time Charles I (1625–49) came to the throne, conditions had improved markedly and a prosperous era had begun.

Plymouth: 1620

The pressure to force uniformity of religious worship and practice on people during the reign of James I had induced "separatists" from the Church of England to emigrate to the Netherlands. It was an unhappy choice for many of the dissenters because they did not understand the Dutch language and they found it difficult to adjust to Dutch customs. A number decided to join separatists in England who planned to emigrate to North America where it was possible to found and fashion an English community of their liking. They were a hardy and independent people who did not ask government for financial aid for the venture. What they did want was freedom to worship, work the soil, and fish and trade as they pleased. They sailed from Plymouth, England on the *Mayflower*, a ship of 180 tons, with a company of 102 men, women and children—poor people, most of them of peasant stock. They arrived off the coast of America in November, 1620 and after examining a number of locations, the *Mayflower* was anchored on December 21 in what came to be called Plymouth Bay in present-day Massachusetts. It became the site of the first permanent European settlement in New England.

Half the settlers died during the first winter, which was severe. Despite this, the New England region continued to draw immigrants anxious to escape the religious and political turmoil that would soon turn into civil war, seeking the freedom to choose their leaders and create their own system of worship. Some came because they were dissatisfied with the high cost of land in the old country—attracted by the ease of acquiring land in the New World. Men and women from more advantaged stations in life—the well-born and well-educated—joined the wave of people who preferred the raw life of the New World to the tiresome strife in the old.

Between 1620 and 1642, roughly 50,000 people came to Anglo-America and the West Indies. It was in marked contrast to the few score settlers that reached New France in the same period—an expression, in part, of the Frenchman's characteristic reluctance to emigrate from his native land.

Early French attempts to colonize Canada: 1598–1605

Cartier and Roberval had failed miserably in the years between 1541 and 1543, to found a French colony on the St. Lawrence River. The cause lay mainly in the opposition of the Iroquois who occupied and controlled the river valley at the time. Cartier had earned the hostility of the Iroquois, a proud and arrogant people, and they forced him out.

For a time after the Cartier voyages, the French did not have the heart to begin again the task of establishing themselves in the valley. They turned instead to lands in the south claimed by Portugal and Spain. They created a base for a colony at the mouth of the Rio de Janeiro River in 1555; five years later the Portuguese captured it. In 1562 they sought to found a Protestant colony in Florida but three years later the Spanish fell on it and massacred the would-be settlers. The lesson of these ventures in the south seemed to be that if the French were going to colonize any part of the New World, it would have to be out of reach of the military might of Portugal and Spain—in the northern part of North America. Cartier's discovery of the St. Lawrence River in 1535 had given France a claim to that part of the continent, a claim that had not been challenged by any other European nation.

Late in the sixteenth century the English had begun showing a renewed interest in the North American continent. In 1576, Martin Frobisher entered the north polar seas on the first of three voyages to resume the search for a Northwest Passage. He was followed by John Davis in 1585. Further to the south, Sir Humphrey Gilbert annexed Newfoundland in 1583 and in the following year Sir Walter Raleigh made a first attempt to found a colony on Roanoake Island, on the eastern coast north of Florida. These English activities helped to revive the flagging French interest in the northern part of the continent and they brought to the fore a Frenchman—Samuel de Champlain—whom history would name the Father of New France.

Champlain was born about 1567 at Brouage on the Bay of Biscay, the son of a sea captain. As a young man he fought in the War of the Three Henrys which led, in 1589, to securing the crown of France for Henry IV (king between 1589 and 1610, often remembered as Henry the Great). Brouage was a thriving port at this time. The sea dominated the lives of its inhabitants and not unnaturally, it influenced Champlain when he considered how to occupy himself after the war. With the fighting at an end, he looked about for adventure and employment and he chose the sea. In 1598, at the age of thirty, he entered the service of the king of Spain and joined an expedition to Spanish America. It was an extraordinary opportunity for the young Frenchman; few foreigners had been able to see and study these territories. In the next two years (1599 and 1600) he visited the principal ports of Spanish America and journeyed inland as far as Mexico City. In Central America, Champlain was intrigued with the idea, talked about for more than fifty years[7], of cutting a canal across Panama to shorten the voyage from the Atlantic to the Pacific Ocean by more than "1,500 leagues."

The experience of the two years gave him a broad overview of Spanish methods of colonizing the southern Americas and a perspective that would prove useful, later, in New France. He reported his impressions to Henry after he returned to France in 1601.

Development of the fur trade

The St. Lawrence River may have been neglected by the French government after Cartier's third voyage, but French fishermen including those from Brittany, Normandy and the Bay of Biscay did not. As the Grand Banks off Newfoundland became crowded, the Bay of Fundy, the Gulf of St. Lawrence and the lower reaches of the St. Lawrence River attracted increasing numbers of fishermen. By the end of the sixteenth century, 500 ships representing a half dozen European nations, fished these waters annually and the Spanish had established a whale fishery in the St. Lawrence River at Tadoussac.

The very early fishermen in the Gulf, even before Cartier's first voyage in 1534, had found an avid interest by natives, in the items the Europeans wore and used in their daily work—hatchets, knives, axes, pots, kettles, woolen clothing and blankets, and trinkets. The Indians developed a passionate urge to acquire wares, such as metal kettles and axes, to replace tools and utensils made from bone, wood, hide and stone. These commonplace European items revolutionized their daily living and they offered fish, meat, vegetables and grain, baked goods, furs, arrows—the articles that were traded among tribes—to obtain them. The fishermen developed, gradually, the art of trading, learning what was most easily bartered. Of the few things of value the natives had to trade, furs were most acceptable to the Europeans; furs required no special care, they survived the long voyage back across the Atlantic and there was a ready market for them in Europe.

When the fishermen began dry-curing their fish on the beaches and harbors to reduce the expense of preserving the catch with salt, the opportunity for contact between fishermen and natives naturally increased. It brought even more natives to the coastal waters carrying furs for barter; the business of fur trading began to take hold.

In the beginning marten was probably the most widely traded fur. Beaver fur had been used in Europe since the Middle Ages to manufacture hats—to such an extent that toward the end of the sixteenth century, the animal became extinct in western Europe. The use of beaver fur expanded steadily in Europe when French fishermen began returning from the New World with thick lustrous pelts and it was discovered there was an almost inexhaustible supply. toward the end of the sixteenth century, the broad-brimmed beaver hat had become an item of fashionable wear and it created a powerful and incessant demand for North American beaver fur. It gave a boost to the fur trade and resulted in an increase in the number of ships entering the Gulf of St. Lawrence.

The earliest French voyagers into the gulf had come for fish. They were followed by government-sponsored explorers who ascended the St. Lawrence River, hoping it was a channel to the Orient; and when this proved false, they came for the gold and jewels said to be abundant in the kingdom of the Saguenay which lay somewhere north of the St. Lawrence. Now, late in the sixteenth century, as seamen realized that the returns from the fur trade could equal the profits from fishing and at less trouble to them, increasingly ships put into New World waters solely for the purpose of trading in furs. Fur trading replaced fishing in economic importance.

Ocean-going ships came as far as Tadoussac at the mouth of the Saguenay, a river used by natives as a route between the St. Lawrence and the headwaters of several rivers that rise in the height of land below Hudson Bay. Tadoussac offered good anchorage for ocean-going ships and it became the favored place for Indians from the interior to meet traders from overseas.

The business of fur trading differed markedly from the fishery and its nature was to have an effect on the French attitude toward Canada. Fishing was carried on over a wide region, by individuals who required little contact with the land or its natives beyond the need for open beaches and staging for drying the catch. In contrast, as the competition for furs grew intense, the industry moved into the interior toward the source of the furs. Trading posts were established on or at the intersection of well-traveled canoe routes. And since the supply of furs was determined by what the Indians brought to the posts, the success of the operation depended on recognizing that both Europeans and natives had a role to play—good working relations were important. The fur trade required a commitment to the land—to the founding of permanent quarters whose first function was to service the traders.

Sable Island: 1598

As the fur trade grew and competition increased, it became apparent to some of its white participants that it would produce better profits for them if it was conducted under the umbrella of a royal monopoly designed to reduce competition. Henry IV of France was willing to grant monopolies but there would be a price. The English presence in Virginia and England's renewed activity in the far north under Frobisher and Davis posed a threat to French territorial claims in the New World. Some of Henry's advisors argued that it was necessary for France to solidify her claims in North America by setting up colonies in New France, otherwise she risked losing out to an aggressive England. Henry was persuaded but he was impoverished by the fighting for his throne. He decided the fur traders would have their monopolies but in payment, they would have to finance and establish his colonies.

Henry chose the Marquis de la Roche, a nobleman from Brittany, to stake France's claim in the New World, granting him control of Canada and the entire east coast of North America (presumably on the basis of Verrazano's voyage in 1523). La Roche sailed in 1598 having selected Sable Island, where Sir Humphrey Gilbert's colonization attempts had foundered in 1583, as the site of his colony. The island, mostly sand but with good pasturage, was twenty-five miles long and one mile wide (40 by 1.5 km.), surrounded by a broad beach, a hundred miles (160 km.) southeast of Nova Scotia. The choice may have been influenced by the expectation of using it as an outpost to warn off nationals of other countries sailing near lands claimed by the French.

The colonists (200 men and 50 women)[8], collected from slums and jails because suitable candidates would not volunteer, were settled on the north shore of the island. La Roche arranged that a ship would call once a year with new settlers and fresh supplies. Unaccountably, the colonists were not serviced in 1602 and when the ship appeared the following year, only eleven people were found on the island. It seems the failure to provision the settlers had created a serious situation. Desperately hungry, they had ransacked the storehouse, killing several officials who opposed them. Then they fled the island. The survivors were taken to France and that was the end of the Sable Island colony.

First attempts to found a colony in the St. Lawrence valley

A second attempt at founding a colony—by Pierre Chauvin, a French fur trader—fared no better. He chose to establish his colony at Tadoussac on the St. Lawrence River. He came out in the spring of 1600 with sixteen men swept up in some French seaport. Pierre Du Gua de Monts, another fur trader and a friend to Henry IV, accompanied the colonists as an observer.

After a profitable summer of trading, Chauvin and de Monts sailed back to France leaving the colonists housed in a cabin. The men were unwilling or incapable of adjusting to the cold primitive winter on the north shore of the St. Lawrence. When they had eaten the food that had been left for them, they seemed unable to fend for themselves and they starved and became sick. Fortunately, the natives had pity and took them in. Those that survived the winter found their way back to France on one or other of the ships that reached Tadoussac in the spring.

Three years later (in 1603), Henry appointed Aymar de Chaste, one of his staunchest supporters and a seaman who had once commanded a French fleet, to the position of lieutenant-general of New France (that is, of all the territory in North America claimed by France). De Chaste immediately sent a small expedition to the St. Lawrence River to do some trading. Samuel de Champlain accompanied the expedition in the role of geographer with instructions to ascend the river beyond Tadoussac and prepare accurate maps for future use.

Champlain's appointment as de Chaste's geographer proved to be of value for French fortunes in America. He went up the St. Lawrence in a small boat manned by five seamen as far as the foot of the St. Louis Rapids near present-day Montreal and he explored the Richelieu and Saguenay Rivers, two important tributaries. He found the valley of the St. Lawrence greatly changed from the time of Cartier. The hostile Iroquois had been driven out and a warm reception was accorded Champlain by the relatively few Indians who lived in their places.

The natives described for Champlain what lay above the St. Louis Rapids—the Ottawa River, Lake Ontario, Niagara Falls and Lake Erie. Above Erie was another body of water which they said was so large, they never had dared to try to cross it. Champlain understood them to say the water of this lake was not drinkable. He assumed this meant the water was salty and that the lake was actually the Western Sea that separated him from Asia. The Indians were referring to Lake Huron.

Port Royal, Nova Scotia: 1605

De Chaste died within the year but Henry was not about to let the new beginning perish with him. He appointed Pierre Du Gua de Monts, who had accompanied Chauvin to Tadoussac in 1600, to the vacant position of lieutenant-general. He granted de Monts a ten-year monopoly of the fur trade on condition that he establish a colony of at least sixty settlers and work at converting the natives in the New World to the Christian faith.

De Monts sailed for New France in 1604, accompanied by Champlain and a large party of soldiers and prospective settlers, some of them skilled artisans. The experience of Tadoussac in 1600 had convinced de Monts that the climate in the St. Lawrence valley was too rigorous. He chose the Bay of Fundy, a region which had been described for him as a fair land with mild winters. Still another reason for abandoning the valley lay with the independent traders who made their summer headquarters at Tadoussac; they refused to honor monopolies granted by the king and competed fiercely for the available furs.

De Monts chose Dochet island in Passamaquoddy Bay at the mouth of the St. Croix River (in the U. S. A.), for his settlement—a small island only about five acres in area. There was little wood and no certain supply of fresh water on the island but it lent itself to easy defense against native attack and this may have been its chief attraction for de Monts.[9]

That winter (1604–5) the snow came early and often, and remained until late in spring. The settlers had been expecting a mild winter and they were totally unprepared for the severe cold. They stayed indoors, huddled before the fireplaces until they were driven out of doors by the necessity to cut firewood. The island could not supply their needs and they had to risk the tides and ice-floes to reach the mainland to replenish firewood and drinking water. They avoided hunting on the mainland for fresh meat, fearing they would draw hostile natives to the sound of their gunfire, preferring to exist on poor salt meat. The cold, the inactivity and the inadequate food took their toll. Inevitably, scurvy ravaged the community and thirty-five of the seventy odd people died of the disease before the warm weather of spring arrived. Most of the survivors declared they would return to France at the first opportunity. All had had enough of the island and it was abandoned late in 1605 in favor of a location across the bay in Nova Scotia, the site of present-day Annapolis Royal. They called it Port Royal.

Champlain had begun mapping the Atlantic coast in 1604 and he used the summer of 1605 to continue the task. He worked south from Cape Breton, looking for an opening to the "Western Sea." He stopped short of the Hudson River which Henry Hudson explored four years later for the Dutch. Had Champlain reached and ascended the Hudson, the French and not the Dutch would have become dominant in this part of New England.

The Port Royal settlement did not fare well. Champlain had some success in persuading the settlers to fish and hunt during the winter with the expectation that exercise and a diet of fresh meat would improve their resistance to sickness. Regardless, the company was again wracked by scurvy—they were not familiar with the cure obtained by Cartier from the Indians of Stadacona. Twelve died in the first winter at Port Royal and another seven succumbed the following year.[10]

The old quarrels over religion, forgotten for a time in the New World, surfaced and split the community. And although de Monts had been granted a monopoly by the king, fishermen who worked the nearby coastal waters refused to respect the monopoly. They moored their ships at convenient places along the Atlantic coast after they had filled their holds with cod, and waited for the Indians to come to them with furs. De Monts did not have the means to police the long coastline and in these circumstances he could not obtain enough furs to meet the cost of founding and maintaining the colony. The final blow came in 1607 when the independent traders succeeded in persuading the king that a monopoly was unjust—that free trade in furs should be restored. In July 1607, the settlers abandoned Port Royal and boarded ship for France.

It was not the end of Port Royal. Three years later, in 1610, one of Champlain's associates settled a new colony into the buildings. Although he planned to finance the operation with the trade in furs, the colonists were expected to contribute to their own subsistence and provide themselves with a more varied diet by tilling the soil and growing grain and vegetables. A priest who accompanied the expedition was intended to be the nucleus of a mission.

It was soon evident that the fur trade could not generate enough income to sustain the colony properly and since the project had been launched without sufficient capital, it suffered from a chronic shortage of financing. In 1611, when two Jesuit priests joined the colony, it became torn by disputes. The Jesuits and a number of dissidents left the site, crossed the Bay of Fundy to the mouth of the Penobscot River (in present-day Maine), and settled on Mount Desert Island.

188

The two French settlements did not escape the attention of the English. The governor of Jamestown, the English colony founded in 1607 on Chesapeake Bay, formed the opinion that the country was not big enough for both English and French. In 1613 he sent a company of Virginians under Sir Samuel Argall to rid the eastern seaboard of the French and take over the territory of Acadie (later Acadia) as the French called the region. Argall was ruthless with the two settlements. In the attack on the closer one—Mount Desert—a Jesuit priest was killed and a number of settlers wounded; he took the others prisoner and leveled the buildings. Then he advanced on Port Royal, fired the buildings, made prisoners of its people and carried them off to Virginia. A handful of men, away when the Virginians attacked, survived the raid. As it turned out, the Argall raids did not expel the French from the east coast.

The raids were another sign of England's growing interest in the Atlantic mainland coastline, all the way north to the St. Lawrence River, and a prelude to more serious conflict over Canada.

Quebec, first permanent settlement in the St. Lawrence valley: 1608

Champlain returned to France after the de Monts settlers abandoned Port Royal in 1607. He was still optimistic about the prospects for a French settlement in the New World but he had concluded Nova Scotia was not the proper location. He persuaded de Monts that a year-round enterprise was feasible on the St. Lawrence River and could provide an opportunity to recoup the money lost at Port Royal. He argued that "the scattered thinness of the coastal fur supply"[11] along the Atlantic Ocean had contributed to the failure of Port Royal, that the country north of the St. Lawrence (present-day Quebec) was very different. It was a vast land—nobody knew how vast—intersected by numerous and intricate waterways, and it was characterized by long cold winters. These were the ingredients for generating an abundant harvest of thick and lustrous furs.

Champlain urged de Monts to petition the king for the exclusive right to maintain a station on the river. He reasoned that a monopoly on the river should be easier to enforce than one in the Gulf of St. Lawrence or on the open coastline of the Atlantic Ocean. De Monts was convinced; he applied for the monopoly and it was granted—but for a period of one year only and it would not apply to the international rendezvous at Tadoussac which was beyond the king's control.

The anchorage at Tadoussac continued to attract many traders—more than enough for the number of furs offered by the Indians—and some of the traders paid the penalty of too much competition. Champlain personally saw the loss which many merchants must suffer, who had taken on board a large quantity of merchandise, and fitted out a great number of vessels, in expectation of doing a good business in the fur-trade, which was so poor on account of the great number of vessels, that many will for a long time remember the loss which they suffered this year.[12]

Greediness of gain...causes the merchants to set out prematurely in order to arrive first in this country. By this means they not only become involved in the ice, but also in their own ruin, for, from trading with the savages in a secret manner and offering through rivalry with each other more merchandise than is necessary, they get the worst of the bargain. Thus, while purposing to deceive their associates, they generally deceive themselves.[13]

The condition that Tadoussac was to be excluded from the monopoly, led Champlain to locate his post well up river—so far up the comparatively narrow and imperfectly charted St. Lawrence River that few traders would be encouraged to sail their ships past Tadoussac into the river and make the journey inland to compete with him.

Champlain entered the river with two ships in 1608 and paused at Tadoussac. There was immediate trouble with the Basque traders who angrily defied any attempt to subject them to law and order. He continued up the St. Lawrence for another 130 miles (210 km.) to a constricture where it narrows to a width of less than a mile and is commanded from the shore by a high promontory. It was the place where Cartier had anchored his ships seventy-three years previously, in September 1535—the location of the Indian village of Stadacona in Cartier's time. This was Champlain's choice for a base in the St. Lawrence valley. He went ashore on July 2, 1608. The founding of Quebec, the cradle of French civilization in North America, is traced back to that day.

In Cartier's time the agriculturally-based Iroquois had occupied the St. Lawrence valley between Stadacona and Hochelaga and controlled the use of the river. The hostility of the Iroquois had caused the northern hunting Indians who traded across the headwaters of the Ottawa, St. Maurice and Saguenay Rivers, to use the tiresome and demanding Saguenay River route to reach the St. Lawrence and the traders waiting at Tadoussac. As the demand for beaver grew, they had become locked in a struggle with the Iroquois for control of the St. Lawrence. By the time of Champlain's first visit to the river in 1603, the conflict was almost at an end; the Iroquois had been driven out of the valley to lands south and southeast of Lake Ontario. Now, in 1608, the formerly well-populated Iroquois villages of Stadacona, Achelacy and Hochelaga were deserted and the Indians of the north were coming down the Ottawa and St. Maurice Rivers at will, using the St. Lawrence to reach Tadoussac. The St. Lawrence was open for commerce and Champlain's agents and Indian middlemen were free to travel it, even to its upper reaches.

The founding of Quebec had an uncertain beginning. A troublemaker, Jean Duval, plotted to kill Champlain and invite the Basques trading out of Tadoussac, to take over Quebec. So degenerate were Champlain's people, that all of them, including his personal servant, came to be privy to the plan but chose not to inform him. Fortunately, Champlain discovered the plot in good time. He had Duval hanged and his head was prominently displayed as a warning to would-be conspirators.

During the first years of its existence, Quebec was essentially a fur trading station. Little thought was given to bringing in people who would farm the land, raise families and settle in to build a future for themselves in the New World. The station consisted of:

> three connected barracks, eighteen feet by fifteen feet [5.5 by 4.6 m.], a large storehouse, and a pigeon loft, all surrounded by a palisade with a cannon mounted at the corners and a fifteen-foot moat complete with drawbridge. In the early years fewer than twenty men wintered at the base.[14]

The men at the station seemed unable to bring themselves to adapt to the life on the frontier and make the best of their lot. They made little effort to improve the original buildings and grew practically no food, depending in the main for their sustenance on supplies shipped in from France. They were forced, of course, to spend much time in cutting firewood. Mentally depressed, they readily fell sick from scurvy and other diseases; fifteen of the original company of twenty-eight men did not survive the first winter.[15]

Soon after the expiration of de Mont's one-year monopoly in 1609, independent French traders began coming up the river and competing with Champlain at the Lachine Rapids (at Montreal). Champlain complained that these traders were unscrupulous and dishonest, anxious to make a profit but unwilling to share in the trouble and expense of creating trade with the Indians:

> ...several others who had forsaken their former traffic at Tadoussac, came to the rapids with a number of small pinnances, to see whether they could carry on barter with these tribes, to whom they affirmed that I was dead, whatever our men might say to the contrary.... They only want people to run a thousand risks in

191

discovering nations and countries, in order that they may keep the profit and the others the hardships. It is unreasonable, when one has caught the sheep for another to have the fleece.[16]

There was sporadic fighting between the Iroquois from south of the St. Lawrence and Champlain's Indian allies—the Algonquins of the Ottawa River valley and the Hurons from the lake of that name. The competing traders generally shirked the fighting but, much to Champlain's disgust, gathered like vultures when the fighting was over to strip the dead Iroquois of their fur robes.[17] Still, a few did join him in fighting the Iroquois and helped to reduce expenses by shipping their provisions with his in the same boat.

In the first years relatively few furs were brought into the station and the enterprise barely paid its way. Champlain perceived that he needed to reach more Indians and establish a closer relationship with them. To this end, he began sending his agents and Indian middlemen into the interior on the St. Lawrence River's tributaries—into the villages to encourage the natives to spend more time hunting animals and to carry their pelts down to Quebec. He instructed his people to learn the language of the Indians so that they could converse without the use of interpreters; he wanted them to become familiar with the geography of the territory and translate the knowledge into maps.

Henry IV, strong and buoyant, a man of vision, a genius who had guided France during Champlain's early years in the New World, was assassinated in May, 1610. Now Champlain had to deal with the regent for the child king, Louis XIII—Henry's widow, Marie de Medicis, a cold, calculating and shallow woman. There was fear that the religious toleration practiced by Henry would give way to another war over religion.

Already by 1612, the natives had become uneasy with the effects of the fur trade. They were anxious to have the French merchandise that eased the burden of their daily lives but they were not pleased at being asked to guide the white men into the interior so that they could learn their languages and map the lakes and rivers. And they did not appreciate being asked to change certain practices, such as the slow torture of prisoners, which the Europeans saw as brutal and barbarous.

Louis Hébert, Quebec's first settler: 1617

The policy of Champlain's backers was to wring the maximum profit out of the fur trade. There was little interest in using some of the returns to bring out proper settlers and establish permanent communities, send missionaries to the Indians and explore the interior. By 1614, six years after the Quebec station was opened, profits were substantial enough that Champlain was able to win support for an appeal to bring out a few peasants who would grow foodstuffs, augment the food supply and thereby decrease the dependence of the operation on supplies from France.

Champlain contended that uncontrolled trade debauched the natives and he suggested it was time to begin converting the Indians to the faith, using the argument that this would "cement their commercial ties with the French as well as save them from eternal hell-fire in the next world."[18]

On one of his trips to France, Champlain visited a community of Recollets near his native town of Brouage and he invited them to send missionaries to Canada. It was arranged that three friars should sail with him to Quebec in the spring of 1615. The fur traders were mostly Huguenots and actively antagonistic to the spread of the Catholic religion. They opposed a Recollet plan to induce Indians to settle near trading posts where they might hear more of the gospel message; they preferred to have the natives continue their nomadic existence and hunt for furs to keep the company profits up.

In 1617 Champlain persuaded his company to assist Louis Hébert, a well known apothecary, to establish himself as a farmer in Quebec. Hébert had come out to Acadia in 1606 and returned to France in 1614 after Argall destroyed the settlement of Port Royal. An adventuresome man, he found his existence back in Paris palling; he missed the raw life of the New World and he was easily induced by Champlain to bring his wife and three children to Quebec. They were the station's first real settlers.

Hébert, unfazed by the severe winters, was determined to till the soil although he had not even a plow to turn the sod. The company did little to encourage him or other would-be settlers who might be interested in following him to the New World. Ten years passed before the first plow, and an animal to draw it, was brought to Quebec. Hébert was informed that he had to perform certain company duties in payment for his support from the company, and for the time that he was drawing support, he could farm only in his spare time and his produce would have to be sold to the company at prices current in France.

Early Newfoundland colonies: 1610–29

Early in the seventeenth century, Newfoundland offered several advantages for founding an English colony in the New World. Except for Greenland, it was the closest part of North America and summer crossings had become relatively routine and could be made in as little as three weeks time. Also, an economic infrastructure based on the cod fishery was already in place. Moreover, interference from Spain was unlikely in this latitude and there was little danger from the natives who lived for most of the year in the interior.

The first English attempt to form a colony on the island, not based exclusively on fishery or the fur trade, was initiated under a charter granted by James I in 1610 to the London & Bristol Company—a company composed for the most part, of merchants from the two cities. The company's land grant consisted of Newfoundland's coastline and off-shore islands, from Cape Bonavista to Cape St. Mary's, an area English fishermen had used for more than fifty years.

In contrast to Virginia and New England, the move to colonize Newfoundland encountered strong opposition in England. A number of ports in England's West Country, particularly in Devon and Dorset, were well placed to take advantage of the export of cod from Newfoundland and had become the centers of an enterprise which reached a national importance and was to endure for two centuries. Ships carrying salt, the essential ingredient for preserving the fish, reached Newfoundland in the spring. The best of the salted fish was carried to the Mediterranean, the poorest to the slave plantations in the West Indies. The ships returned to England in the autumn with wine, oil and other products from the Mediterranean, and bullion from the Indies. Early in the seventeenth century, West Country merchants were sending several hundred ships annually to Newfoundland.

The merchants who carried on this trade actively resisted the establishment of permanent settlements in Newfoundland and even discouraged fishermen from wintering there. They garnered the greatest custom for themselves by insisting that the merchant and fishing fleets and their crews, be based in the English West Country ports. The policy naturally had the effect of retarding the economic, social and political development of Newfoundland. But it produced important economic benefits for England and resulted in a pool of hardy experienced English seamen that were available in the event of a national emergency. Not surprisingly then, the West Country merchants had powerful friends in government.

The London & Bristol Company had been careful to avoid including a request for a fishing monopoly on any part of the coast of Newfoundland, knowing it would generate additional antagonism among the West Country merchants to their plans.

Cupids on Conception Bay: 1610

The company chose John Guy, one of its members, to head its venture.

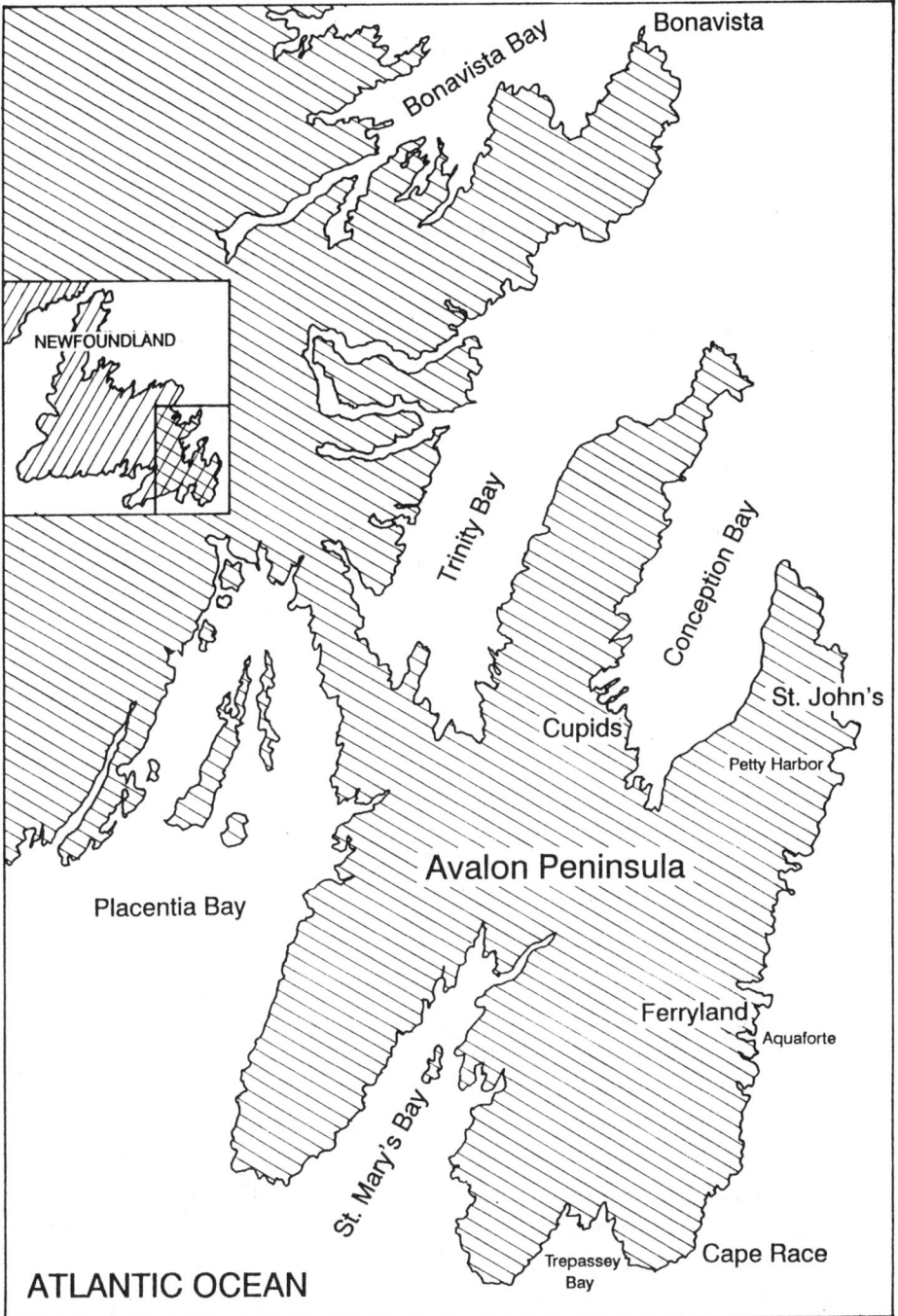

Figure 36. Cupids and Ferryland—early Newfoundland settlements in the Avalon Peninsula.

He had come out in 1608 and selected Cupids, well down the west side of Conception Bay, as the site for his settlement. He arrived in the summer of 1610 with forty well-qualified settlers. They went to work with a will, clearing land, planting grain, and building houses and a storeroom. Fortunately, that first winter was mild; the livestock did not want for food and the settlers were able to get about and explore the region around Conception Bay.

In 1611, Guy brought out additional settlers including skilled artisans and sixteen women, and the following year he arrived with still more settlers, livestock and items of hardware. The settlement was not free of problems—each winter a number of colonists sickened and died, food for people and livestock was sometimes in short supply, and some settlers complained incessantly. But these difficulties in themselves were not serious enough to condemn the colony. "Pirates were...the one great threat to the prosperity of the Newfoundland trade."[19] The pirates—outlaws mainly from England, France and Spain and particularly one Peter Easton—robbed the settlers and plundered the Newfoundland fishing fleet of food, guns, ammunition and ships. Most significantly, they took men to replace those who had deserted, been killed in action or died of disease. Guy argued in England that with some help from the navy and proper coordination, his settlers and the Newfoundland fishing fleet could overcome the pirates. He got no help; England did not have control of the North Atlantic in the first half of the seventeenth century and the pirates did much as they pleased.

In the spring of 1613 Guy announced, unexpectedly, that he was returning to England to stay; apparently the accumulation of problems had finally overwhelmed him. His departure had serious consequences for the Cupids colony; the settlers began drifting away and by the end of the summer, only thirty were left. The colony still had some presence during the 1620s, but it was fading and early in the third decade, Newfoundland's first colony ceased to exist. In truth, it had never shown any evidence of returning a profit for the company. Not one or any combination of industries—agriculture, fur trading, lumbering, mining and sundry indigenous occupations—promised to repay the company's investment of thousands of pounds.

It is reasonable to agree with historians who claim[20] that the permanence of the colony might have been ensured had it been sponsored jointly by the West Country and the London-and-Bristol merchants. The two groups had much to gain from each other's existence but there was a lack of trust on the part of the West Country people. They feared that the ultimate goal of the other merchants was to force them off the Newfoundland cod banks, that their intent was to fashion a monopoly of the fishery for themselves. They were not prepared to entertain that possibility.

Ferryland in the Avalon peninsula: 1621

To recoup some of its outlay of capital on the Cupids venture, the company sold blocks of its land. Sir William Vaughan, a Welshman, was the first to acquire a lot. He sent out a small party of mainly Welsh colonists in 1617 and again in 1618. The venture failed for want of dynamic leadership—apparently Vaughan never visited his colony and most of his people lacked the initiative and industry required for life in a primitive land. Those colonists that did not return to the old country moved to other sites nearer St. John's.

Vaughan sold part of his land to Sir George Calvert, an influential Englishman who became the first Lord Baltimore. Calvert subsequently applied for more land and the king responded by giving him title to the entire island but later he reduced this to a block on the southeast coast extending from Petty Harbor south to Aquaforte, and west to the shores of Placentia and Conception Bays. Calvert called it Avalon and in time the name was applied to the whole of the peninsula which is the most easterly section of Newfoundland. Calvert's charter made him a virtual dictator of Avalon except over the off-shore fishery; the traditional rights of the West Country merchants were preserved.

Calvert's first twelve colonists came out in 1621 and were settled at Ferryland on the Atlantic coast. They built a stone house for the governor, and for protection they surrounded it with a palisade. They were followed in the second year by twenty-five men and seven women. The first years passed easily for the colonists; the grain and vegetable crops did well, game and fish were plentiful, they found edible fruits growing wild, and the winters were mild. Calvert visited the colony for the first time in 1627. There was as yet no prospect of a profit large enough to repay his outlay but he was so pleased with the prospects that he brought out his wife and family, and some relatives the following summer with the intention of living there permanently.

12

The First War Over Canada
1628–9

The Company of New France: 1627

In 1625 the strength of the French base at Quebec was augmented by the arrival of five Jesuits, members of the Society of Jesus. Willing to endure hardship and pain, dedicated to converting the Indians to their faith, loyal to the monarchy, they soon became a powerful force in New France.

The Jesuits found that the population of Quebec, seventeen years after its founding, still numbered less than a hundred French. In all of Canada, there were only seven French families and six white children.

The competition to acquire furs had been so intense that the merchants employed in the trade had suffered losses and they began demanding some form of monopoly. They were supported by Champlain and in 1613 he was able to arrange a kind of cooperative monopoly among them. At the time the Jesuits arrived in 1625, a company composed of Huguenots had gained control of the monopoly. The principal interest of the company—almost its only interest—lay in improving the profits of the fur trade. It saw no advantage in spending money to promote settlement except where it benefited the fur trade. It felt that permanent settlers might even reduce their profits for, in time, they would probably compete with the company for furs. The company's salaried employees were serviced, in large part, from France and the company was content in the knowledge that they would retire to France when they had completed their term of employment. As a consequence of this policy, Hébert and the missionaries who had come out with him had succeeded in cultivating only about fifteen acres of land in the New World.

The Jesuits became convinced the trading monopoly of the Huguenots must be ended and a new company formed. They reported their findings to Cardinal Richelieu. At the time, the Huguenots were in open rebellion in France and it took little persuasion to convince Richelieu that he should suppress them in New France. He acted swiftly and annulled their charter in 1626. The next year, just two years after the Jesuits came to New France, he moved to lay the groundwork for the colonization of New France by founding the Company of New France with himself as president. The company would have a hundred shareholders—The One Hundred Associates—each subscribing 3000 *livers*. He granted it ownership of all of the St. Lawrence River region from Newfoundland to the source of the river; a monopoly in perpetuity of the fur trade; and a fifteen-year monopoly of other trade except in the cod and whale fishery. The Company would be obliged to bring out two to three hundred settlers in 1628 and four thousand by the year 1643 when the fifteen-year monopoly expired.

Richelieu assigned responsibility for the religious conscience of New France to the Society of Jesus; the implication was that only French Catholics would be acceptable as colonists.

Profit was not a strong motive for investing in the company; its prospective shareholders proved to be more interested in promoting the missionary work of the Jesuits and in founding a French colony in the New World. There was no difficulty in finding the hundred men and women to pledge the desired 300,000 *livers* (equivalent to 12,000–13,000 English pounds). It was a very small amount of money for the task; the English spent fifteen times that amount in founding their New England colonies. Still, the act of establishing the company promised to become a turning point in the history of New France.

The Kirke brothers capture Quebec: 1629

The seeds of war between England and France were germinating on the Atlantic coast in 1627 when the Company of New France was formed. It was not the best of times to begin bringing out the 4000 French colonists required by the company's fifteen-year trade monopoly. Six years previously, King James I of England had granted the coastal territory from the St. Croix River (the present boundary, at the coast, between Maine and New Brunswick) north to include the Gaspe peninsula, to a fellow Scotsman, Sir William Alexander. The grant was renewed by Charles I (1625–49). It totally disregarded the fact that it included Acadia which was partly occupied by the French. The region of the grant—Alexander called it Nova Scotia (that is, New Scotland)—was intended to act as a buffer between New France and New England. It was also meant to serve as a base for English ambitions in the Gulf of St. Lawrence and play a part in the large design of forcing France out of North America. To further this end, Alexander organized a company which was known as the Adventurers of Canada. One of its principal members was Gervase Kirke, a wealthy London merchant.

In 1625, Charles I, newly-crowned king of an intensely Protestant England, had married Henrietta Maria, sister of Louis XIII of France and passionately Catholic. It might have seemed an omen for peace between the two countries but both Charles and Henrietta were intolerant of religious opinions that differed from their own. The marriage did nothing to improve relations between the French and English.

As a precursor to war with France over Canada, England began issuing letters-of-marque to privateers in 1628. The most notable recipients were the sons of Gervasc Kirke—David, Lewis and Thomas—who, with financial backing from the Adventurers, outfitted three fighting ships and sailed for New France in March, 1628.

About the same time, Richelieu's One Hundred Associates were collecting the first group of colonists, assembling a fleet of about twenty vessels, and loading the ships with supplies for the settlement in New France. The Kirke brothers reached Tadoussac on the St. Lawrence river in July. They captured a number of Basque trading vessels and set up a blockade of the river. Then they sent a demand to Champlain to surrender Quebec. The fort was desperately short of food and could offer little resistance but Champlain refused to surrender. His bold front induced the Englishmen to rely on their blockade to starve Champlain into submission.

The Kirke brothers had received word that the French fleet had entered the Gulf of St. Lawrence through Cabot Strait and could be intercepted off the Gaspe. Although their three ships were badly outnumbered by the French fleet, they found and attacked it. As it turned out, the French ships were mainly heavily-loaded, poorly-protected transports. They were no match for the swift English privateers. The Kirkes forced the surrender of eighteen French ships. They took 600 prisoners including 200 settlers. They captured the settlers' building supplies, household effects, food and livestock, as well as cannon to protect the fort and supplies for Champlain. The prisoners were taken back to England where they were released and returned to France.

After their labors, the Kirke brothers retired to England, certain that Champlain would be ready to surrender when they returned next year. And indeed, when three English ships appeared before Quebec on July 19, 1629, Champlain and his men—weary after a winter of sickness and food shortages, with no help in sight—quietly gave up the post. Canada and Acadia had been lost to the English and Champlain was carried to London as a prisoner. It seemed a total and devastating defeat for France in North America, one from which she could not recover.

When Champlain reached Europe he found that an agreement was in place that had ended hostilities between England and France. It had been signed on April 24, 1629—almost three months before he surrendered Quebec. Champlain was free to return to France where he immediately set about persuading Richelieu that it was important to retain New France—that an empire was at stake. Charles I was governing England without Parliament at the time and badly in need of money. One source of funds was the large dowry of his French queen; only half of it had been paid. When Charles asked for the remainder, Richelieu told him he would have to give up Canada and Acadia to collect it. Charles agreed to the condition and the Treaty of St. Germain-en-Laye was concluded on March 29, 1632. By its terms, Canada and Acadia were restored to France and Charles received a dowry payment of 400,000 *crowns*.

Champlain returned to Quebec in 1633 to find that the Kirkes had burned some of the buildings and stripped others of furniture, doors, even window frames, and they had made off with the spring's trade in furs. Although the French had to make a new start at Quebec, the climate for improvement was at hand. Champlain was now the king's commander in New France; the French government actively supported him; and the Jesuits were established and preparing to carry the faith deep into the interior. Next year a party of colonists arrived at Quebec bringing a herd of cattle and soon another settlement was founded further up the river, at Three Rivers.

In October 1635, Champlain, now sixty-eight and tired, was stricken by paralysis. He died on Christmas day. His insistence that New France should not be totally abandoned to the fur traders had resulted in a commitment by France to the idea of forming French colonies in North America but the pace of colonization was agonizingly slow. At the time of Champlain's death, only about 200 French people lived in New France. In 1643, when Richelieu's agreement with the Company of New France called for a total of 4000 settlers, the population still numbered less than 300.[1]

The effect of the war on Newfoundland

The 1628–9 war over Canada had brought a bleak turn to the fortunes of the Ferryland colony in Newfoundland. In the summer of 1628, French warships began raiding the Newfoundland coastline. Calvert was kept busy warding off the attacks and he undertook some raids of his own. The winter of that year (1628–9) was very severe and the colonists, lulled by the gentle winters of previous years, had insufficient stocks of food and firewood. Lady Baltimore, a woman of frail health, found the climate too rigorous and she moved to Virginia with her son in 1629. Calvert, depressed by the loss of the fortune he had expended on his colony and its recent misfortunes, decided to follow her. He appealed to the king for a grant of land in Virginia and returned to England to press the request. It was 1632 before the king granted him a charter—in present-day Maryland—too late to enjoy it for he had died before it was signed.

Cecil, Calvert's eldest son, inherited the Newfoundland charter and family title. He appointed a Captain Hill to act as governor of Ferryland and taking a number of Ferryland colonists with him, he founded a successful settlement on the Maryland land grant. (The name of the state's capitol, Baltimore, is a reminder of the family.) Roughly half of the original settlers remained in the colony after the departure of Calvert and they became a part of the continuing permanent population of Ferryland.[2]

The Treaty of St. Germain-en-Laye which formally ended the war between France and England in 1632, required the Kirkes to restore to France all they had won. It left Sir David Kirke considerably out of pocket. The transitory conquest of New France had helped Charles obtain the final payment of his wife's dowry. He may have felt he owed Kirke a favor for when Kirke applied for a charter to found a colony in Newfoundland, it was granted in 1637, presumably to compensate him for the loss of his war gains. Charles' ready compliance may also have been motivated by a wish to bolster opposition to French encroachment on the island following the near-demise of the Calvert enterprise in 1629.

The charter gave Kirke the right to license the exploitation of natural resources, including the fishery; it granted him the privilege of collecting a tax from all foreign (non-English) ships using Newfoundland facilities; and he was given the authority to make laws and enforce their obedience. There were some exemptions to his powers. The West Country merchants retained their traditional fishing privileges; any taxes or laws devised by Kirke would not apply to them; and they could reserve for themselves the best and most convenient beaches to carry on their fishing operations. A peculiar clause in the charter denied Kirke the right to cut wood and erect buildings, except as needed for local fishing, within six miles (10 km.) of the sea on the mainland, and within thirty miles (48 km.) of the sea on the off-shore islands, in the region between Cape Bonavista and Cape Race. The clause, if enforced, would prevent the founding of a colony on this coastline because any settler in this region must necessarily live near the sea. It seemed to indicate that the colonization of Newfoundland had a low priority with the English king and that he expected the taxing and licensing authority would enable Kirke to earn an adequate profit. The clause may have been merely a sop to the West Country merchants who still opposed the formation of colonies, with little expectation that a man of Kirke's stature and temperament would obey the restrictive clause.

The first contingent of Kirke's people arrived in Ferryland in 1637, and

Kirke and his family followed them the following year, bringing another hundred men. Almost immediately a dispute arose with the Calvert family who claimed that its grant of land in the Avalon peninsula, which coincided with Kirke's grant, had been given in perpetuity. The English government ruled that the Calverts, in transferring their interests to Virginia, had deserted the Ferryland colony and forfeited their rights in Newfoundland. The ruling ignored the presence of the governor, Captain Hill, who was still in residence in 1638 and in charge of the Calvert property.

Kirke settled into the Calvert property and set about zealously using his powers to tax and license Newfoundland life for everyone, from ordinary settler to foreign-ship's captain. He antagonized the West Country merchants and they complained so bitterly about him that within a year (in 1639) the English government began an investigation of his activities and his London associates tried to recall him.

Kirke was difficult to dislodge and he was still actively pursuing his inclinations in Newfoundland ten years later when, in 1649, his enemies charged that he was fashioning a center at Ferryland for Prince Rupert's royalist fleet. It was too much for Cromwell's Commonwealth government. Kirke was arrested and carried to England, but he had powerful friends and he was acquitted of the charges. He returned to Ferryland in 1653 but thereafter his fortunes declined. The Calvert family had continued its efforts to regain the Ferryland property and in 1654, Kirke was jailed for a short time in England as a consequence of a suit they brought against him. He died soon after he was released.

Ferryland was restored to the Calverts by the courts in 1661, but their interest in the colony had faded with the years. Fortunately, the people of the colony and the nearby regions remained to become permanent residents of Newfoundland. Nevertheless, the death of Kirke and the collapse of his colony brought an end, for a time, to efforts to establish settlements. The social and political development of Newfoundland gave way again to the cod fishery that had dominated its existence from the beginning of European occupation. As late as 1683 there were only 120 permanent residents on the island and by 1800 the number had increased to a mere 20,000.

The brief but colorful participation of Sir Humphrey Gilbert in the life of Newfoundland was not in vain. His annexation of the island marked the beginning of what was to become a commanding although not an exclusive role by the English, in the history of Newfoundland. Certain place names along the coast—Norman's Cove in Trinity Bay, Spaniard's Bay and French's Bay in Conception Bay; Biscay Bay and Portugal Cove in Trespassey Bay; Breton and Frenchman's Cove in Fortune Bay—are a reminder of the on-shore activities of fishermen from other parts of Europe.

The colonization of New France fared little better. The Company of One Hundred Associates founded by Richelieu to begin the colonization failed to bring out the number of settlers required by their fifteen-year monopoly of trade in the St. Lawrence valley. And the grants of land given to seigniors on condition that they settle their holdings with tenants failed. In 1660, New France was populated by only about 2300 Europeans.

The French King, Louis XIV, canceled the Associates' charter and converted New France to a Royal Province with a governor. Thereafter, in the 1660s, more than 3000 settlers were sent out from France, including girls of marriageable age. Only a few followed them but the multiplication of families produced a natural increase. Within a hundred years the population of New France numbered more than 50,000 people.

The colonization of Canada by way of a steady migration from France never did take hold. Most of the six million living Canadians whose mother tongue is French can trace their ancestry back to a few thousand[3] French who followed Louis Hébert, over the years, across the Atlantic to settle in Canada—an indication of how slight was French interest in the colonization of Canada. The growth in population of Canadians of French descent is almost entirely by natural increase, aided by an inclination on the part of the early settlers to have large families.

Appendix

Whole earth data

Earth is almost a sphere; there is a slight bulge about the equator and the polar regions are slightly flattened.

Equatorial circumference	24,896 mi. = 40,090 km.
Polar circumference	24,814 mi. = 39,958 km.
Average circumference	24,869 mi. = 40,046 km.

The oceans and seas cover 71 percent of earth's surface; exposed land occupies about 28 percent.

Latitude and longitude

A common method for defining the location of a street is to superimpose a grid or network of squares on a map of the city and assign coordinates to the squares (say, numbers for counting left to right and letters, top to bottom). Accompanying the map is an alphabetically ordered list of the streets with the coordinates of the square (the number and letter, e.g. 5B, that lead to the square) in which the user must search for a street.

Gridding the surface of earth is somewhat more complex because of earth's sphericity. Still, the basis for the method in use today for defining the location of any place on its surface was worked out about two thousand years ago by Greek scholars. One element of the grid is a system of north/south lines called *meridians*, running around earth from pole to pole. Because earth is spherical, these lines are half-circles that share earth's axis as a common diameter. The other element is a system of parallel circles centered on earth's axis and appropriately called *parallels*. The equator is the most prominent parallel.

The location of any place, P, can be defined by the parallel and the meridian that intersect in P. The coordinates of that intersection are called its *latitude* and *longitude*.

Latitude is the angular distance measured along a meridian, north or south from the equator, to the parallel that passes through P. The distance

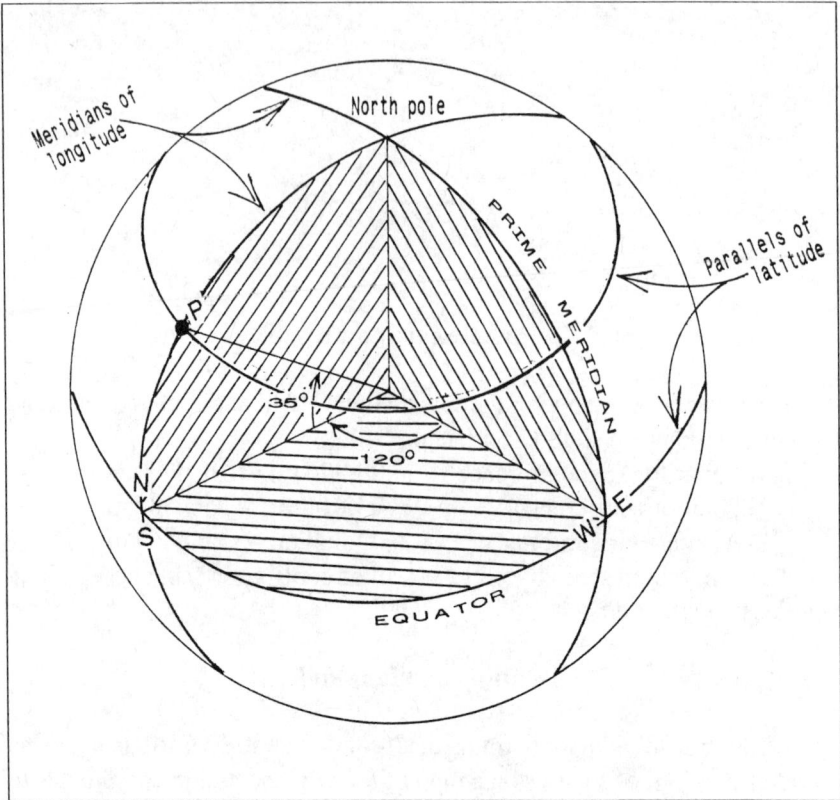

Figure 37. The geographical coordinates, latitude and longitude. The location of the place, P, on the surface of the earth, is specified by its latitude (35°N) and its longitude (120°W).

from the equator to either pole is 90° (¼ of earth's circumference) and hence latitude ranges from 0° at the equator to 90°N and 90°S at the poles. Since the polar circumference of earth is about 24,814 miles, 1° of latitude is equivalent to a linear distance of 24,814/360 = 68.9 miles (111.0 km.).

The equator is a natural zero quantity for latitude but there is no similar "middle" meridian of longitude. The meridian that passes through Greenwich, England is taken, by general agreement, as the zero meridian. Thus longitude is the angular distance measured along the equator, east or west from this "prime" meridian to the meridian that passes through P. Since meridians converge at the poles, the linear distance between two meridians varies with the latitude. At the equator, 1° of longitude is equivalent to a linear distance of 24,896/360 = 69.2 miles (111.4 km.); at latitude 60°, the linear distance is about 34.5 miles (55.6 km.); and at the poles it is zero.

Glossary

archipelago: an island group in a large body of water.

Arctic Ocean consists of the North Polar Sea (the waters north of approximately 80°N) and associated waters such as the Greenland, Norwegian, Barents, Kara, and Laptev Seas; Baffin Bay and the waters of the Canadian archipelago.[1]

barque: a three-masted vessel with fore and main sails square-rigged.

Breton: a native of Brittany, an ancient province and duchy of France.

fjord: a long, relatively narrow arm of the sea, bordered by steep cliffs, as on the coast of Norway.[2]

Genoa: an Italian city at the head of the Ligurian Sea.

Helluland (Flatstone Land): Erik the Red's first landfall (on Baffin Island) in North America after leaving Greenland.

Hop: Thorfinn Karlsefni's temporary camp in North America, possibly at L'Anse aux Meadows on the northern tip of Newfoundland.

knot: a unit of speed equivalent to a nautical mile per hour.

league: the marine league is equivalent to three nautical miles.

Leifsbudir: Leif the Lucky's encampment in North America, probably at L'Anse aux Meadows in Newfoundland.

letters-of-marque: a license or extraordinary commission granted by a government to a private person to fit out an armed vessel to cruise as a privateer or corsair at sea and plunder the enemy.[3]

letters-patent: written authority from a government or sovereign conferring a grant upon a person for a limited period.

Macedonia: an ancient country at the head of the Aegean Sea including parts of modern Greece, Bulgaria and Yugoslavia.

magnetic north pole: the direction in which the needle of a compass points; the direction differs in most places from true north.

Markland (Wood Land): Eric the Red's second landfall in North America (the first on the mainland), probably at Hamilton Inlet in Labrador.

Mesopotamia: an ancient country in Asia between the Tigris and Euphrates Rivers; modern Iraq includes much of Mesopotamia.[4]

mile: a statute mile consists of 5280 feet; a nautical mile is equivalent to 6080 feet.

ness: a headland, promontory or cape.

Normandy: an ancient duchy, later a province of northern France along the English Channel.

Norse: belonging or pertaining to Norway, or to ancient Scandinavia generally.[5]

Phoenicia: an ancient kingdom on the eastern Mediterranean shores including modern Lebanon and parts of modern Israel and Syria.

pinnace: any of various kinds of ship's boats capable of being propelled with sails or oars.

port: the left side of a ship facing the bow.

privateer: a privately owned and manned armed vessel, commissioned by a government in time of war to fight the enemy, especially his commercial shipping.[6]

Scandinavia: the collective name of Norway, Sweden, Denmark and sometimes also Iceland and the Faeroe Islands.[7]

shallop: a small light boat.

Spanish main: the mainland of America adjacent to the Caribbean Sea, especially between the mouth of the Orinoco River and the Isthmus of Panama.[8]

starboard: the right side of a ship facing the bow.

strait: a narrow passage of water connecting two large bodies of water.

Straumfjord: Thorfinn Karlsefni's main encampment in North America. The most likely locations are the northern tip of Newfoundland and near Sandwich Bay in Labrador.

Tartar: a member of any of a mingled host of Mongolian, Turkish and other tribes who, under the leadership of Genghis Khan, overran Asia and eastern Europe during the Middle Ages.[9]

Toledo: a city of very remote origins and the capital of the Spanish province of the same name.

ton: as a unit of displacement of ships, it is equivalent to 35 cubic feet of salt water.[10]

Viking: a Scandinavian rover or sea robber of the type that infested the seas around northern and western Europe during the eighth, ninth and tenth centuries.[11]

Vinland: the coastal region from Newfoundland (or perhaps southern Labrador) on the north, to the southern limits of Norse travel in North America.

Notes

Part 1, Chapter 1
1. *Encyc. Brit.*, vol. 2, pp. 698–9.
2. *Ibid.*, vol. 21, pp. 1095–6.
3. *Ibid.*, vol. 3, pp. 360–1.
4. *Ibid.*, vol. 4, pp. 132–3.
5. *Ibid.*, vol. 2, p. 68.
6. *Ibid.*, vol. 4, p. 152.
7. L. F. Hannon: *The Discoverers*, p. 32.
8. E. Wahlgren: *The Vikings and America*, p. 156.
9. *Ibid.*, p. 152.
10. *Landnamabok*, p. 16.
11. *Ibid.*, p. 16.
12. *Ibid.*, p. 17.
13. *Ibid.*, p. 17.
14. *Ibid.*, p. 18.
15. *Ibid.*, p. 15.
16. *Ibid.*
17. G. Jones: *The Norse Atlantic Saga*. p. 14.
18. *Ibid.*, p. 58.
19. *Ibid.*

Chapter 2
1. G. Jones: *The Norse Atlantic Saga*.
2. *Ibid.*, p. 82.
3. *Ibid.*, p. 172.
4. *Ibid.*, p. 173.
5. L. F. Hannon: *The Discoverers*, p. 38.
6. G. Jones: *The Norse Atlantic Saga*, p. 149.
7. H. Ingstad: *Westward to Vinland*, 250 p.
8. G. Jones: *The Norse Atlantic Saga*, p. 152.

9. *Ibid.*, p. 90.
10. *Ibid.*, pp. 181–2.
11. *Ibid.*, p. 184.
12. *Ibid.*, pp. 91–2.
13. *Ibid.*, p. 185.
14. *Ibid.*, p. 186.
15. *Ibid.*, p. 186.
16. G. Lanctot: *A History of Canada...1663*, p. 29.
17. G. Jones: *The Norse Atlantic Saga*, p. 152.
18. *Landnamabok*, p. 61.
19. G. Jones: *The Norse Atlantic Saga*, pp. 69–70.
20. *Ibid.*, p. 68.
21. *Ibid.*, p. 70.

Part 2, Chapter 3
1. *Encyc. Brit.*, vol. 16, p. 520.
2. *Ibid.*, vol. 19, p. 33.
3. *Ibid.*, vol. 8, p. 46.
4. M. Komroff: *The History of Herodotus*, p. 138.
5. *Ibid.*, pp. 216–7.

Chapter 4
1. S. E. Morison: *The Great Explorers*, p. 379.
2. *Ibid.*, p. 422.
3. J. N. Wilford: *The Mapmakers*, p. 59.

Chapter 5
1. C. Hibbert: *Venice, the biography of a city*, p. 81.

Chapter 6
1. L. A. Vigneras: *The Cape Breton...John Day*, p. 219.

2. H. P. Biggar: *The Precursors...Canada*, p. vii.
3. *Ibid.*, p. 28.
4. *Ibid.*, p. 11.
5. *Ibid.*, p. 6.
6. *Ibid.*, pp. 8–10.
7. L. A. Vigneras: *The Cape Breton...John Day*, p. 228.
8. M. H. Jackson: *The Labrador...reconsidered*, p. 125.
9. *Ibid.*, p. 126.
10. H. P. Biggar: *The Precursors...Canada*, pp. 8–10.
11. *Ibid.*, pp. 12, 16–7.
12. *Ibid.*, pp. 14–5.
13. *Ibid.*, pp. 15–6.
14. *Ibid.*, pp. 19–21.
15. L. A. Vigneras: *The Cape Breton...John Day*, pp. 219–28.
16. *Ibid.*, p. 227.
17. H. P. Biggar: *The Precursors...Canada*, p. 12.
18. *Ibid.*, p. 20.
19. L. A. Vigneras: *The Cape Breton...John Day*, p. 227.
20. H. P. Biggar: *The Precursors...Canada*, p. 20.
21. M. H. Jackson: *The Labrador...reconsidered*, pp. 127–8.
22. *Ibid.*, p. 128.
23. H. P. Biggar: *The Precursors...Canada*, p. 120.
24. L. A. Vigneras: *The Cape Breton...John Day*, p. 227.
25. *Ibid.*, p. 227.
26. H. P. Biggar: *The Precursors...Canada*, p. 14.
27. L. A. Vigneras: *The Cape Breton...John Day*, p. 227.
28. H. P. Biggar: *The Precursors...Canada*, p. 14.
29. *Ibid.*, p. 20.
30. L. A. Vigneras: *The Cape Breton...John Day*, p. 227.
31. H. P. Biggar: *The Precursors...Canada*, p. 20.
    Tanais, now Azov, was the ancient name of a Greek colony at the mouth of the Don River on the Sea of Azov.
32. M. H. Jackson: *The Labrador...reconsidered*, p. 139.
33. L. A. Vigneras: *The Cape Breton...John Day*, pp. 227–8.
34. H. P. Biggar: *The Precursors...Canada*, p. 29.
35. *Ibid.*, p. 20.
36. *Ibid.*, pp. 26–7.
37. *Ibid.*, p. 21.
38. *Ibid.*, p. 14.
39. L. A. Vigneras: *The Cape Breton...John Day*, p. 228.
40. F. Bacon: *The History...Henrie the Seventh*, p. 188.
41. H. P. Biggar: *The Precursors...Canada*, p. 28.
42. B. C. Hoffman: *Cabot to Cartier...1497–1550*, p. 8.
43. *Ibid.*, p. 8.
44. H. P. Biggar: *The Precursors...Canada*, pp. 23–4.
45. *Ibid.*, p. 20.
46. *Ibid.*, pp. 28–9.
47. *Ibid.*, pp. 30–1.

Chapter 7
1. B. C. Hoffman: *Cabot to Cartier...1497–1550*, p. 13.
2. *Ibid.*, p. 13.
3. H. P. Biggar: *The Precursors...Canada*, p. 101.
4. B. C. Hoffman: *Cabot to Cartier...1497–1550*, p. 14.
5. H. P. Biggar: *The Precursors...Canada*, pp. 50–1.
6. B. C. Hoffman: *Cabot to Cartier...1497–1550*, p. 14.

7. H. P. Biggar: *The Precursors...Canada*, p. 190.
8. *Ibid.*, pp. 99–100.
9. B. C. Hoffman: *Cabot to Cartier...1497–1550*, p. 17.
10. H. P. Biggar: *The Precursors...Canada*, p. 35.
11. *Ibid.*, p. 35.
12. B. C. Hoffman: *Cabot to Cartier...1497–1550*, p. 27.
13. H. P. Biggar: *The Precursors...Canada*, pp. 63, 66.
14. *Ibid.*, p. 63.
15. *Ibid.*, p. 69.
16. *Ibid.*, pp. 63–5.
17. *Ibid.*, p. 64.
18. *Ibid.*, p. 64.
19. *Ibid.*, pp. 66–7.
20. *Ibid.*, pp. 97–8.
21. B. C. Hoffman: *Cabot to Cartier...1497–1550*, p. 21.
22. *Ibid.*, p. 20.
23. *Ibid.*, p. 21.
24. *Ibid.*, p. 18.
25. *Ibid.*, p. 34.
26. *Ibid.*, p. 34.
27. H. P. Biggar: *The Precursors...Canada*, pp. 196–7.
28. B. C. Hoffman: *Cabot to Cartier...1497–1550*, p. 35.
29. *Ibid.*, p. 127.
30. *Ibid.*, p. 128.
31. H. P. Biggar: *The Precursors...Canada*, pp. 147–8.
32. *Ibid.*, p. 157.
33. *Ibid.*, p. 159.
34. *Ibid.*, p. 193.
35. *Ibid.*, pp. 192–3.
36. *Ibid.*, pp. 125, 130.
37. W. C. Eccles: *The Canadian Frontier, 1534–1760*, p. 12.
38. B. C. Hoffman: *Cabot to Cartier...1497–1550*, p. 107.
39. *Ibid.*, p. 108.

Chapter 8
1. B. C. Hoffman: *Cabot to Cartier...1497–1550*, p. 113.
2. *Ibid.*, pp. 112–3.
3. M. Trudel: *The Beginnings...1524–1663*, p. 12.
4. B. C. Hoffman: *Cabot to Cartier...1497–1550*, pp. 113–4.
5. M. Trudel: *The Beginnings...1524–1663*, p. 12.
6. H. P. Biggar: *The Voyages of Jacques Cartier*, p. 56.
7. *Ibid.*, p. 65.
8. *Ibid.*, p. 71.
9. *Ibid.*, p. 78.
10. *Ibid.*, p. 92.
11. *Ibid.*, p. 93.
12. *Ibid.*, p. 85.
13. *Ibid.*, p. 101.
14. *Ibid.*, pp. 103, 106.
15. F. McFadden: *Origins, a History of Canada*, p. 119.
16. H. P. Biggar: *The Voyages of Jacques Cartier*, p. 309.
17. *Ibid.*, pp. 106–7.
18. *Ibid.*, p. 113.
19. *Ibid.*, p. 120.
20. *Ibid.*, pp. 121–2.
21. *Ibid.*, p. 141.
22. *Ibid.*, p. 168.
23. *Ibid.*, p. 177.
24. *Ibid.*, p. 204.
25. *Ibid.*, p. 218.
26. *Ibid.*, pp. 210–1.
27. *Ibid.*, p. 229.
28. *Ibid.*, p. 143.
29. W. J. Eccles: *The Canadian Frontier, 1534–1760*, p. 16.
30. H. P. Biggar: *The Voyages of Jacques Cartier*, p. 249.
31. B. C. Hoffman: *Cabot to Cartier...1497–1550*, p. 144.

32. W. J. Eccles: *The Canadian Frontier, 1534–1760*, p. 16.
33. H. P. Biggar: *The Voyages of Jacques Cartier*, p. 254.
34. *Ibid.*, p. 255.
35. H. P. Biggar: *The Works of...Champlain*, vol. 1, pp. 151–2.

Chapter 9
1. H. P. Biggar: *The Precursors...Canada*, p. 173.
2. *Ibid.*, p. 176.
3. *Ibid.*, p. 167.
4. *Ibid.*, p. 167.
5. *Encyc. Brit.*, vol. 8, p. 496.
6. D. A. Young: *According to Hakluyt*, p. 7.
7. J. Hampden: *Richard Hakluyt...Adventurers*, p. 114.
8. *Ibid.*, p. 114.
9. *Ibid.*, p. 116.
10. I. R. Blacker: *"Hakluyt's Voyages...1600 Yeares,"* p. 177.
11. *Ibid.*, p. 178.
12. *Ibid.*, p. 179.
13. *Ibid.*, p. 180.
14. D. A. Young: *According to Hakluyt*, p. 10.
15. I. R. Blacker: *"Hakluyt's Voyages ...1600 Yeares,"* p. 187.
16. *Ibid.*, p. 187.
17. D. D. Hogarth: *priv. comm.*
18. *Ibid.*
19. D. A. Young: *According to Hakluyt*, p. 25.
20. *Ibid.*, pp. 25–6.
21. D. D. Hogarth: *priv. comm.*
22. J. Hampden: *Richard Hakluyt...Adventurers*, p. 119.
23. D. A. Young: *According to Hakluyt*, pp. 35–6.
24. *Ibid.*, pp. 36–7.
25. J. Hampden: *Richard Hakluyt...Adventurers*, p. 204.
26. *Ibid.*, pp. 204–5.

27. *Ibid.*, p. 205.
28. D. A. Young: *According to Hakluyt*, p. 44.
29. *Ibid.*, pp. 45–6.
30. J. Hampden: *Richard Hakluyt...Adventurers*, p. 205.
31. D. A. Young: *According to Hakluyt*, p. 53.
32. *Ibid.*, p. 59.
33. I. R. Blacker: *"Hakluyt's Voyages...1600 Yeares,"* p. 395.
34. *Ibid.*, p. 397.
35. D. A. Young: *According to Hakluyt*, p. 75.
36. I. R. Blacker: *"Hakluyt's Voyages...1600 Yeares,"* p. 380.

Chapter 10
1. *Encyc. Brit.*, vol. 11, pp. 806–7.
2. I. R. Blacker: *"Hakluyt's Voyages...1600 Yeares,"* p. 409.
3. *Encyc. Brit.*, vol. 11, p.806.
4. L. Powys: *Henry Hudson*, p. 134.
5. *Ibid.*, p. 157.
6. *Ibid.*, p. 160.
7. *Ibid.*, p. 164.
8. *Ibid.*, p. 166.
9. E. M. Bacon: *Henry Hudson...Voyages*, p. 212.
10. *Ibid.*, p. 213.
11. *Ibid.*, p. 214.
12. L. Powys: *Henry Hudson*, p. 186.

Chapter 11
1. F. W. Rowe: *A History of Newfoundland and Labrador*, p. 95.
2. *Ibid.*, p. 65.
3. I. R. Blacker: *"Hakluyt's Voyages...1600 Yeares,"* p. 287.
4. *Ibid.*, p. 299.
5. *Ibid.*, p. 301.
6. J. Hampden: *Richard Hakluyt...Adventurers*, pp. 213–4.
7. H. P. Biggar: *The Precursors...Canada*, p. 194.

8. M. Trudel: *The Beginnings...1524–1663*, p. 63.
9. D. Creighton: *Canada: The Heroic Beginnings*, p. 32.
10. *Ibid.*, p. 35.
11. J. B. Brebner: *Canada, a Modern History*, p. 29.
12. H. A. Innis: *The Fur Trade in Canada*, pp. 32–3.
13. *Ibid.*, p. 33.
14. W. J. Eccles: *The Canadian Frontier, 1534–1760*, p. 23.
15. G. M. Wrong: *The Rise...New France*, vol. 1, p. 173.
16. H. A. Innis: *The Fur Trade in Canada*, p. 32.
17. G. M. Wrong: *The Rise...New France*, vol. 1, p. 182.
18. W. J. Eccles: *The Canadian Frontier, 1534–1760*, p. 26.
19. F. W. Rowe: *A History of Newfoundland and Labrador*, p. 137.
20. *Ibid.*, pp. 83–4.

Chapter 12
1. M. Trudel: *The Beginnings...1524–1663*, pp. 187, 191.
2. G. M. Wrong: *The Rise...New France*, vol. 1, p. 244.
3. F. W. Rowe: *A History of Newfoundland and Labrador*, p. 89.

Glossary
1. *Encyc. Brit.*, vol. 2, pp. 341–2.
2. C. L. Barnhart: *American College...Dictionary*, p. 455.
3. P. B. Gove: *Webster's Third...unabridged*, p. 1298.
4. C. L. Barnhart: *American College...Dictionary*, p. 763.
5. *Ibid.*, p. 827.
6. *Ibid.*, p. 964.
7. *Ibid.*, p. 1082.
8. *Ibid.*, p. 1157.
9. *Ibid.*, p. 1240.
10. *Ibid.*, p. 1274.
11. *Ibid.*, p. 1357.

References

Bacon, Edgar Mayhew: *Henry Hudson, His Times and His Voyages.* G. P. Putnam's Sons, New York, 1907.

Bacon, Francis: *The history of the reign of King Henrie the Seventh,* 1st edition, 1622.

Barnhart, Clarence L. (editor): *American College Encyclopedic Dictionary.* Spencer Press, Inc., Chicago, 1956.

Bartholomew, J. G.: *The Comparative Atlas.* Meiklejohn & Holden, London.

Biggar, H. P. (editor): *The Precursors of Jacques Cartier, 1497–1534. A collection of documents relating to the early history of the Dominion of Canada.* Publications of the Public Archives of Canada, no. 5, Ottawa, 1911.

Biggar, H. P. (general editor): *The Works of Samuel de Champlain* in six volumes; volume 1 for the period 1599–1607 translated and edited by H. H. Langton and W. F. Ganong, 1922. The Champlain Society, Toronto.

Biggar, H. P. (editor): *The Voyages of Jacques Cartier.* Publications of the Public Archives of Canada, no. 11, Ottawa, 1924.

Blacker, Irwin R. (editor): *"Hakluyt's Voyages: The Principal Navigations, Voyages, Traffiques & Discoveries of the English Nation Made by Sea or Over-land to the Remote and Farthest Distant Quarters of the Earth at any time within the compasse of these 1600 Yeares."* The Viking Press, New York, 1965.

   Note: Richard Hakluyt, born to a London leather merchant about 1553, was a clergyman who traveled throughout England, collecting the journals, accounts, charts and stories of English seamen who took part in the historic voyages and events in Elizabeth I's reign—the time of Sir Francis Drake and Sir Humphrey Gilbert, the founding of Virginia, the voyages of Martin Frobisher and the battle with the Spanish Armada. *Hakluyt's Voyages* is the published account of this research. It is basically an anthology, a collection of materials written by others that has been an essential source for historical writers since it first appeared. For a more complete account of the life of Hakluyt and his contributions, see Young: *According to Hakluyt,* and Blacker: *Hakluyt's Voyages.*

Brebner, J. Bartlet: *Canada: A Modern History.* The University of Michigan Press, Ann Arbor, 1960.

Burpee, Lawrence J.: *An Historical Atlas of Canada.* Thomas Nelson and Sons, Limited, Toronto, 1927.

Cottrell, Alvin J. (general editor): *The Persian Gulf States—A General Survey.* The John Hopkins University Press, Baltimore, 1980.

Creighton, Donald: *Canada: The Heroic Beginnings.* Macmillan of Canada, Toronto, 1974.

Eccles, W. J.: *The Canadian Frontier, 1534–1760.* Holt, Rinehart and Winston, New York, 1969.

Encyclopaedia Britannica, twenty-three volumes plus Index and Atlas, 1969. William Benton, Publisher.

Gove, Philip Babcock (editor in chief): *Webster's Third New International Dictionary of the English Language unabridged.* G. & C. Merriam Company, Springfield, Mass., 1971.

Hampden, John (editor): *Richard Hakluyt: The Tudor Adventurers.* The Folio Society, London, 1970.

Hannon, Leslie F.: *The Discoverers.* McClelland and Stewart Ltd., Toronto, 1971.

Hibbert, Christopher: *Venice, the biography of a city.* Grafton Books, London, 1988.

Hoffman, Bernard C.: *Cabot to Cartier. Sources for a Historical Ethnography of Northeastern North America, 1497–1550.* University of Toronto Press, Toronto, 1961.

Hogarth, D. D., P. W. Boreham, and J. G. Mitchell: *Mines, Minerals, Metallurgy —Martin Frobisher's Northwest Venture, 1576–1581.* Canadian Museum of Civilization, Hull, Quebec, 1994.

Ingstad, Helge: *Westward to Vinland*, trans. Erik J. Friis. St. Martin's Press, New York, 1969.

Innis, Harold A.: *The Fur Trade in Canada.* The University of Toronto Press, Toronto, 1970.

Jackson, Melvin H.: *The Labrador Landfall of John Cabot: The 1497 Voyage reconsidered.* The Canadian Historical Review, vol. 44, 1963, pp. 122–141.

Jóhannesson, Jón: *Islendinga Saga: A History of the Old Icelandic Commonwealth*, trans. Haraldur Bessason. University of Manitoba Press, Winnipeg, 1974.

Jones, Gwyn: *A History of the Vikings*, sec. ed. Oxford University Press, Oxford, 1984.

————: *The Norse Atlantic Saga.* Oxford University Press, 1964.

Kerr, D. G. G.: *Historical Atlas of Canada.* Thomas Nelson & Sons (Canada) Limited, Toronto, 1975.

Komroff, Manuel (editor): *The History of Herodotus*, trans. George Rawlinson. Tudor Publishing Company, New York, 1947.

Lanctot, Gustave: *A History of Canada*; vol. 1: *From its Origins to the Royal Régime, 1663*, trans. Josephine Hambleton. Clarke, Irwin & Company Limited, Toronto, 1963.

Landnámabók: The Book of Settlements, trans. Hermann Pálsson & Paul Edwards. University of Manitoba Press, Winnipeg, 1972.

Note: The principal source books about the Norse discoverers of Iceland and the early history of Icelandic (and to a lesser extent, Greenlandic) society are the *Islendingabok* or "Book of the Icelanders" and the *Landnamabok* or "Book of Settlements."

The *Islendingabok* was written about 1125 by Ari Thorgilsson (Ari the Wise) who lived from about 1067 to 1148. It appears to be a revision of an earlier work he composed for two bishops. It is preserved in two transcripts dating from the seventeenth century (Jones: *The Norse Atlantic Saga*, p. 224).

The *Landnamabok* traces the discovery of Iceland by the Scandinavians and the emergence of the Icelanic nation during the Viking period. Ari Thorgilsson was probably the author of an original *Landnamabok*, with the help of other learned men and many informers. There exist five versions of the *Landnamabok*, dating from the thirteenth to the seventeenth century, all derived from a lost version prepared by Stymir the Learned who was born about 1170 and died in 1245. Only two of the five versions, one composed by Sturla Thordarson about 1275 and the other at an unknown time by Hauk Erlendsson who died in 1334, are complete; they are not identical (Jones: *The Norse Atlantic Saga*, pp. 224–5). The recent publication of a translation into English by Hermann Palsson & Paul Edwards, of the Sturla Thordarson version has made this Old Icelanic manuscript available to the English-reading public.

Lopez, Barry: *Arctic Dream*. Charles Scribner's Sons, New York, 1986.

Marquis, Thomas Guthrie: *The Jesuit Missions*. Glasgow, Brook & Company, Toronto, 1916.

McFadden, Fred (general editor): *Origins: A History of Canada*. Fitzhenry & Whiteside, Markham, Ontario, 1989.

Morison, Samuel Eliot: *The Oxford History of the American People*. Oxford University Press, New York, 1965.

———— *The Great Explorers—The European Discovery of America*. Oxford University Press, New York, 1978.

Nuffield, Edward W.: *The Pacific Northwest*. Hancock House Publishers Ltd., Surrey, B. C., 1990.

Powys, Llewelyn: *Henry Hudson*. John Lane The Bodley Head Ltd., 1927.

Quinn, David B.: *The Argument for the English Discovery of America between 1480 and 1494*. The Geographical Journal, vol. CXXVII (1961), pp. 277–85.

Roos, Willy de: *North-West Passage*, trans. Bruce Penman. Hollis & Carter, London, 1979.

Roesdahl, Else: *The Vikings*, trans. Susan M. Margeson & Kirsten Williams. Penguin Books, London, 1991.

Rowe, Frederick W.: *A History of Newfoundland and Labrador*. McGraw-Hill Ryerson Limited, Toronto, 1980.

Trudel, Marcel: *The Beginnings of New France, 1524–1663*, trans. Patricia Claxton. McClelland and Stewart, Toronto, 1973.

Vigneras, L. A.: *The Cape Breton Landfall: 1494 or 1497; note on a letter from John Day*. The Canadian Historical Review, vol. XXXVIII, no. 3, September 1957, pp. 219–28.

Wahlgren, Erik: *The Vikings and America*. Thames and Hudson Ltd., London, 1986.

Whiteley, George: *John Cabot's Voyage of Discovery*. The Newfoundland Quarterly, vol. LXXXII, no. 1, Summer, 1986, pp. 13–4.

Wilford, John Noble: *The Mapmakers*. Alfred A. Knopf, New York, 1981.

Wrong, George M.: *The Rise and Fall of New France*, vol. 1. Octagon Books, New York, 1970.

Young, Delbert A.: *According to Hakluyt.* Clarke, Irwin & Company, Toronto, 1973.

Index

219